SESAME STREET

and the Reform of Children's Television

SESAME STREET

and the Reform of Children's Television

ROBERT W. MORROW

The Johns Hopkins University Press

Baltimore

© 2006 The Johns Hopkins University Press
All rights reserved. Published 2006
Printed in the United States of America on acid-free paper
2 4 6 8 9 7 5 3 1

The Johns Hopkins University Press
2715 North Charles Street
Baltimore, Maryland 21218-4363
www.press.jhu.edu

Library of Congress Cataloging-in-Publication Data
Morrow, Robert W., 1954–
Sesame Street and the reform of children's television / Robert W. Morrow.
p.   cm.
Includes bibliographical references and index.
ISBN 0-8018-8230-3 (hardcover : alk. paper)
1. Sesame street (Television program) 2. Television and children. I. Title.
PN1992.77.S43M67 2005
791.45'72—dc22   2005004535

A catalog record for this book is available from the British Library.

For Stephanie, Johanna, and Katherine

Contents

Illustrations appear following page 84

Preface

■■

I did not first watch *Sesame Street* as a preschooler. My siblings and I, we were all too old for it when it premiered in 1969. Instead, I watched it when my daughters were preschoolers in the mid-1980s. By the time they reached the age of four or five, it was clear that I liked the show more than they did. Years later, I began the research for this book. It began as a doctoral dissertation at the University of Maryland, home of the Children's Television Workshop archives. During the research portion of this book, my adviser James Gilbert kept telling me, "You must watch the show." And I kept answering, "I will. I will. I have watched the show. I know what it looks like." To my mind, after all the reading, that part of the research was like dessert. At the suggestion of another member of my dissertation committee, Douglas Gomery, I decided to sample thirty randomly chosen episodes from the first ten years.

When I finally sat down to watch the sample shows, I found that, as usual, Gilbert was right. Watching the show opened my eyes. What I saw was a child's primer on popular culture: game shows, westerns, news reports ("Hi, ho, Kermit the Frog here"), vaudeville acts, pop music, ballet and opera (mercilessly parodied from a populist perspective), public television, and, of course, commercials. I came to appreciate the unsung parts of the show: the films and cartoons. An entire story about the struggle for self-expression and love, told with a hand (and arm up to the elbow) as its only character. The Mad Painter series, in which a mischievous misfit paints numerals in inappropriate places and is pursued by his nemesis, a bald man, who is always trying to stop him. The stop-action animation Teeny Little Super Guy parables of childhood conflict and striving. The countdown cartoons in which the rocket almost never takes off. The prim know-it-all Alice Braithwaite Goodyshoes. These are the parts of the show that I believe have been neglected and forgotten by the public in its adulation—wholly deserved—for Jim Henson's Muppets.

This book is about *Sesame Street*'s serious side, the idea of using television to prepare children for school and to spread a message of tolerance for diversity. At the time of this writing, *Sesame Street* is no longer the most popular children's program on PBS, let alone all of television. This book takes the reader back to a time when, though the show could not match the ratings of top Saturday morning programs, it was a cultural sensation. For people who worried about television's effects on children, it stirred hope that a good example might convince the TV networks to change their shows to match *Sesame Street*. The debate that raged around it and around television in general reveals a lot about how Americans think about the relationship between the medium and its youngest viewers. Although *Sesame Street* and TV were different then, these ideas endure.

The book has three parts: *Sesame Street*'s roots, its development, and its place in public discourse. Chapter 1 covers the source of the original impetus for the show: public discontent and debate about television, commercialism, and children. The second chapter describes the program's other wellspring, the preschool moment, when social developments combined with those in child development psychology to produce a climate of optimism about social reform through early education.

Following these are three chapters about the program's development, form, and content. The founding of Children's Television Workshop, the funding and organizational groundwork for *Sesame Street*, is the subject of chapter 3. Chapter 4 explains the workshop's distinctive production system, the CTW model, and describes its creation between early 1968 and the end of the show's first season in 1970. Chapter 5 relies, in part, on an analysis of thirty episodes from *Sesame Street*'s first ten seasons (1969–79) to illustrate the form and content of the show and examine its distinctive contribution to educational TV.

Public reaction and the show's place in public discourse are described in the final two chapters. I have structured each of these chapters around the three subjects for debate: reform, education, multiculturalism. Chapter

6 describes the months before the premiere and the first two seasons when the program became the apotheosis of children's television through its promotional campaign and subsequent popularity. This chapter also introduces the Action for Children's Television reform debate and the show's place in it. The final chapter completes *Sesame Street*'s early history, including the demise of the reform campaign, the press's ambivalent endorsement of the show, and the workshop's response to rising multiculturalism. Though it did not remain at the pinnacle of esteem it had achieved, it became the icon of worthy children's television and an idealized vision of a diverse, tolerant America. The conclusion revisits the major views of Sesame Street and adds several important stories from the years since the mid-1970s. These last stories show how the program has continued to be important thirty-five years after its premiere.

A book like this never gets written without a lot of help from other people. Gilbert taught me a lot about writing and history and pointed me in many fruitful directions. Gomery guided me at key points, especially prodding me at a crucial juncture to find the story's endpoint. David Sicilia wisely advised me on several interpretive issues. My thanks also to my dear friend Holly Shulman for her suggestions and support. Saverio Giovacchini kindly read a recent draft and made encouraging suggestions. In the later drafts, Heather Hendershot's close reading helped me correct many potentially embarrassing errors and forced me to solve the largest interpretive problem left over from the dissertation.

Among the founders of the Children's Television Workshop, Robert Davidson served as the organization's unofficial historian, organizing the archives and creating essential oral histories. His advice and perspective were invaluable to me. I appreciate the time of all of those whom I interviewed: Davidson, Lewis Bernstein, Gerald S. Lesser, Lloyd N. Morrisett, Edward L. Palmer, Leona Schauble, and James Thurman. I particularly thank Joan Ganz Cooney for her generosity with her time. Her secretary, Janet Wolf, put me in touch with people and turned up information for me at the workshop. I also appreciate the help of Ken Schwab at CTW and Paul Arnsberger at the Internal Revenue Service for assistance with financial figures. My thanks also go to Robert Schuman at the workshop for making tape copies of episodes and to CTW for granting its permission. James Thurman kindly gave me access to David Connell's papers.

Every historian owes a debt of gratitude to archivists. Thomas Connors, Karen King, Michael Henry, and the entire staff of the National Public Broadcasting Archives and the Library of American Broadcasting have not only helped with research but have become dear friends and colleagues.

I would also like to thank my editor, Robert J. Brugger, at the Johns Hopkins University Press for his patience and unfailing good judgment.

My mother-in-law, Janice Fain, helped by carefully reading a late draft and, like all mothers-in-law, was great at finding the little errors. Most of all, I thank my wife, Stephanie, who endlessly encouraged me and patiently read draft after draft. For years she has stood in for the thoughtful reader I hope to reach with this book.

Of course, even with all this help, any errors that remain are mine.

SESAME STREET

and the Reform of Children's Television

Introduction

A puppet skit from *Sesame Street:* In a small living room, Bert is watching the television and moaning. His roommate Ernie enters and asks, "What're you watchin'?" Bert whines, "I was watching my favorite program, *The Wonderful World of Pigeons*, and all of a sudden this 'H' comes on." A capital letter "H" flashes on the screen as a voice repeatedly drones "H" and the set buzzes. Ernie says that he can fix the set and turns it off; Bert unplugs it. Through the front of the set—where the screen would be—Ernie reaches in and says, "Aha. Here's your problem, Bert. You had a hat in there, Bert. 'Hat' is an 'H' word." Bert is dumbfounded. "How'd you do that?" he asks. Then, in succession, Ernie removes from the set a hammer, a bicycle horn, a toy house, a hamburger, and a hamster, identifying each as "a good 'H' word." By the end, Bert's protests have turned to numb bewilderment. The two plug the set back in and turn it on. Now, an "I" flashes on the screen just as the "H" had before. Ernie immediately apologizes: "Oh, Bert, I'm sorry. I thought I had it all fixed." But before Ernie can turn the set off to resume his repairs, Bert says, "Hold it." It turns out Bert is *delighted* by the flashing "I." He exclaims, "It's new! It's brilliant! It's unique! It's new television talent! What we needed all along!"[1]

This book is about the creation of *Sesame Street* and its early history. Unlike Ernie, the show's creators did not so much take things out of TV; instead they combined stylish, popular elements of televisual art with an educational apparatus of goals and testing. They created the show to demonstrate a new, better way to make educational programs for children. This book is about the ideas, techniques, organization, and funding it took to create *Sesame Street*.

But it is also about what happened when *Sesame Street* became a subject for public debate. A viewer watching Bert and Ernie's encounter with the unruly television could understand it as a comment about the very show on which the two were starring. *Sesame Street* evoked a reaction from many Americans not unlike Bert's reaction to the flashing letter "I." When the new children's program premiered in late 1969, many television critics hoped that it would change the entire medium—that it would be "what we needed all along." For instance, Les Brown wrote: "Not until the closing weeks of 1969 did television offer a program series that really answered the long-standing criticism of the medium—namely that it takes of a viewer's time without giving anything in return—and held out hope for a more substantive future." After its first season, teachers were reporting that it had affected the incoming kindergartners. Polled by an educators' magazine, one teacher in Cleveland said, "Besides the knowledge about letters and numbers, the kids seem to have a different attitude about school, as if they've already learned what school is for and what to do there. And they're excited about it." Some parents hoped that it would bring more racial understanding. Jim Fiebig, a newspaper columnist, wrote: "When our white-skinned 3-year-old sits down for the magic hour each day, a darker shade of 3-year-old is doing the same in someone else's living room. And they both see the same thing: people—not races. Those two 3-year-olds will continue to see things that way—in the spirit of *Sesame Street*—even on the day they meet face to face." The show created a public sensation, and within a few years a huge majority of the nation's preschoolers—along with many older Americans—were watching it regularly.[2]

Sesame Street had its detractors, as well. Advertising and broadcasting industry executives agreed with Quaker Oats's Robert Thurston that *Sesame Street* was not "commercially competitive with other programming." It simply was not as popular as entertainment programs and was therefore not going to convince the broadcasters to change their programs. Not everyone agreed that it was *too* educational, though. Minnie Perrin Berson, a columnist in an academic journal, was so disgusted by the elements of popular entertainment in the show that she asked, "Why debase the art form of teaching with phony pedagogy, vulgar side shows, bad acting, and layers of smoke and fog to clog the eager minds of small children?" And not everyone, at least in the first seasons, celebrated the show as a model of multiculturalism. When the producers of the show asked for advice, a group of Hispanic activists called them "racist" and told them that the bilingual aspects of the show were of "poor quality and patronizing." Controversies over the show did not disappear after these early years, either. For writer Marie Winn, TV was the "plug-in drug," and *Sesame Street* served an important "role in promoting television viewing even among parents who might feel an instinctive resistance to plugging such young children in."[3]

Looking at these reactions decades later, they seem surprisingly intense. To explain this passion requires consideration of the place of children in American society and the controversies about television's effects on them. The thinking about youngsters' position in American society largely originated with the rise of the middle class during the nineteenth century. Middle-class parents tried to prepare children for a life of work and citizenship but also to shield them within the family from the perceived immorality of the larger world. Nurturing children's self-discipline, character, and education in the home also meant keeping out books and magazines that might undercut those values. Censorship campaigns in the late nineteenth and early twentieth centuries showed the political power and energy with which the middle class sought to protect its children. Though these actions seem distant from *Sesame Street*, those who praised and those who condemned the show echoed this earlier drive to shield children.

If these efforts and ideas seem quaint, it is because in time child-rearing practices and ideas change. By the 1930s and 1940s, social scientific ideas about child development began to displace moralistic ones, and advice manuals suggested that parents accept many childhood behaviors as natural. Children had an innate desire to explore, which was crucial to their growth. Parents were urged to insure that pleasure always be a part of the parent-child relationship. Sociologist Martha Wolfenstein called this line of thought "fun morality," a replacement for "goodness morality." But, in time, the quest to inject fun into every activity became oppressive, boredom seemed to drive children's exploration as much as stimulation, and the experts began to warn against letting children dominate family life. In a similar way, manufacturers first marketed television sets as a source of family fun, and many parents initially embraced the new medium. Within a few years, they also started to complain that the advertisements were teaching children to importune their parents to buy particular products. American reactions to television reflected general oscillations in the culture between a permissive, development-oriented set of ideas and older, moralistic concerns about self-discipline.[4]

These powerful concerns about children explain the intense efforts to control TV, but they also beg the question of why children are so often the focus of social controversy. Fears about children frequently have served as an opening for the expression of wider anxieties. As sociologist Viviana Zelizer has shown, the middle class has placed high, sentimental value on children as the embodiment of the desire that some parts of society be kept free of the intrusions of an increasingly commercial society. In the first decades of the twentieth century, this sentimental view of children displaced a working-class view that a child earned wages to contribute to the family's income and to prepare for adult work. Middle-class reformers pressed for laws that banned child labor and set limits on the legitimate occupations for youngsters. Unease about the intrusion of money into all aspects of life became focused on children.[5]

Similarly, those who sought to regulate television did so from adult ideas about its effects on children. As communications scholar Heather Hendershot put it, "Debates about children's entertainment inevitably reveal what *adults* need or desire *for* themselves and *of* children." Hendershot analyzed producers, network censors, and reform groups who shaped children's TV on the basis of their ideas about children. Many saw children as innocent and helpless before television's powerful force. Few saw youngsters as active, capable viewers who used television for their own social and emotional needs, as researchers like Ellen Seiter have demonstrated them in fact to be. Adults project onto children their own fears about the pervasive and powerful influence of television on everyone's lives. The general intensity of emotion invested in the debates about television in general, and about *Sesame Street* in particular, can be understood in the long-term desires to protect children, to preserve a sanctuary from commercial culture, and to reform society more easily through concern for children.[6]

As much as the drive to protect children, the hope that *Sesame Street would inspire better TV* needs explanation too. Why were these critics of TV so hopeful that the show's example could change commercial TV? One practical answer might be that the entertainment industry imitates any new, popular program, but the times, the 1960s, offer a more compelling explanation. Historian David Farber has called that decade "the age of great dreams," and one of the most noble of those dreams was the creation of a society free of racism, free of poverty. Many people shared the energy, optimism, and determination that produced the civil rights movement and the Great Society programs, even if they were not directly involved in these struggles. To these familiar stories—central to the 1960s—this book adds another dimension. Like the popular Head Start program, *Sesame Street* grew in part from new insights about intellectual growth from developmental psychology. Scientists began to believe that changing early education could tap stifled potential, nurture greater cognitive growth, and liberate poor children from poverty. The culmination of these trends in the mid-1960s—what I have called the "preschool moment"—meant that early education took on a new significance. *Sesame Street* drew not only on scientific ideas but also on a utopian undercurrent that Farber identified: "Many Americans saw in their rush to consume, a push toward a richer world, a limitless world in which people would be free to create themselves anew." Like so many others, *Sesame Street*'s creators embraced the hopes of the time without necessarily considering consumer culture antithetical to social reform. It made sense to teach letters of the alphabet through advertising-style cartoons to poor children in the hopes that later academic success would lift them from poverty.[7]

Another reason that *Sesame Street* seemed able to propel change in the TV industry lay in the reform campaign already in motion. Intermittently throughout the 1950s and 1960s, many middle-class parents, clergymen, politicians, and psychologists expressed anger with television's violence and commercialism and became concerned about its long-term effects on young viewers. After congressional investigations and government pressure, the industry remained largely unresponsive. With the failure of these efforts, a new wave of activists, among them Action for Children's Television (ACT), advocated the removal of all advertising from children's programming. The reformers believed that without the profit motive, other incentives could shape the content of network programs. Their proposal came just weeks after *Sesame Street* premiered, and the new show seemed to prove that a noncommercial educational program could attract a large audience. Construing *Sesame Street* as important evidence for ACT's petition thrust the show into the political arena.

Naturally, *Sesame Street* itself kindled many of the reformers' hopes. It came from the Children's Television Workshop (CTW)—a new nonprofit subsidiary of National Educational Television, the predecessor of the Public Broadcasting Service. CTW brought together talented producers and writers from commercial TV with child psychologists and educators to create the show. Through their dialogue, these disparate professionals systematically melded educational content and current popular television. And it worked. The show not only entertained, it also taught children things that they could show off to their parents. With a professional promotional campaign, the workshop built a sense of anticipation, and the press covered the show extensively. After its first year on the air, Educational Testing Service validated the educational results of the show through a study of children who watched during the first season. With ACT's reform campaign gaining momentum, *Time* magazine put *Sesame Street* on its cover, calling it "TV's gift to children."[8]

Americans nevertheless debated the value of *Sesame Street* during the early 1970s. They did so in three ways. First, as it became central to consideration of ACT's petition, that group needed to persuade the television industry that a more rigorous educational show could be popular and serve as an example worth emulating. Second, many educators, psychologists, journalists, and researchers asked whether it taught preschoolers—particularly impoverished ones—the appropriate lessons in the best way. Could television really teach? Third, activists demanded that it serve the needs of all of the children in its diverse, national audience, particularly black, Hispanic, and female preschoolers. Could *Sesame Street* help convince each of its young viewers that he or she could succeed? Could it be multicultural when multiculturalism was just emerging?

Sesame Street met these challenges with a fresh and exciting face. It was a "new bloom on the [television] wasteland," and it held great promise. Looking back years later, it is no longer as popular as it once was. It has aged despite its producers' earnest efforts to keep it growing with new goals and new characters and new formats. Other new children's programs have aspired higher than the bottom line and have challenged *Sesame Street* for its place in the spotlight. For example, when *Blue's Clues* (Nickelodeon, 1996–present) premiered, *New York Times* reporter Lawrie Mifflin warned, "Move over, Big Bird; a new blue dog is in town." In the long run, however, *Sesame Street* achieved more than popularity and longevity; it set a standard against which each new educational children's program was judged. By the mid-1970s *Sesame Street* had grabbed a unique place in American culture. This book tells that story.[9]

CHAPTER 1

The Problem of Television
and the Child Viewer

Television in 1948 was new, exciting, and a little scary. In the *New Yorker* magazine, Leonard Lyons told readers about his four-year-old son Jeffrey's experience with the new medium. Unaware of the many baseball games that Jeffrey had watched on TV, Leonard took him to Central Park to show him how to play the game. To the father's amazement, his son already knew how to hit the ball and run to first base. The boy also could mimic New York Yankees star Joe DiMaggio's every mannerism, even ones his father had never noticed. When Leonard asked him what else he had learned, Jeffrey showed him that he could wave a baton like a symphony conductor and frisk a suspect like an experienced detective. The child had learned from television. In telling the story, the *New Yorker*'s columnist called the story "a minor saga that we pass along as a glimpse of what, in the dawning age of television, may soon be the experience of all parents."[1] In a sweet and intimate way, this story held a portent of the delight, awe, and anxiety that American parents would feel as this new force entered their families' lives.

Only thirteen years later, Newton N. Minow, President John F. Kennedy's newly appointed chairman of the Federal Communications Commission (FCC), spoke to the National Association of Broadcasters. The commission regulated broadcasting—television and radio—on behalf of the American people, and Minow's audience included the leaders of the commercial broadcasting industry, assembling at a time when the industry's prestige had fallen. The commission chairman did not offer reassurance or encouragement; he outraged them. If they watched their own programs—as he had just done for hours on end—he assured them that they would "observe a vast wasteland" of predictable, escapist shows leavened with too little news or cultural programming. Like a newspaper that carried only the comics, the television networks and stations were ignoring the public interest, he said. They were neglecting viewers who wanted something other than "Westerns and private eyes." Turning to children's television, he decried the "massive doses of cartoons, violence and more violence." "Search your consciences," he implored his listeners, "and see if you cannot offer more to your young beneficiaries, whose future you guide so many hours each and every day." Minow spoke for the millions of Americans who no longer looked upon television with delight and awe but with distaste and anxiety. His complaints echoed those of many, who were, if not a majority of Americans, a vocal minority. Not long before, Walter Lippmann, the most prominent newspaper columnist in America, identified the "problem" of TV: it had become "the creature, the servant, and indeed the prostitute, of merchandising."[2]

What had gone wrong with American television? The answer must include both long-term and more recent historical contexts. Unquestionably, the early history of TV as a new industry and as a cultural force explains much of the discontent articulated by Minow. But over the previous hundred years or so, a middle-class culture developed that focused on the protection of children as a part of class survival and that sought to prevent popular culture from compromising that protection. By the time of television's advent, Victorian-era book censorship by the federal government had given way to industry self-regulation as the primary means of social control in film. Those who were uneasy about the impact of films and television on children had to compel the entertainment industry to conform its product to their standards. To do this, TV's detractors had to convince the politicians and the public to join in pressuring the industry. They sought to do so, in the two decades preceding *Sesame Street*'s premiere, by proving that television taught children to behave violently and did so for crass commercial purposes. Their reliance on social science departed from earlier censorship campaigns based on moralistic arguments, but they still found it difficult to convince the broadcasters to change profitable programming. From this history, *Sesame Street* emerged and similarly used social science to demonstrate its value. It offered a way to break the cycle of fruitless campaigning for self-regulation by offering instead a positive model for broadcasters to copy.

The twentieth century's ideal family, the middle-class family, had emerged a hundred years earlier. During the first decades of the nineteenth century, the market revolution and cultural trends promoted changes among both rural and urban families, but it was among those in the cities that the new middle class began to form. Most basic to this new social stratum was a shift to fathers working outside of the home, mothers confining themselves to domestic and child-rearing work, and children living at home until their late teens or twenties. Previously, the farm family had required the labor of all to survive. When children did leave the home, they went to work as servants or apprentices. With the creation of the middle-class family, children no longer had to work; instead they stayed within the shelter of their families to learn what they needed to be independent adults and to develop moral character. What might have seemed a great improvement in material well-being—only fathers had to work—also provoked anxiety. Parents worried that their children would not have either the education to succeed professionally or the character to resist the temptations of the larger world. If children failed, they could slide downward on the social scale into the working class and poverty.

For nineteenth-century parents, avoiding this fall in status demanded that they inculcate moral values like self-control, diligence, and moderation. They began from an acceptance of the philosopher John Locke's idea that children were born innocent, not sinful and depraved. To this, evangelical Christianity added the hope that children would grow into their spiritual salvation if parents nurtured them correctly. They began to eschew physical punishment in favor of correction that prompted self-reflection and shame in their children. Francis Wayland, a minister and later president of Brown University, sought to stop his fifteen-month-old son's defiant behavior. Instead of beating him, Wayland confined the child to a room with no food until he would take bread from his father's hand and embrace him. It took more than a day before he repented of his disobedience. More often, the nurture of children fell to mothers, rather than to fathers like Wayland; in either case, parents could not carry the entire burden. Society had a part to play in the nurture of children despite the insularity of the middle-class family. So much of parents' happiness and satisfaction—a sense of their life's work continuing after them—depended on their children's futures that society's role naturally became an important concern for them.

Public education spread throughout the northern states in the first half of the nineteenth century to provide the preparation for employment and the shaping of character that middle-class parents demanded for their children. With the public school movement before the Civil War, education shifted from simple literacy and religious training to include the rudiments needed by a professional middle class, including history, geography, math, and science. Though the home remained the center of moral education, parents still expected the schools to inculcate self-discipline and Protestant Christian faith. For their part, the schools also responded to social concerns that children be prepared to be good citizens within a democratic society with an increasingly divisive class system. The *McGuffey* reader cautioned that "It is God who makes some poor and others rich" and that "the rich have troubles which we know nothing of; and . . . the poor, if they are good, may be very happy."[3] Catholic parents objected to Protestant Bible lessons and other parts of the emerging public school curriculum. From the time that society began to shoulder some of the burden of children's upbringing, there arose contention over values and social class.

Commercial popular culture also developed in this same era and quickly became a point of class conflict. In the early nineteenth century, theater, such as the plays of William Shakespeare, attracted rich, middling, and poor alike, each seated in its own section and all participating in the performance. Audiences maintained control of the show by demanding encores of favorite parts, throwing vegetables, and even leaping onto the stage to interact with the actors. As middle- and upper-class Americans became more uncomfortable mixing with the lower classes, they began to demand separate theaters in which the audience remained passive and silent. Tensions between the classes became so intense that in 1849 two rival actors—one an outspoken opponent of elitism and the other a darling of the elite—sparked a confrontation over a performance of Shakespeare's *Macbeth*. In response to shouts of "Burn the damned den of the aristocracy," a crowd stoned the Astor Place Opera House. The New York militia fired and killed twenty-two.[4] By the end of the nineteenth century, Shakespeare, along with opera, classical music, and museum art exhibitions, became high art forms, and popular commercial culture emerged as entertainment opposed, and separate from, "high brow" culture. Minstrel shows, circuses, vaudeville, and sporting events amused those who lacked the education, inclination, or class identity to pursue more elite entertainment.

Conflict over popular culture did not end with this "highbrow-lowbrow" division, and children became a particular flashpoint for battles over censorship in the late nineteenth century. The man most closely identified with censorship in America, Anthony Comstock, focused much of his efforts on protecting children from violent criminal newspapers and sexually arousing literature. In his 1883 book *Traps for the Young*, he oscillated between, on the one hand, crimes described in popular books and newspapers and, on the other, tales of youthful criminals imitating criminal acts. "In the department of murder," he wrote, "the instruction given by the dime-novel writers is all that could be desired. There is not a possible method of murder that is not fully described and illustrated by brilliant examples in these admirable educational works." He appealed to his largely upper-class supporters' concerns that their own children would be corrupted by reading obscene newspapers and books, become sexual deviants or criminals, and fall from respectable society. In an age of economic booms and busts, like those of the 1870s and 1890s, parents' worries about their children's futures were understandable; Comstock's explanation of how culture corrupts individuals seems irrational now, but it established a middle-class unease about the effect of popular culture on their children. With the authority of federal law behind him, Comstock prosecuted distributors of objectionable literature and pressured postmasters to interdict its passage through the postal system. Aggressive efforts to control popular culture forms in the name of protecting *all* children became another enduring pattern in American culture, despite the class segregation of theaters and the emergence of highbrow entertainment, especially for the middle and upper classes.

Censorship was not the only response by middle-class Americans to the perceived cultural threat; didactic and moralistic books and magazines offered a positive alternative. In one novel called *Home*, Catherine Sedgewick wrote, "Mr. Barclay [a father] . . . believed the only effectual and lasting government—the only one that touches the springs of action, and in all circumstances controls them, is *self*-government."[5] Nurturing self-control was preferable to sole reliance on physical punishment. Similarly, substituting entertaining but didactic books and magazines for objectionable literature enhanced the effectiveness of censorship, or so the Women's Christian Temperance Union (WCTU) believed. In their magazine *The Young Crusader*, they offered children short fiction in which children modeled the virtues of temperance and perseverance. Even if the women added a positive approach to Comstock's book burning, they ironically shared his understanding that children simply imitated actions they read about without any intervention of moral sense or self-control. The WCTU activists objected to stories about the exploitation of women and the lynching of black men. Contrasting this more liberal position to Comstock's conservatism underlines the diversity of the censorship advocates. The women also felt freer to criticize high art depictions of nude women than Comstock did because he relied on the support of wealthy men who were also patrons of that same art. Divisions along class and gender lines attest to the breadth of censorship's support within the middle and upper classes.

Although these nineteenth-century roots seem distant from *Sesame Street*, in fact they do not lie far beneath the surface in the debates about TV in the 1950s, 1960s, and 1970s. The concept of the home as an inviolable refuge from a harsh capitalist society carried over into education, which became an oasis from commercial culture. So important did many critics of popular culture consider the classroom's isolation that, when *Sesame Street* attempted to use elements of that culture to educate, those who might have applauded its educational ends instead condemned its popular means. Concerns about self-control and diligence emerged when critics of TV worried about its effects on younger viewers. Violent or sexual acts might be mimicked by vulnerable children, these same observers feared in much the same way that Comstock and the WCTU had decades before. Their censorship crusades continued into the twentieth century, and the focus would turn to controlling the effects of movies. But government censorship gave way to the entertainment industry's self-regulation in radio and television as well as film. For purposes of understanding *Sesame Street*, self-regulation involved negotiation between entertainment producer and would-be censor, processes that are the antecedents of *Sesame Street*'s innovative marriage of artistry and child development expertise.

Motion pictures began as a rudimentary and working-class entertainment around the turn of the twentieth century but quickly became popular with a broad spectrum of American society; soon it was a potential competitor with family, church, and community in the formation of children's moral values. Early films like *The Kiss* ran for only seconds and did little more than demonstrate the moving image technology. More elaborate storytelling would come slowly with films like *The Great Train Robbery* (1903), which brings together several sequences to tell of a western gang's daring crime. Much more elaborately, pioneer filmmaker D. W. Griffith brought together multiple plotlines, a large cast, and an epic style to create the first truly modern motion picture, *The Birth of a Nation* (1915). As the art form matured, films flickered in peep show machines, then amused Vaudeville audiences between stage acts, and, by the 1920s, filled large screens in grand movie palaces. By that time, children began coming to films in large numbers, often unaccompanied by adults. Film became a focus of social controversy. *The Kiss* caused some moral reformers to worry about movies arousing lust in children. African Americans and Progressives protested that Griffiths's glorification of the Ku Klux Klan during Reconstruction spurred racism in its viewers. With crime and romance as prime movie subjects, Progressive-era moral reformers quickly became concerned that children would simply mimic the behaviors they saw on the screen.

In response, Progressives soon urged censorship of movies; with these early efforts came all of the problems of controlling culture for a diverse audience. By the early twentieth century, American cities had large immigrant populations, people who did not entirely share the values of the native-born middle class. In 1908, Mayor George B. McClellan closed all of New York City's 550 movie theaters; in response, theater owners proposed that a well-respected reform organization, the People's Institute, view and approve all films to be shown. The Institute's National Board of Censorship fulfilled this role for New York City as well as for much of the rest of the country. Not only did the reviewers' cultural standards vary from those of more conservative rural viewers, but problems arose when filmmakers attempted to deal with social problems, even when these efforts came from a point of view similar to that of the censorship board. With the creation of local and state boards of censorship, the process of film production and distribution took on a complexity unimagined today. The 1913 film *The Inside of the White Slave Traffic* treated a social issue of great concern at the time: the seduction of respectable young women into prostitution. Popular press reports were telling lurid tales of women drugged or tricked into lives of prostitution. More honest accounts added that they had become trapped because respectable society—even their own families—would not accept them back. Despite the rarity of such situations, the popular film *Traffic in Souls*, also 1913, told a tale of women heroically rescued before they fell. The board preferred these simple moral lessons. *The Inside of the White Slave Traffic*, on the other hand, attempted to tell a more complex story of women drawn into sex and slowly declining into a life of misery, unable to escape due in part to their subsequent rejection by upright society. After several rounds of changes, the board still refused to pass the film. San Francisco's censors allowed *The Inside of the White Slave Traffic* to play to large audiences, but many local and state boards refused to approve even the white slave trade films that the board had passed. Film censorship was not a simple process. It demanded cooperation between censors and producers, but ultimately it allowed filmmakers to confront America's cultural diversity as they attempted to reach the profitable national audience.[6]

With so much at stake for the major film studios, the industry created, at first, a weak system of self-regulation and later a much stronger one in response to continued criticism. By the 1920s, a few major studios controlled the production and distribution of films, and, in 1922, a series of sex scandals and the ensuing public outrage forced the movie moguls to promise to clean up the industry. They established the Motion Picture Producers and Distributors Association under a prominent conservative Republican named Will Hays, who functioned more as a public relations man than as a true censor. While Hays developed relationships with religious groups, his Studio Relations Committee encouraged filmmakers to follow guidelines with injunctions like "Don't" and "Be Careful." But in the 1920s the cultural diversity of the United States had only grown since the years before World War I, and the values of rural fundamentalists clashed with the tastes of urban audiences.

In the 1930s, the industry put in place a stronger system of self-censorship, but only after a campaign brought together a diverse group of conservative viewers. When the Great Depression slashed studio revenues, the industry responded by producing racier and more violent films. In 1934, the Roman Catholic church led a campaign to boycott all movies that united millions of working-class and middle-class, Catholic, Protestant, and Jewish moviegoers. Hollywood capitulated. Joseph Breen, a prominent Catholic layman and film critic, took over the Motion Picture Association's Production Code Administration with new powers to force producers to hew to conservative social values in their films. Breen's staff closely supervised every phase of production, attending not only to explicit meanings but also to implication and innuendo. They shielded children from any hint of sexual behavior. For more than two decades, the most successful censorship system in American history helped create a distinctive style that attracted large audiences and consistent profits.

Ironically, it is around this time that censorship began to take on the oppressive image it has today. While Hollywood struggled to please diverse audiences in the 1920s, the same organizations that had worked with Comstock continued to censor books and magazines. However, new authors with a hostile outlook toward Victorian-era culture and new publishers in sympathy with them challenged the moralistic reformers. No longer uniformly supported by publishing industry insiders, many attempts to stop the publication of a book ended up in court. Judges began to consider the larger social and artistic merits of a work as well as the risqué passages. Censorship advocates moved to strengthen New York State's obscenity laws and enable prosecution on the basis of a single passage in a book without regard to the rest of the work. Lawyers, writers, newspaper editors, and others came out strongly against the law and turned the tide against the idea of censorship. By the late 1920s, books no longer seemed a threat to women and children; in fact, books seemed much less significant as film and radio became more pervasive. Nazi book burners in the 1930s made censorship seem even less appealing. As H. L. Mencken wrote: "To be a censor today, a man must be not only an idiot; he must be also a man courageous enough in his imbecility to endure the low guffaws of his next-door neighbors."[7] Hollywood's system lasted more than thirty years after this ridicule, but once the courts recognized film as an art form worthy of constitutional protection, filmmakers increasingly defied the censors. The Motion Picture Association abandoned the system in the 1960s.

Radio, too, was adopting a self-censorship approach while the barriers to expression in print were falling. During the 1930s and 1940s, before television eclipsed radio, programming included drama, comedy, variety, and children's shows in addition to the more familiar music and news programs heard on radio today. Because several of these genres could offend various segments of the audience, the networks established continuity acceptance departments. The censorship staff would preview scripts and request changes in material that listeners might consider immoral, such as sexual innuendo. For example, one script called for the following line from comedienne Fanny Brice, speaking on the telephone: "Hello Mrs. Greenberg—this is Mrs. Cohen—oy, am I sick. I was in bed all day with three doctors and two nurses."[8] However, the network censors had quite limited power because advertising agencies produced almost all of the programs for corporate sponsors, who provided the revenue for the radio networks and stations. Agency production staffs and casts had the additional advantage that the shows were produced live, making it difficult for the broadcasters to stop offending lines from getting on the air.

Each instance of film or radio censorship was a process of negotiation between censor and producer, and the results ultimately hinged on the relative power of each side. These systems differed significantly from those involving print media, in which a government agency could bring suit against a publisher or bookseller and thus suppress a work entirely. By contrast, when several private organizations negotiated among themselves in a self-censorship system, commercial pressures favored editing a work to make it acceptable, thus salvaging the investment already made in production. The story of censorship before *Sesame Street* is an important context for the show because its production process also involved negotiations— albeit completely internal to the organization. However, there the similarity ends. The Children's Television Workshop created a process that put its child experts—in a position analogous to that of the censors—in a more positive and effective position than those who in earlier decades had sought to protect children's morals. And an intense public debate rooted in this long history swirled around the workshop when *Sesame Street* came to the small screen.

Television's history before *Sesame Street* explains in large measure the impetus behind the workshop's experiment and the discontent that made the show both possible and successful. Radio critics and other writers who anticipated television's arrival had done so with great ambivalence. One such critic, Harriet Van Horne, imagined that, along with the soap operas, educational programs on the arts would appear on television. "Ideas know no boundaries," she wrote in 1945, speculating that the new medium might unify the country.[9] Others were less sanguine. Few expected it to raise the cultural level of the great bulk of Americans or to provide a new channel for democratic debate and dialogue. In fact, many expected it to follow radio's lead and deliver popular entertainment with plenty of commercialism.

Isolating American families in their homes, in the family circle, became a specific appeal that manufacturers made to consumers. In countless advertisements, television manufacturers depicted mothers, fathers, and children gathered in a semicircle around the set, absorbed in the action on the screen. Drawing the family closer together, the set promised to strengthen the domestic haven by giving the family members entertainment to share. In a 1951 survey, one parent remarked, "It keeps us together more." After the children went to bed, some women thought that it brought them and their husbands closer: "Until we got that TV set," one remarked, "I thought my husband had forgotten how to neck."[10] American families bought their first televisions, and, even more quickly than movies and radio had, television became a part of millions of Americans' lives. In 1948 only 0.4 percent of American households had televisions; by 1960, that percentage had risen to 87.[11]

Generally, parents appreciated the new medium. In 1954 the National Council of Churches of Christ sponsored a study by the Communications Research Project. Though the study was otherwise critical of TV, it found that 69 percent of parents approved of children's programming; only 26 percent objected. In 1961, two professors of human development, Robert Hess and Harriet Goldman, found that 91 percent of mothers they polled agreed with the statement that "television is a great educational influence." When Columbia Broadcasting System, Inc. (CBS) commissioned a large survey of TV viewers, 75 percent of parents said that children are "better off" with television than without it—outpolling adults who had no children. Thirty-five percent of parents claimed that they knew of a child who had "benefited from television," and a majority said that education was the primary benefit of TV. By 1960, children had settled into watching an average of twenty hours of TV per week.[12]

Initially, middle-class parents worried only about the amount of time their children spent watching television. "Television is a new invader of children's time," proclaimed Paul Witty and Harry Bricker at the beginning of their *Parents* magazine article in 1952.[13] Witty became a frequent adviser to the magazine's readers in the years that followed, and he recommended that they carefully regulate the amount of television that their children watched. As Witty and others illustrated in their advice columns, some feared that children would become addicted to TV and that they would allow it to supplant schoolwork and outdoor play. In keeping with long-held middle-class values, parents sought to instill self-discipline and focus their children's lives on learning. Television "invaded" the sanctum of family life, but parents could cope. Or so was the message of Witty and others. *New York Times* critic Jack Gould, one of the most important voices on the subject at the time, counseled calm: "It takes a human hand to turn on a television set."[14] Though concerns about TV addiction continue to this day, parents' apprehensions shifted to commercialism and violence in the late 1950s and 1960s.

The critique of commercialism began with changes in programming and in advertising, changes that occurred in both evening prime time and children's programming. During the 1950s, adult prime time television changed in ways that alarmed and disgusted those who influenced literate public opinion. Critics like Gould and Gilbert Seldes contended in the early 1950s that TV had a natural artistic superiority over Hollywood films because it lent itself to intimate, socially valuable drama, an outgrowth of legitimate theater. Beginning around the middle of the decade, however, the live shows they so valued gave way to filmed westerns and action-adventure programs from Hollywood. Print journalists covering television, major critics writing about the medium, and some writers, actors, and directors working in TV rejected the new telefilms (TV programs recorded on film) as violent, cheap, mediocre, or homogenous. How large a segment of the American viewing public these discontented voices influenced is hard to determine. Judging by the volume of such criticism and its appearance in many newspapers and magazines, its impact seems likely to have reached beyond the tiny intellectual elite to the larger group of well-educated, middle-class viewers.

Children's programming changed in analogous ways, moving critically acclaimed shows to more marginal time slots and switching to cartoons. In 1949, *Time* magazine remarked that not only did prime time shows directed to children quiet them down for bed, but "the fact that TV children's programs are so generally good is regarded by most parents as a happy byproduct." Among programs for children, there was initial approval for shows like *Kukla, Fran, and Ollie* (NBC, 1948–54, ABC, 1954–57, PBS, 1970–71), a witty puppet show that appealed to adults as well and introduced many families to TV. After four years, however, two of its sponsors withdrew in favor of programs that attracted more adult viewers. The National Broadcasting Company (NBC), which had been carrying it, shortened its time slot from thirty to fifteen minutes, later cancelling it altogether. The networks dropped other children's shows to make room for adult programs until they discovered that youngsters could be reached on Saturday mornings, a time when no more lucrative audience could be found. They also moved most of their educational programs to Sundays, which, into the 1960s, remained a marginal segment of the programming schedule. Just as telefilms displaced live shows in the evenings, cartoons first began their long domination of children's TV with the broadcast of old cartoons originally shown in movie theaters. Production costs were minimal. Much more expensive was the creation of new cartoons. But the development of limited animation techniques in the late 1950s reduced the cost of new ones, cementing their place in the TV schedule.[15]

Advertising trends coincided with these changes in programming. The critically acclaimed anthology drama programs disappeared over roughly the same period in the mid-1950s that advertising shifted from single- to multiple-sponsorship. In television's early years, broadcasters continued the prevailing practice in radio that a single sponsoring corporation paid the cost of production and air time, put its name on a program, and thus identified its image with the show. Producers of small consumer goods replaced corporate image advertisers, and this new group of sponsors did not care about a program's content as long as it attracted a large audience for their product-specific sales messages. Because filmed action-adventure shows received larger audiences than did prestigious live programs, these consumer goods companies chose to sponsor telefilms. And the networks used this trend to increase their control of the broadcast schedule and displace the power of advertisers over programming. When the quiz show scandal in 1958 revealed the venality of the companies that sponsored programs like *Twenty-One* (NBC, 1956–58) and *The $64,000 Question* (CBS, 1955–58), the networks claimed to have been ignorant of what sponsors and their production companies had done. This scandal, along with bribery and corruption revelations at the Federal Communications Commission, led to denunciations from many commentators, including Walter Lippmann.

Ironically, despite these censures, the most visible institutions in the industry—the networks—increased in power through not only advertising control but also through self-censorship. In response to the first wave of public concern in the early 1950s, the networks created standards and practices departments to uphold the National Association of Broadcasters' Code of Good Practice. Each internal censorship office watched for violations of commercial law in the advertising carried by its network and for commercial messages woven into programs. More significantly, the standards staff censored shows by examining scripts, negotiating with program producers, and demanding changes in much the way that Breen's office had done in the movie industry. In the wake of the quiz show scandal, the censors' power increased, but it apparently never approached the influence of its predecessors in the film industry. In the two decades after the scandal, critics of TV searched for ways to force the networks to exclude violent content more strictly.

While the scandals and programming changes exposed the industry's crassness, advertisers discovered how effectively children could be reached through television. Much print advertising for toys and other children's products had addressed parents, leaving them relatively in control of their youngsters' access to consumer goods. Ads in magazines like *Parents* often included parents in tableaux of children at play, implying parental awareness and approval of their youngsters' toys. As children became the majority of viewers during the late weekday afternoons and Saturday mornings, television advertising could reach them without parents looking on. With age-segregated audiences, advertisers of toys, candy, and sugared cereals, who had previously not found television an economical medium, increased their sponsorship of children's shows. By advertising to youngsters without their parents present, TV could prompt children to be the advertiser's advocate within the family. The instruction directed to young viewers to "tell your mother to buy" became notorious in the eyes of parents sensitive to the way that TV intruded on the domestic sanctuary. Commercials also began to portray a child's world free of parental authority, a realm of fantasy and fun. In this way, television began to speak to children in ways that concerned middle-class parents.

The Christmas season soon came to show off the medium's power. In 1955, the Mattel toy company took a risk with expensive advertisements on a promising new program, Disney's *Mickey Mouse Club* (ABC, 1955–

59). Showing a boy, armed with his toy burp gun, hunting big game in his living room, the commercial "made the child [viewer] and his imagination [its] message."[16] That Christmas, the toy became such a fad that there were shortages in the stores. By the early 1960s, children's television had become profitable for the networks and proven itself an effective medium to boost sales dramatically.

Though these developments did not prompt as much public comment as the quiz show scandal had, the experience of two early children's programs illustrates an emerging popular aversion to commercialism. In 1952 a new children's program, *Ding Dong School* (NBC, 1952–56), went on the air, and its educational consultant soon became its host. Dr. Frances Horwich, a one-time nursery school teacher and professor of psychology, read stories to her young viewers, showed short films, and demonstrated craft projects. To keep kids engaged, she would include exercises or active games. At the end of each show, she asked the children to bring a parent to the TV set for a special message. She then briefed the parents about what she had covered during the show. As it quickly became popular, the program attracted sponsors, for whom Horwich delivered advertisements as a part of the show. Jack Gould complained: "the integration of what amounted to delightful kindergarten school work on television with hardhitting salesmanship continued throughout much of the program, even to blatant coercion of unsuspecting small children to persuade mother to buy the product."[17] By 1956 the show went off the air, for two reasons. The controversy spurred by Gould's continuing criticism of the show's commercialism crystallized concerns that many parents apparently had about advertising's effects on their children. But the show also went off the air when sponsors abandoned it for evening family programs that reached children in larger numbers. To many parents at the time and to some of *Sesame Street*'s early planners, *Ding Dong School* was an educational program that had fallen prey to the medium's commercialism, though few observers decades after *Sesame Street* would still consider it "educational."[18]

Outlasting *Ding Dong School* by decades, *Captain Kangaroo* (CBS, 1955–84) also won parental and critical approval for its mixture of entertainment and education. Robert Keeshan created and hosted *Kangaroo* after performing on *The Howdy Doody Show* (NBC, 1947–60). Although lacking Horwich's credentials, he created an educational program for young children. Like *Ding Dong*, his show followed a variety format that mixed cartoons and puppets with his own antics as the bumbling, grandfatherly captain. A 1957 Peabody Award citation lauded the program: "*Captain Kangaroo* is almost the only genuine children's program on network television, certainly the only one which puts the welfare of the children ahead of that of the sponsor, which instructs children in safety, in ethics, in health, without interrupting the serious business of entertaining them at the same time."[19] On other occasions, the Captain attempted to explain how a congressional bill became law and to teach about modern art. In 1957, Keeshan explained to a reporter that his approach would be to point out to a child that the artist "didn't want to paint only what he saw with his eyes but how he saw these things with his mind and feelings, too." He hastened to add, "We're not trying to educate children in great art. We feel, though, that they have innate good taste."[20]

Unlike *Ding Dong School*, *Captain Kangaroo* avoided the problems of commercialism and won the enduring esteem of middle-class parents, in part because Keeshan refused to accept certain sponsors. For example, he rejected advertisements for certain vitamins, a major focus of anger with Horwich, and for the Johnny 7 toy gun, which had interchangeable parts to make seven different kinds of weapons. Undoubtedly, other elements, like the lack of violence, contributed to the show's popularity with middle-class parents as much as Keeshan's sponsorship scruples. Whatever the source, this approval became dramatically clear when a rumor of the program's cancellation brought ten thousand letters of protest in one week. By 1963, when CBS's survey asked parents to name the "best programs" for their children, they mentioned *Captain Kangaroo* far more than any other show.[21]

At first, it seems ironic that *Ding Dong School*, designed and hosted by an expert in early education, failed, while *Captain Kangaroo*, designed and hosted by a clown from *The Howdy Doody Show*, succeeded. Keeshan's skill as an entertainer no doubt made a difference, as did his inclusion of nonviolent cartoons created to meet his standards. *Captain Kangaroo* also had a marginal time slot from which CBS initially expected little because it aired opposite the highly rated adult program *Today*. Once established, its ratings might have remained weak, but *Captain Kangaroo*'s prestige sustained it. Nevertheless, CBS executives moved to cancel it several times. The program's precarious position seems to have served only to establish it more firmly as a lone symbol of beneficial—or at least benign—children's programming because it underscored, for its supporters, the tenuous status of all such programming in a commercially driven medium. Keeshan's more sensitive control of sponsorship had played an important role in establishing the program's image at a time when commercialism was becoming a primary complaint of outspoken parents.

Captain Kangaroo survived in spite of the central reality of commercial television's programming system: ratings data almost always determined what a viewer saw on the three networks. Network executives sought to maximize revenues and profits during each part of their broadcast schedules. They did so by trying to reach the largest number of people at any given time and to reach the people considered most desirable by advertisers. Crafting programs to attract demographically specific viewers had begun, but such targeting did little to improve or increase the programming for children. Generally, the largest total "circulation" remained the objective. Network concerns about audience flow—keeping viewers tuned to the same channel from the end of one show to the beginning of the next—put even more pressure on programs to draw the largest total viewership. If a program's ratings dipped below those of the one that immediately preceded it, the networks considered those viewers lost for the subsequent show as well. Low-rated shows hurt not just their own advertising revenue; they depreciated adjacent programs as well. In the wake of the quiz show scandal, a congressional committee investigated the ratings systems and their impact on programming between 1960 and 1964. Hearings prompted broadcasters to question the validity of the rating services' methods—but not the use of their numbers as the ultimate measure of success. Ratings maximization meant that any viewer who wanted to watch something different from what the networks believed the majority wanted had no alternative but to turn the TV set off. Though well-educated adults with higher incomes probably made up most of that disgruntled minority, children—though less prone to discontent—were also a minority audience not specifically served by the programming they saw at the times that they watched.

For parents, commercialism did not stand alone as their only major complaint about television; after 1960, the controversy about the effects of violent television programming on children eclipsed commercialism. The fear that children would imitate violent acts went all the way back to Comstock's day. But it grew more intense and widespread during the years after World War II with the national debate about the causes of juvenile delinquency. Religious activists, social scientists, politicians, and others actively seeking a public response to adolescent criminality laid part of the blame on television, as well as on comic books and movies, for directly causing the misbehavior of children and youths. A belief in direct media effects gained fresh scientific authority from the work of psychologist Albert Bandura and others, but politicians could not translate this evidence into pressure for stronger industry self-censorship. This debate not only sets the immediate context out of which *Sesame Street* grew but also illustrates the persistence of simple ideas about television and children, ideas whose impact the show diminished.

Bandura and his generation of researchers were not the first social scientists who tried to demonstrate experimentally that media directly affected children's behavior and thus should be controlled. In 1928 a Congregationalist minister, the Reverend William Short, hoped to arouse the public to the dangers that movies posed for children through a series of research projects called the Payne Film Studies. Four years later, the researchers had completed most of their studies, but they could not present the clearcut evidence for the direct-effects theory for which Short had hoped. For example, sociologist Paul Cressy studied whether movies abetted juvenile delinquency in Harlem and found that other influences, such as the darkened theater and the youths' social situation, determined their behavior far more than what appeared on the screen. Direct media effects that seemed so self-evident and well-established to middle-class parents and moral reformers became less persuasive when scientists tried to substantiate the connection between the media cause and the child's behavior or attitudes. Short commissioned a popularization of the findings, *Our Movie-Made Children*, to use the ambiguous evidence to polemical ends. It backfired, as critics like philosopher Mortimer Adler punctured the book's credibility. The Legion of Decency used other means to force self-censorship, leaving the Payne Studies in relative obscurity.

Beginning in the 1940s, media researchers proposed an alternative to the popular direct-effects theory. Trained as sociologists or social psychologists, these scientists considered viewers to be active agents who chose what to watch as it suited their psychological needs. This "uses and gratifications" school of thought emerged from the work of Paul F. Lazarsfeld, the dean of communications researchers, and others like Wilbur Schramm, the lead author of the first comprehensive study of children and television in 1961. Schramm, for instance, articulated the view that media played a distinctly secondary role in the development of juvenile delinquency, surpassed in importance by some "great lack in the child's life," such as a "broken home" or a "feeling of rejection by parents or peer group." Elihu Katz and David Foulkes offered a formal version of the uses and gratifications theory a year later. Postulating that viewers came to television "deprived and alienated," the authors suggested that the audience sought out dramas featuring a hero with whom they could identify. Finding their conclusions supportive, the broadcasting industry often employed these scientists to do audience research. When Congress held hearings on the causes of delinquency, those who blamed the media and urged self-censorship had to confront media experts whose work undercut the scientific basis for their demands.[22]

In 1954, Senator Estes Kefauver led a special committee to investigate delinquency and the sources of youthful criminality. Middle-class parents, Protestant clergymen, and others wrote to urge him to seek the cause in the mass media, including TV. One mother blamed her son's delinquency on "what they see on the screen in movies, on TV, reading those foul [comic books]." Kefauver held a more tentative view of the media's effects on society, and his hearings presented a wide variety of opinions from others, like Children's Bureau and broadcast industry witnesses, who did not support the direct-effects concept. Nevertheless, the committee did conclude that violent TV could "teach techniques of crime" and cause a "hostile child . . . to imitate these acts in expression of his aggression" or become insensitive to "human suffering and distress."[23]

After Kefauver gave up leadership of the committee, Senator Thomas Dodd took up the gavel; in 1961, he aggressively shifted its focus to television violence as a cause of delinquency. This later round of hearings featured new research that lent fresh scientific authority to the belief in the direct-effects theory. Albert Bandura, a psychologist, was then creating his "social learning theory," which would make him a major figure in the field. He testified before Dodd's committee that "exposure to filmed aggression" explained delinquency better than the social causes cited by the uses and gratifications researchers. After he laid out his evidence, Dodd enthusiastically endorsed this new research and hoped that it would "produce a response from the citizens of this country." After this appearance before Dodd's committee, Bandura's experimental and theoretical work took on central importance for the controversy over media's effects on children.[24]

Bandura's influence grew from a single simple, compelling experiment. It involved a group of children from Stanford University's preschool and a Bobo doll. The doll was an inflated clown figure with a round base; when punched, the toy rocked and then popped back up. Each child in the experimental group watched a film in which an adult attacked the doll. Those in the control group watched a nature film. In the violent film, the adult model used mallets and kicks to attack the doll, sat on it, and made exclamations like, "Sock him in the nose." Having demonstrated aggressive behavior for the children to copy, Bandura next created in his subjects the drive to be aggressive. After viewing the film, the child entered a room full of attractive toys; when the child settled in to play with them, a researcher ushered the child out of the room with the somewhat insulting admonishment that they were the researcher's "very best" toys and that the researcher would not "let just anyone play with them." Finally, the child arrived in a play room that included, among other toys, a Bobo doll. The experimenter observed the child and scored the ensuing play for aggressive behaviors. Bandura and his partners summarized their findings: "The results of the present study provide strong evidence that exposure to filmed aggression heightens aggressive reactions in children. Subjects who viewed the aggressive human . . . models on film exhibited nearly twice as much aggression than did subjects in the control group."[25]

After this experiment and his testimony before Dodd's committee, Bandura further popularized his findings in an article in *Look* magazine in 1963. The dramatic power of the original experiment lay in the fact that children closely imitated the filmed model's aggressions against the Bobo doll depicted in the film. Control group children, who did not see the violent film, may have punched the doll—it was made, marketed, and sold for that purpose—but they were unlikely to reproduce the exact behaviors portrayed. Just as his committee testimony had included screenings of hidden camera footage showing the youngsters' behavior, from which his *Look* article included still photos. He lined up the photos of the model and two subjects, one boy and one girl, so that photos of each of the model's actions—such as hitting the doll with a mallet—were juxtaposed with ones of each of the children doing likewise. The visual power of these photos supported his point that children learn "*forms* of aggression" that they retain for later use. Bandura used this seemingly unmediated evidence to bolster his contention that his research "directly examine[d] the children's attitudes and social behavior." Like believers in the direct-effects theory, he leaped from evidence of social behavior to underlying attitudes without imputing any thought in between. At no point did he consider the possibility that, for example, children who had watched toys advertised on television might take the filmed aggression as suggestions for fun—and appropriate—things to do with a Bobo doll.[26]

In the article Bandura also made a theoretical point. He juxtaposed the implicit credibility of his research to "several widely circulated survey studies [that] contend that televised violence has neither harmful or beneficial effects, except perhaps on highly insecure and emotionally disturbed children . . . based on little more than findings from public opinion polls and survey questionnaires." With his compelling evidence, his sweeping conclusions seemed quite plausible, and his theory made a deep impression on the public, overwhelming the uses and gratifications alternative. He contended that viewing aggression on TV breaks down inhibitions against aggressive behavior. Once children learned forms of violent action, even a television show's moral ending, in which a villain ultimately was punished, did nothing to erase the behaviors that youngsters had assimilated. Bandura apparently had created clear and convincing evidence of direct media effects. Other researchers repeated his study and created ones based on similar premises, most of which bolstered Bandura's case.[27]

Although Dodd's committee ultimately produced nothing more than another round of admonitions to the industry, he helped cement in the minds of some middle-class parents the relationship between violent programming and commercialism. After the first round of hearings, promising still more embarrassing revelations in a second round, Dodd suddenly changed direction. He took campaign contributions from broadcasters, used them for personal purposes, and abandoned the inquiry. Revelations of these actions destroyed his political career. The committee released only a preliminary report, and even that came two years after the end of the hearings. It recommended closer FCC supervision of a strengthened industry code, systematic opinion polling about television programs, and more research into the effects of TV on children's behavior. The committee also released industry memos, which the press picked up. *U.S. News and World Report* included in its coverage quotations under a headline itself taken from one memo: "I Like the Idea of Sadism . . . ." In these quotations, network executives pressured writers and producers to increase the violent action—and also the sexual innuendo—to improve the ratings and, thus, the revenues. In a related practice, when a serious dramatic series, *Bus Stop* (ABC, 1961–62), received disappointing ratings, the network extensively promoted a more violent episode starring an actor popular with teenagers. The ratings went up.[28]

Four years after the Dodd committee report, in 1968, assassins gunned down Martin Luther King Jr. and Robert F. Kennedy. Many observers took these tragedies to symbolize the pervasive violence in American society. President Lyndon Johnson created the National Commission on the Causes and Prevention of Violence, popularly known as the Eisenhower Commission. Network executives began to pressure producers to reduce violence in their programs, telling them that a deluge of letters of complaint had come from mothers all over the country. Whether this claim was true or not, it became a legend within the industry that it was the murder of Robert F. Kennedy—perceived to be an advocate for children—that brought a new sensitivity to broadcasters. The presidential commission's final report was less decisive. It emerged as a catholic mix of the competing scientific views, combining Bandura's view that a child "learns by vicarious reinforcement" with the idea, from the uses and gratifications school, that children seek "entertainment, relaxation, or relief of boredom and loneliness" from TV. Ultimately, the commission wrote: "We believe it is reasonable to conclude that a constant diet of violent behavior on television has an adverse effect on human character and attitudes. Violence on television encourages violent forms of behavior, and fosters moral and social values about violence in daily life which are unacceptable in a civilized society." Beyond recommendations for self-regulation, the commission made one novel recommendation: "adequate and permanent financing" for the newly created public television system. Its report became public two years after the creation of that new network and just days before *Sesame Street* premiered.[29]

Frustration with perceived industry inaction and with the Eisenhower Commission's tepid findings led to the effort that became the culmination of the direct-effects critique of TV. Senator John O. Pastore chaired the committee responsible for broadcast regulation and had become the most powerful member of Congress on such issues. He thought more definitive scientific studies might prompt action after others had failed. He convinced President Richard Nixon's incoming Secretary of Health, Education, and Welfare Robert Finch to create the Surgeon General's Advisory Committee on Television and Social Behavior in April 1969. Implicitly modeled on the 1964 report in which the Surgeon General had conclusively linked cigarette smoking and lung cancer, the project symbolized the degree to which TV had become defined, especially with regard to children, as a social problem or even as a health threat. After receiving forty-three proposals, the committee funded twenty-three studies and prepared a report in late 1971.

Avoiding the Reverend Short's mistake with *Our Movie-Made Children*, the commission's summary cloaked its conclusions in cautious language, but its partisans made the most of what was there. Poorly written, its most succinct conclusion appeared in the letter transmitting the document to the Surgeon General: the research had established "a preliminary and tentative indication of a causal relation between viewing violence on television and aggressive behavior."[30] In his committee's hearings, Pastore sought to maximize the report's impact and called it "nothing less than a scientific and cultural breakthrough." "We now know there is a causal relation between televised violence and antisocial behavior which is sufficient to warrant immediate remedial action." In an article after the release of the report, one of its editors, Eli Rubinstein, asserted that Bandura's theory that children's imitation of television violence "has now been clearly demonstrated." There was "no evidence that television binds the family together"; indeed, it led to "quarreling about program selection." A year after receiving the report, the surgeon general advocated that parents do more to control what their children watched, that the government monitor the level of violence on television, that the Federal Communications Commission create a family viewing refuge in the early evening hours, and that parents demand better programs. Though the FCC did try to broker a "family hour" by the TV networks, critics failed to force the industry to adopt self-censorship as the Legion of Decency had done with Hollywood in the 1930s. However, Rubinstein proposed a "viable alternative": "expanding the role of television for positive child development rather than merely restricting the negative influences." *Sesame Street*, the only program he mentioned by name, had shown the way, he wrote.[31]

Rubinstein could have found support for his idea in an unexpected place if he had reread the Kefauver Committee hearing transcripts from 1955. Ironically, communications researcher Paul Lazarsfeld, father of the opposing uses and gratifications school of researchers, offered just such an alternative. "The aridity and the negativism of much of the discussion which takes place today," he told the senators, "can be overcome only if it is shown that there is something like a good [television] program, that there are people who can be trained to write and produce them, and that children are willing to listen [*sic*] to them." The idea of positive alternatives was not new; the WCTU had explored this avenue around the turn of the century. But Lazarsfeld's proposed combination of research and production could truly be considered the beginning of *Sesame Street*. When Gerald Lesser, who had been instrumental in developing the show's educational design, wrote a book about it, he quoted Lazarsfeld's words as an epigraph.[32]

Public television might have been expected to provide such an alternative, but it had attempted little in the way of a research-production partnership until Fred Rogers began to explore the idea. The educational television system had grown from noncommercial radio, a medium that struggled to survive since the 1920s. During the 1950s National Educational Television (NET) moved from shows that starred only a professor and a blackboard to cultural and public affairs programming intended to attract an educated, adult audience that could contribute to the system's financial support. However, none of NET's children's programs attracted much attention until Rogers brought his show, *Mister Rogers' Neighborhood*, from Canada to the United States in 1968. He created his program in consultation with psychologists and often thought and spoke in developmental terms. Children needed specific kinds of nurture and instruction depending on their age, he argued. By making his program developmentally specific, Rogers limited the size of his audience and created a distinct alternative to commercial programming. While the industry avoided narrowing its audience to maximize advertising circulation, Rogers could direct his show more clearly to young viewers' needs and not to those of advertisers, stations, and networks. As he was bringing his show to the United States, *Sesame Street* was also drawing extensively on expert advice and directing its show to a fairly narrow age range.

Though Rogers's program broke new ground with its approach, its style and philosophy followed that of *Captain Kangaroo.* "Because adults in our society aren't always available to children who are watching television, a caring adult must be on the screen," he told a Senate committee in 1969.[33] He inherited the fatherly mantle and sympathetic press coverage of the Captain as well. And like his predecessor, Rogers attracted the children of well-educated, middle-class parents, the same people that public broadcasting courted. These parents, some of television's most disgruntled critics, became some of the new public system's most loyal backers. The Public Broadcasting Service replaced NET around 1970 and brought with it bright hopes that a truly alternative system could balance a commercial industry that refused to regulate itself. Although President Richard Nixon's efforts to strangle the governmental system dimmed those hopes, *Sesame Street* became PBS's symbol and its best justification.

Protecting children from the harsh world outside, shaping their characters, and projecting middle-class values had motivated moral reformers to use censorship. A consensus no longer existed for censorship by the 1950s when television began to take hold, but the old impulses remained. *Sesame Street* drew support from those who had become alarmed by the commercialism and violence on TV but, in time, it also encountered problems with those supporters because it blurred a treasured boundary between education and mere entertainment. A middle-class desire to shield children from the ill effects of TV fueled the enthusiasm for a program that meant that youngsters did not need to be protected. Just as parents had done with *Captain Kangaroo* and *Mister Rogers' Neighborhood,* they could allow their children to enjoy *Sesame Street* free of the anxieties that popular culture had aroused in their parents and grandparents for decades. But, apart from television, the show also drew on just as strong a cultural impetus, the hope for a more fair and equal America, one from which none of its people were excluded.

CHAPTER 2

The Preschool Moment

The September 1966 issue of *Science* magazine included an editorial by Lloyd N. Morrisett, vice president of the Carnegie Corporation foundation. At the time, under the auspices of the Carnegie foundation, Joan Ganz Cooney, an educational television producer, was working with Morrisett on the early planning of *Sesame Street*. The Carnegie foundation is now better known for its support of the Killian Commission, which recommended the creation of public television the following year, but the foundation had long supported education research as well. In his *Science* piece, Morrisett made an oblique reference to Cooney's project—a reference only she and a few others would have recognized—but, in the main, he described the confluence of trends that had led to "a climate highly favorable to research and action" on early childhood education. Several decades of research had suggested that preschools like Head Start could help their impoverished students "to break out of the cycle of inadequate education, low occupational skill, [and] low pay." But Morrisett insisted that early education held hope for all young children, not just the poor. "People are asking why children cannot acquire significant intellectual skills," he wrote, "before entering first grade and thus accelerate their progress." The government's new Head Start preschools and the proposed funding for nationwide public preschools were steps in the right direction; Morrisett added that "television is an untapped resource, and its potential for early education should be fully tested."[1]

This preschool moment—when early education seemed to offer the possibility of solving great social problems—helped launch *Sesame Street*, but it also foreshadowed some of the resistance it would face. Enthusiasm for using early education and child development science to prepare poor children for success in school made *Sesame Street* attractive both to the public and to the professionals. Although the preschool's power to change American society still has its believers forty years later, this faith held much stronger sway when President Lyndon Johnson's administration created Head Start. Urgent demands to include poor and minority Americans in the American dream made Johnson's War on Poverty politically possible. But politics alone did not usher in the preschool moment. Long-term trends in early education and child science lent credence and momentum to the antipoverty aspirations. Poverty, not racial inferiority, explained low intelligence scores and poor school performance, leading experts said. Fix the learning environments of poor, black children, this line of thinking held, and they too will rise in society, beginning with success in school. This dream of upward mobility for America's most obvious outsiders excited not just federally funded preschool educators but Morrisett, Cooney, and the rest of the group that started *Sesame Street*. But there was a hitch. Experts could not agree on the specifics of what in poor children's environments hampered their intellectual development. They also wondered what the best techniques to compensate for these "deficits" in children's worlds could be. These were controversial questions, and *Sesame Street* would later become entangled in them. In short, the preschool moment gave the show momentum and engendered controversy.

Optimism about preschool was a small part of the general mood arising from economic prosperity and scientific progress. The American gross national product grew 250 percent between 1945 and 1960, while unemployment remained at or below 5 percent. The standard of living for most rose, and automobile ownership doubled. Presidential candidate Adlai Stevenson proclaimed that the nation stood "on the threshold of abundance for all." Having survived the nation's two worst crises of the twentieth century—the Great Depression and World War II—a generation of working- and middle-class Americans felt an almost unbounded confidence in the future. Feeling economically secure, young couples had children at record rates, creating a "baby boom"—a 20 percent growth in the population during the 1950s. Science and technology reinforced national confidence, as well. As an example, Jonas Salk's vaccine assured parents that this new generation would not face the threat of polio.[2]

Prosperity also seemed a vindication of "American universalism," a set of ideas that undergirded the preschool moment's optimism. These ideas began with the belief that every citizen was equal and had natural rights within a government of rational laws. Universal equality also meant that each individual had a right to rise socially and economically within a society that many Americans often boasted lacked the rigid class structure present in so many other nations. Beneath civic equality and social mobility, however, lurked a dynamic tension between these ideals and a dominant class, of British and northern European extraction, that reserved these rights and opportunities to itself. Slowly, over decades of American history, they admitted various ethnic minorities into the fold. By the mid-1950s the European ethnic groups that had immigrated between 1880 and 1920—the Italians, the Poles, and others—had moved up the social scale and joined the civic community. Like national pride in broad affluence, this social accomplishment reassured many Americans, confirming the justice of their system, at a time when the Soviet Union's putative egalitarianism was challenging it all over the globe.[3]

In the face of universalism's triumphs, African Americans, after three hundred years, had still not attained real equality, and the civil rights movement dramatized this national failure. In the 1954 *Brown v. Board of Education of Topeka* decision, the United States Supreme Court recognized that segregated schools destroyed the real and psychological potential for equality. With the support of research by Kenneth and Mamie Clark, the National Association for the Advancement of Colored People showed not only that segregated schools were inferior at educating children but also that black children had internalized a sense of personal inferiority. In the years immediately after the decision, Southern white citizens resisted the mandated remedy for inequality—integration of schools—and dramatically illustrated the paradox that beset American universalism. The Montgomery Bus Boycott, sit-ins, voting rights marches, Freedom Rides, and the March on Washington further highlighted the dimensions of civic life that equality encompassed, and these protest actions heightened the crisis. As Martin Luther King Jr. put it, "Democracy transformed from thin paper to thick action is the greatest form of government on earth."[4] Captured in press photos or, later, television footage, the violent Southern response brought Northern white sympathy for the civil rights activists. Press coverage and rhetorical eloquence, like that of King, engaged the whole nation in the struggle and helped redefine American nationalism as multiracial. The challenge posed to the nation's definition of itself galvanized action, such as the Civil Rights Act of 1964 and the Voting Rights Act of 1965. The desire to take positive action to bring about equality became a reservoir upon which the creators of *Sesame Street* also drew.

Parallel to the movement but linked to it in subtle ways, the rediscovery of poverty also worked to shatter postwar complacency and dramatize an unjust class structure. In 1963 Michael Harrington wrote in *The Other America:* "The American poor . . . are dispossessed in terms of what the rest of the nation enjoys, in terms of what the society could provide if it had the will. They live on the fringe, the margin. They watch the movies and read the magazines of affluent America, and these tell them that they are internal exiles. . . . This sense of exclusion is the source of pessimism, a defeatism that intensifies the exclusion." As with the denial of civil rights, poverty excluded particular groups of people from the national community, and Harrington specified who these groups were: "the unskilled workers, the migrant farm workers, the aged, the minorities, and all others who live in the economic underworld of American life."[5]

This "invisible land" started to become visible to the wider American public. In a popular series of anthropological studies, Oscar Lewis described a "culture of poverty" that set the poor apart and kept them impoverished. Although in this and other works he focused on Latin American peoples, he did identify "some universal characteristics which transcend national differences." Among these cultural traits, "resignation and fatalism" seemed amenable to change. Lewis and others prescribed social activism by the poor to give them a sense of control over their own destinies. On television, the 1960 CBS documentary *Harvest of Shame* revealed an isolated world of migrant workers, unknown to most of the middle-class suburbanites who consumed the produce picked by the migrants. To break out of this isolation, their children needed education. From two sociologists came another indication that poverty was trapping its victims and causing a major social problem, juvenile delinquency. Lloyd Ohlin and Richard Cloward concluded that impoverished adolescents adopted behaviors contrary to social norms because poor education and other obstacles blocked them from achieving life goals and joining the mainstream. In each of these instances, social scientists or journalists revealed sharp social divisions and their social and psychological costs. These accounts sometimes touched the sympathy of comfortably affluent Americans who had been unaware of the plight of their fellow citizens.[6]

Addressing himself to universalism's crisis, President Johnson, propelled by the postwar optimism, translated this new awareness into action with his War on Poverty. Presidential aide Eric F. Goldman polled intellectuals before the president's first State of the Union message in 1964 and found a strong consensus for an antipoverty program. Typical of the responses he received was that given by Polaroid camera inventor Edwin

Land: "Those of us who should feel responsible are for the most part completely preoccupied with the exciting, brilliant, and effective segment of American life. The [poor population] is as far away as occupants of some distant land." In the speech that followed, the president echoed the language of exclusion: "Many Americans live on the outskirts of hope—some because of poverty, and some because of their color." Our "failure to give our fellow citizens a fair chance to develop their own capacities" had been the cause of poverty, and "a lack of education" was the first way in which the nation had shortchanged the poor. He proposed the Economic Opportunity Act, which the Congress passed in August 1964. The new law created the Office of Economic Opportunity (OEO) to involve the poor in Community Action Programs (CAPs), to train the poor for private-sector jobs through the Job Corps, and to send Volunteers for America (later VISTA) into poor urban and rural areas.[7]

The president apparently struck a chord with many Americans. After his speech, President Johnson visited impoverished areas and spoke through the press to arouse sympathy for the poor. A substantial part of the public responded. As Johnson's biographer Doris Kearns put it, his enormous popular majority in the 1964 election confirmed that "the people were pleased with their president and shared his confidence in the almost limitless capacity of the American nation." The president's own private polls at the time of the Economic Opportunity Act's passage indicated general approval of between 60 and 74 percent in several northeastern states. Johnson also courted interest groups, in particular organized labor. The executive council of the AFL-CIO responded by applauding his "forthrightness and courage" in telling "affluent Americans to face up to the fact that one-fifth of the families in the richest and most productive nation of the world still live in poverty." Popular support for the "war" was general, but pollsters had not queried citizens on particular programs. Nor had Johnson won over Republican conservatives, but they resisted any antipoverty effort.[8]

A part of the support for the War on Poverty, though, also came from the fact that the president's larger reform agenda, the Great Society, included many programs for the middle class. Contrary to later memory of Johnson's efforts, they were not all directed at the poor and minorities. The Medicare program has remained popular for decades since its inception because it serves middle-class retirees as well as more impoverished ones. Environmental protection served the needs of everyone and began with Johnson's Clean Air and Water Quality Acts of 1965. When many motorists became alarmed that their automobiles might be "unsafe at any speed," they appreciated the new National Highway Traffic Safety Administration, which forced manufacturers to fix safety-related defects.[9] Subsidies for the arts and a revitalization of federal conservation also appealed to those who were not poor in America. Indeed, what most closely ties *Sesame Street* to the Great Society is the way it served different social classes and cultural constituencies. It was a program for discontented middle-class parents, but it also made blacks and Hispanics visible on children's television.

After OEO had begun to create the CAPs, the Job Corps, and VISTA, it added the Head Start preschool program. When OEO Director Sargent Shriver found he had a budget surplus in January 1965, he created a committee to design a summer school to prepare poor children for first grade. Among the eminent psychologists and pediatricians who made up the committee, Mamie Clark served as a personal link to the social science that had undergirded the *Brown* decision. Head Start emerged from the same roots as the rest of the War on Poverty. Structured like the CAPs, Head Start relied not on a central bureaucracy in Washington but on local groups across the country who applied for federal grants to run their own local programs. Unlike the CAPs, however, Head Start became more popular and less controversial because it helped innocent, poor children and because it generally became less embroiled in politics. As with film and television censorship, government expenditures could be more easily justified to help children than to help others.

Head Start also shared founding principles with the rest of the War on Poverty. A member of the planning committee, psychologist Edward Zigler, brought with him a theory like the one Ohlin and Cloward developed from research with juvenile delinquents. As with alienated youths, Zigler believed that little children faced repeated frustrations that discouraged them and prepared them for a life on the margins of society. To arrest this process, Zigler "emphasized the need for successful experiences to improve motivation." Its designers also intended Head Start to "prepare poor children for first grade by helping them overcome any fears they might have of school," according to Zigler. Like the other antipoverty programs, Head Start attempted to undo the isolation of poverty and the disabling psychology that went with it.[10]

Urie Bronfenbrenner, a child development psychologist and another member of the committee, also brought with him a theory compatible with the "maximum feasible participation" principle articulated for the CAPs. Much like Oscar Lewis, the architects of the War on Poverty believed that if the poor participated actively in efforts to improve their own lives, they would gain the sense of personal competence needed to join the social mainstream. In principle, all of the federal projects maximized this benefit as much as possible. Bronfenbrenner had conducted cross-cultural studies and created his "ecological" theory over the several years before he joined the planning committee.[11] Taking into account their health and their lives at home, his holistic approach prescribed that Head Start preschools include health care and invite parental involvement. Children would emulate their actively involved parents, the planners hoped, and would then be empowered, as Lewis predicted. More clearly than any other event, the creation of Head Start symbolized the preschool moment.

Before the antipoverty campaign of the 1960s, early education had no such ambitions. In the nineteenth century, kindergarten educators had first sought to instill morality and character in the children of the middle class. Only later did they turn their attention to socializing and Americanizing the youngsters of the immigrant poor. In short, kindergarten emerged from the larger forces of Victorian-era moral reform and Progressive child-saving. By the first two decades of the twentieth century, kindergarten—school preparation for five-year-olds—had become a common part of most large public school systems. Experimentation with education for still younger children, conducted by psychologists and educators, began at universities in the 1920s. Otherwise, children so young stayed home or went to day care. Only when the Great Depression of the 1930s made public nurseries a necessity did the government become involved with children below the age of five. Nurseries of the Works Progress Administration focused more on employing teachers and staff than on educating children. These schools suffered the stigma of any program specifically designed to care for the poor. During World War II, federal preschools cared for and educated the children of mothers working in war production. Ending with the war, these schools remained a temporary measure. Not until Head Start did the federal government again fund preschools.

With the preschool moment, early education was transformed from an unfortunate necessity to an instrument of social reform. This revolution arose not only from the larger 1960s reform impulse but also from a broad stream of social science. Though researchers did not always make the connection explicit, they undoubtedly pursued ideas in response to universalism and the civil rights movement. Their research, much of it in developmental psychology, yielded a scientific basis for the idea that preschool could enhance the intellectual growth of children enough to make a substantial difference to society as a whole. Though Head Start and other applications of this line of research addressed poor children, these scientific findings led some observers to suggest that *all* youngsters should attend school before kindergarten.

Until the 1950s the consensus in child development recognized no hope of overcoming inborn cognitive limitations. Two ideas made up the fundamentals of this earlier consensus. First, developmental psychologists believed that genetics determined intelligence. G. Stanley Hall, one of the field's founders, established this idea. Henry Goddard and Lewis Terman confirmed it through intelligence quotient (IQ) testing that showed that any individual remained in roughly the same relative position to others over the course of his or her life. Second, almost all developmentalists believed that genetics determined both the rate of growth and the ultimate level of maturity for each individual. Hall believed that the development of each individual replicated the development of animal species from lower forms to higher ones. Hall carried this idea still further. As education historian Barbara Beatty put it, he held that "human embryos went through a fish stage, young children's play repeated the social organization of 'primitive' tribes, and schoolchildren should study the Greeks, then the Romans, and so on." Though Hall's students, like Arnold Gesell, were less enamored of recapitulation, they relied every bit as much on biological and genetic explanations. Their consensus left only a limited role for environmental explanations.[12]

By the mid-1960s virtually no one in the field still held this older view, as a great many researchers had demonstrated the importance of environmental influences. The change began with the establishment in the 1920s of child development research centers at four major state universities, financed by the Laura Spellman Rockefeller Memorial Foundation. Working at the Child Welfare Research Station, Herbert Skeels and a colleague removed three listless orphan babies from a local orphanage. In a desperate attempt to find some better place for them, they placed the babies in a home for mentally retarded teenage girls. "What happened was that the fourteen-year-olds took a motherly interest in the babies and showered them with [the] attention missing in the orphanage where the infants had spent day after day in cribs with little stimulation from people or things."[13] Further research found that orphans who left the orphanage by the age of two and a half years reached an IQ approximating their adoptive parents. Those left behind suffered a steady decline in their intelligence scores. Between 1930 and 1960, a host of researchers found that animals raised in different environments developed or learned differently. Biology alone could not explain the plethora of anomalies that researchers found.

Psychologists at the Iowa center were not alone in noting the implications of this kind of research for social policy. If intelligence and learning could be affected by environment, children who seemed destined to follow their parents' lot in life could escape that fate. Contemporaneous with the orphan and animal studies, others searched for environmental factors that retarded children's development. Otto Klineberg found in 1935 that African Americans in the North outperformed those in the South on IQ tests. Earlier psychologists had postulated that only genetically superior blacks migrated, but Klineberg concluded that better education in the North had raised the migrants' scores. Further research confirmed this finding, adding that stultifying social environments and deprived home lives contributed to later poor performance in school. Additional proof came during the late 1950s and early 1960s when the state of Virginia closed its schools in defiance of federally mandated school integration. During the closure, black school children's IQ scores declined, suggesting to researchers that, without education to alleviate social deprivation, the students' intellectual growth slowed.

Psychologists Benjamin Bloom and J. McVicker Hunt carried environmental explanations to their logical conclusion in the early 1960s, setting the scene for the preschool moment. *Stability and Change in Human Characteristics*, Bloom's 1964 survey of over a thousand studies, built a convincing case for the importance of early education for the full development of human potential. Most famously, he concluded that "in terms of intelligence measured at age 17, about 50% of the development takes place between conception and age 4, about 30% between ages 4 and 8, and about 20% between ages 8 and 17." He lost no time in stating the implications of his findings: "A society which places great emphasis on verbal learning and rational problem solving and which greatly needs highly skilled and well-trained individuals to carry on political-social-economic functions in an increasingly complex world cannot ignore the enormous consequences of deprivation as it affects the development of general intelligence." Not only could deprivation be avoided, but normal development could also be enhanced. "It is hoped that we can drastically reduce the incidence of low levels of intelligence and increase the proportion of individuals reaching high levels of measured intelligence." Hunt concurred: "It is reasonable to hope to find ways of raising the level of intellectual capacity in a majority of the population." Their work had implications for ameliorating the disabilities of the poor and for nurturing the intellectual potential of all children.[14]

President Johnson and other national figures spoke publicly, not about the needs of growing children, but in terms of the nation's needs. For example, CBS Chairman William S. Paley wrote: "The dimensions of the task before education today are more demanding than ever before. Population projections as well as scientific, technical, and social developments clearly show that a whole new burden of substance and quality will be imposed." President Johnson's 1964 task force on education articulated "special contemporary reasons why education is of overriding importance to us," that is, "the crucial role of educated talent in modern society, the rise of automation, increased leisure, the umemployability of untrained men, and the knowledge explosion." The Educational Policies Commission (EPC) of the National Education Association (NEA) connected these general social needs for improved education with preschool. It endorsed "early education at public expense" because "the nation would benefit in the greater development of its people's talents and in the reduction of the need for expensive remedial work and of the incidence of dropout with its attendant economic and social ills."[15]

On the other hand, early educators who spoke in broad terms expressed more concern for the children than the nation. Cornelia Goldsmith, a professor of early education, spoke for many in her field when she wrote: "Every child has a built-in inner mechanism for exploration, finding out, trying out, testing, learning. If he doesn't use it, can't use it, is prevented from using it, it atrophies, and a human potential diminishes." Another professor of early childhood education, Norma R. Law, communicated greater anxiety. Like Goldsmith, she primarily expressed concern for the "individuality and developmental strengths" of preschoolers. But she also derided the nation's "discovery" of young children for "the federal subsidy and public goodwill they represent to many school people, or for the status-by-proxy they represent to many parents, or for the national jump-ahead they represent to many other citizens." She expressed her fear that hastily planned new preschool programs could alienate children and warned that they "could lose us our children if we don't watch out." All these leaders and educators spoke in universal and classless terms; all credited education with the power to change every child's life, not just those who had suffered deprivation. Law's discordant note signaled how quickly the preschool consensus could encounter conflicts over nurture when national action moved beyond schooling poor children to including their middle-class peers. What prompted Law's admonition was a short-lived campaign to make preschool available in all the country's public schools.[16]

Optimistic forecasts, like those of Bloom and Hunt, triggered this effort. Before the EPC made its recommendations, earlier National Education Association (NEA) panels had used the language of universality, which led naturally to public preschools for children not in poverty. In its 1963 report, the Project on Instruction called for "opportunities for developing the individual potentialities represented in the wide range of differences among people."[17] Though this statement appeared in the context of an ongoing struggle against segregated schools, the group envisioned no conflict between the universal and the individual. In 1966 the EPC took the same logic to its next step:

> Early education is advisable for all children, not merely because of the need to offset any disadvantages in their background, but also because they are ready by the age of four for a planned fostering of their development and because educators know some of the ways to foster it through school programs. Early education has long been available to the well-to-do, and it is commendable that governments are now acting on the need to make it available to some of the poor. But the large middle group should have the same opportunities.
>
> The opportunity for early education at public expense should therefore be universal. The nation would benefit in the greater development of its people's talents and in the reduction of the need for expensive remedial work and of the incidence of dropout with its attendant economic and social ills.[18]

Ironically, universality in this context did not mean to assimilate previously excluded minorities but meant instead to offer all children public preschool, which previously had only been offered to disadvantaged youngsters.

Both the federal government and the NEA followed up on the EPC's report. President Johnson endorsed universal preschool. Congressman Roman Pucinski proposed to provide $350 million of aid to local school districts to handle the additional students. At its convention in the summer of 1966, the NEA voted to include in its list of continuing goals, under the rubric "educational opportunity for all," a "provision for the educational needs of children before the age of entrance to the first grade." But the NEA, in plenum session, refused to endorse specific action on universal preschool, and no bill ever left committee in Congress.[19]

Resistance from school administrators may have played a part in the NEA's rejection of the idea. Right after the commission released its report, a poll of sixteen thousand administrators indicated that only 9 percent expected to start a new preschool program and 22 percent a new kindergarten during the following year. Their most common problems in starting the new programs were finding sufficient classroom space, money, and staff. The proposed federal government aid might have eased these problems, but Arthur H. Rice, a commentator in the journal of the school administrators' association, pointed out that federal aid would bring with it "guidelines" to be met. Support for preschools would have come on the heels of the Elementary and Secondary Education Act (ESEA), a massive program of federal grants to local school districts to promote desegregation and other improvements, passed just the previous year. Wary of another intrusive program so soon after passage of ESEA and jealously guarding their autonomy, administrators may have voted against the preschool resolution at the NEA convention.[20]

But more salient for debate at that meeting—and more emotional— was the stigma that marked preschools in the eyes of some educators. Rice wrote that universal preschool "is not desirable now, and I hope the American home never deteriorates to the point where very young children are put into a lock step through any form of public education." At the convention, Mabel M. Mitchell, a high school English teacher from Boulder City, Nevada, offered a substitute resolution that endorsed an expansion of universal education and compensatory preschool for deprived four-year-olds. However, it did not sanction preschool for *all* children. Instead, her proposal asserted "the principle that the home and family are the basic unit in our free society and that parents have prime responsibility for the character development of their children." The resolution implied that preschool was unnecessary for middle-class children and that it threatened to disrupt their nurture within the family. For the middle class, the home remained a haven to be protected from intrusions by educators as well as by television. Early education apparently remained, for these NEA members, an extraordinary, child-saving measure for the poor.[21]

Fueling the debate over that idea was a broader dispute over the purpose of early education. Much of the environmentalist research had focused on the "deficits" that poor children brought to school with them. Following the lead of these researchers, preschool designers attempted to compensate for these handicaps. But the knowledge of these youngsters' disadvantages remained fragmentary, forcing educators to work from incomplete theories of "cultural deprivation." Some researchers concluded that authoritarian parenting styles delayed language development and, with it, cognitive development. Others concluded that children lacked self-esteem or motivation to succeed in school. Those who worked to apply these insights created a variety of curricula to compensate for the various deficits in the children's environments. Researchers often began from middle-class norms; racial and social class biases shaped their thinking. By the early 1970s, psychologists like Kenneth Clark and Herbert Ginsburg denounced the entire concept of cultural deprivation and put the blame squarely on an educational system designed for the middle class. The *Sesame Street* project, in its earliest planning, turned to experts to plan its curriculum and found itself in quandary similar to those who ran preschools: how to help prepare poor children for schools when the research suggested compensation for deficits that might be real or simply misconceptions.[22]

The same environmentalist research that led to notions of cultural deprivation just as readily justified the attempt to achieve full realization of every child's potential, even those from middle-class backgrounds. As the universal preschool debate illustrated, a great many Americans were not willing to put little children in school for any reason less compelling than profound social problems, like inequality. Even if compensation became the consensual purpose for preschools, educators could still not untangle this mission from related questions of curriculum. Should schools solely nurture the youngsters' emotional resources and social skills, or should they begin teaching the academic rudiments? Diverse preschool curricula emerged from the various constructions of early education's purpose.

When Head Start began, the predominant philosophy and approach had emerged from Progressive education principles. Preschool curricula had been developing for nearly two hundred years. Until the end of the nineteenth century, America's scattered kindergartens had followed the pioneering German system created by Friedrich Froebel, which principally developed children's intellects. By 1920 Progressive educators such as Lucy Sprague Mitchell, a colleague of philosopher John Dewey, supplanted the Froebelian approach with a more holistic one. They sought to encourage a child's physical, emotional, social as well as intellectual development and concentrated on the interaction of teacher and child rather than on the child's interaction with curricular materials, as Froebel had. The Progressives also concerned themselves more with practical curriculum development than with theoretical elaboration, using naturalistic observation more than formal testing. Although they dominated preschool practice by the 1960s, they had not created a single, cohesive system but more a broad philosophy and approach.

Educators and theorists at the Bank Street College of Education in New York City began to systematize the Progressive methods which, by the 1960s, had become known as "traditional" nursery school. These schools had long taken as curricular goals cooperation, self-esteem, and self-expression. Barbara Biber, the college's primary theorist in the 1960s and 1970s, further elaborated these objectives. Even with systematizing, the

Progressive, holistic, and humanistic philosophy endured. Unlike others who would teach specific skills, Biber advocated for "the earlier ideal image of a curious, creative, problem-solving, socially sensitive individual." Nurturing the child's free inquiry and self-expression dictated a classroom in which children could choose their own activities and play with a wide variety of developmentally appropriate toys. Teachers were to establish trusting relationships with their students and plan activities—like craft projects, songs, stories, and games—to further develop children's creativity and social adjustment.[23]

Though the Bank Street approach became the model of choice for Head Start, the preschool moment and the deprivation theories opened the door for alternative models. Among them was Susan Gray's Early Training Project in Tennessee, which modified a traditional school to serve the needs of disadvantaged children more closely. Her preschool tried to motivate its students to succeed in school, "to stimulate language development, [and] to encourage the child to order and classify the objects and events of the world." Another prominent model for Head Start was Cynthia and Martin Deutsch's Institute for Developmental Studies. Like Gray, the Deutsches used formal testing to plan instruction and to evaluate effectiveness. They also began with a traditional setting and focused on verbal interaction, "sensorimotor stimulation," "perceptual discriminations," "positive self-identifications," and "task perseverance." They trained their teachers to lead traditional small-group discussions to teach letters and letter sounds more methodically in the hope of improving expressive language skills. Dividing children into tracked groups and using teaching machines, the Deutsches went beyond the traditional format to create a cognitively oriented program. Edward Zigler took a leading role in designing Head Start and preferred the Bank Street approach to these more cognitive ones.[24]

Head Start took a holistic approach encompassing a cognitive, motivational, and social curriculum along with providing health care. Pediatricians involved in the program's planning insisted that children could not learn unless they received the basic medical attention they were not already getting. Bronfenbrenner and others pointed to the importance of involving the students' parents. A 1965 "Handbook for Head Start" from the Urban Child Center at the University of Chicago gives a glimpse of an early curriculum for the preschools. Like Gray and the Deutsches, it focuses on "verbal communication" and "visual abilities." It explains to the teacher accustomed to middle-class children that "these children do not use speech as we know it to communicate." The booklet's "suggestions" are designed

Teacher: [*Presents picture of rifle*] This is a _____ .

Child B: Gun.

Teacher: Good. It is a gun. Let's say it: This is a gun. This is a gun. Again. This is a gun. This is a weapon.

Child D: No, it ain't no weapon.

Teacher: [*Presents pictures of knife, cannon, pistol*] This is a weapon. This is a weapon. This is a weapon. These are weapons. Say it with me. This is a weapon. This is a weapon. This is a weapon. These are weapons. Let's hear that last one again. Make it buzz. These are weaponzzz.

[*Refers to knife picture*] This weapon is a _____. Who knows?

Child E: A knife.

Teacher: Yes, a knife. Let's say it. This weapon is a knife. Again. This weapon is a knife.

[*Refers to cannon*] This weapon is a _____. Who knows?

Child C: Battle.

Teacher: That's pretty good. You use this thing in a battle, but it's called a cannon. This weapon is a *cannon.* Say it everybody. This weapon is a *cannon.*

Is this a *battle*? . . . No, this is *not* a battle. This weapon is a _____. Come on, tell me.

Children A and D: Cannon.

Teacher: Here's the rule: [*Claps rhythmically*] If you use it to hurt somebody, then it's a weapon. Again. If you use it to hurt somebody, then it's a weapon. Say it with me. If you use it to hurt somebody, then it's a weapon. One more time. If you use it to hurt somebody, then it's a weapon. And if it's a weapon, what do you do with it? Do you tickle somebody with it?

Children: No.

Teacher: Well if it's a weapon, do you use it to hurt somebody? Yes. What do you use a gun for?

Child A: Shoot.

Teacher: That's good, A. And do you hurt somebody when you shoot him?

Child C: Maybe kill 'im dead.

Child D: That hurt.

Teacher: Yes, you use a gun to hurt somebody. And what's the rule?

[*Dialogue continues*]

Fig. 1. Sample classroom dialogue from Bereiter-Engelmann method. Adapted from Carl Bereiter and Siegfried Engelmann, *Teaching Disadvantaged Children in Preschool* (Englewood Cliffs, N.J.: Prentice-Hall, 1966), 105–9.

"to help children become skillful at observation." But it goes beyond these cognitive rudiments to "building a sense of self," "creativity and self-expression," and "developing curiosity through science." Though the booklet stresses distinctive traits of disadvantaged youngsters, it also presumes a more traditional style of classroom, too, instructing teachers to "use the same techniques . . . used in many excellent preschool programs for middle-class children." This short curriculum closes with an encouraging note to new teachers: "contact with a single, dedicated, committed and understanding teacher can make a difference." A later, more official and fully elaborated Head Start curriculum confirms that Bank Street's holistic philosophy endured.[25]

More at odds with the conservative Head Start designers than Gray and the Deutsches were Carl Bereiter and his partner Siegfried Engelmann. They "drilled [their students] like marines," according to one approving observer. Bereiter and Engelmann shared the general consensus that a major stumbling block for poor children when they reached school was their lack of standard English language skills. To teach them the syntax and logic of language, these two educators put their students through repetitious drills. For these a teacher had the children stand in rows and instructed them through an exchange like the one in figure 1. Some of their "basic teaching strategies" included "use questions liberally," "use repetition," "clap to accent basic language patterns and conventions," and "encourage thinking behavior." Their curriculum also covered colors, counting, rhyming, and some letter and word recognition. Bereiter later explained, "We cared about the children . . . [and] their emotional stability was the justification for such careful programming of skills—to make learning a less frustrating experience." Many children enjoyed this approach; many parents approved of it. Writer Maya Pines, who enthusiastically endorsed it, noted that after a year of such instruction, children had reached the first grade level in language and second grade level in math.[26]

Many preschool theorists and practitioners did not share this enthusiasm for Bereiter's system. To some in the early education field, his school set up "work and play . . . [as] polar opposites" and created "an atmosphere of puritanical zeal" in which "delight in original expression" was "a devil's pleasure." Other opponents elaborated on this theme. In their view, his method utilized "operant conditioning," treated the student "as passive and non-purposive," and left "no place for feelings, sensitivities, creativity, or a sense of autonomy in learning." In a similar vein, others questioned whether Bereiter's students had not really learned to speak and think but only to parrot full sentences back like a child learning a nursery rhyme. If given a chance, children would learn the rules that lay behind language usage, such as how to form plural nouns, one of Bereiter's opponents wrote.[27]

On the other hand, Cooney was impressed when she visited Bereiter's school in 1966, as a part of the research that led to *Sesame Street*. "I went out to see his classes," she later remembered. "He believed that you really had to discipline [the students] and teach them and make them memorize the ABCs, learn to speak up. [The instructors] would shout at the kids; the kids would shout the answers back. It was a very interesting thing and had a profound impact on me." Cooney included Bereiter's fifteen "minimum abilities needed by a child about to enter first grade" in her first planning report for *Sesame Street*. The show itself later used some of the same principles, such as repetition, rhythm, and rhyming.[28]

Just as *Sesame Street* emerged as a positive solution to the problem of children and television, Cooney and her collaborators wanted to use TV to reach the children Head Start could not. In doing so, the show entered into the controversies surrounding preschool curricula. Bank Street's nurturing and self-directed style of preschool could not be reproduced on television, but certain elements of Bereiter's drill could be. If entering the world of early education brought controversy, it also promised public enthusiasm. Head Start was popular because it held out the hope that poverty could be overcome through education. Any show that could bring the "boob tube" into such noble work could expect support from much of the public. The dream of real social equality was one Americans would let themselves dream in the 1960s. But the dream had at its heart changing the poor and not the economic system. This approach avoided powerful opponents, but it also led into the realm of deprivation theories, which during *Sesame Street*'s first seasons came into disrepute because they blamed the poor for their own plight. Riding the energy of social reform while not being dashed on the controversies challenged the show's planners from the beginning.

CHAPTER 3

"A New Bloom
on the Wasteland"

In the winter of 1966, Joan Ganz Cooney invited a few friends to her apartment for a dinner party. She and Lewis Freedman, her boss at the local educational TV station, and her friend Lloyd N. Morrisett, a executive at the Carnegie Corp. foundation, soon fell into conversation about children and television. Freedman waxed eloquent about the educational potential of television. Morrisett wondered whether it could teach basic cognitive skills. He and Cooney became intrigued with TV's potential to reach quickly and cheaply far more poor children than Head Start and experimental preschools, with their limited funding, ever could. The kind of programs that Freedman was talking about would be a big improvement over what children had to watch, Morrisett thought. The father of two young children, he awoke one morning to find his daughter Sarah staring at a test pattern on the television screen waiting for a program—any program—to come on. Cooney, Morrisett, and Freedman agreed to talk some more about an educational show for children.[1]

With a willing television station to produce a show and an interested foundation to fund it, bringing their idea to reality seemed within reach. Freedman and Cooney met with Morrisett at the Carnegie foundation's offices and discussed the possibilities for a television show to be produced by Channel 13. They suggested to the Carnegie foundation that the show have a variety format with crafts, puppet shows, and visits to firehouses, zoos, libraries and such. It ought to be broadcast twice a day five days a week and "have a live quality to it, i.e. be taped instead of filmed," they recommended. It "would be entertaining and attractive to the children and, at the same time, educational." However, by the end of the year, Freedman was no longer program director at the station, and Cooney quit Channel 13 a few months later when its management rejected the proposed show. For his part, Morrisett knew that Carnegie was unwilling to finance the project on its own, and he and his staff sought other sources of funds. Two years ensued during which Cooney, Morrisett, and others searched for the means to bring *Sesame Street* to the air.[2]

Between 1966 and 1968, they worked to reinvent educational children's television and struggled to keep control of the project and its meaning. They settled basic questions to shape that new vision. What would the show teach? Who would produce it and broadcast it? Who would pay for it and make sure children learned from it? Which children would be in its intended audience? Above all, why pursue the project at all? Defining the show's larger purpose—fighting poverty, improving television—made it possible to obtain funding from federal agencies and the Ford Foundation as well as from the Carnegie foundation. But it also brought more players into the game of defining who the program's audience would be and how it would be produced. Ironically, a longtime commercial broadcasting executive, Louis Hausman, represented the government and sought to maximize its control of the project. He also tried to shape it in accord with the industry from which he had come. Cooney and Morrisett outmaneuvered Hausman to gain a great degree of independence to pursue their vision. Though they retained control of the project, larger questions of audience and mission remained open to debate among the funding agencies and the public.

Between June and October 1966, Cooney took a leave of absence from Channel 13 to research and write a feasibility study for Carnegie. When she and Morrisett began work on the project, they represented two compatible but distinct sides of the *Sesame Street* ethos. She had been working in television for twelve years. During the 1950s, she had worked as a publicist for the *U.S. Steel Hour* (ABC, 1953–55; CBS, 1955–63), an anthology drama praised by the critics. An ambitious career woman and an idealistic Catholic, she was working in television to "make a difference." In 1962, she heard that New York would soon have an educational station. She left commercial TV to produce public affairs and cultural programs at Channel 13. Once there, she became disappointed with the small size of the station's audience.

Nevertheless, two of her productions gained some attention. In her documentary about Cynthia and Martin Deutsch's preschool, Cooney described a program that became a prototype for Head Start. OEO adopted her *A Chance at the Beginning* as an orientation film for its teachers. Later she and Freedman created *Poverty, Anti-Poverty, and the Poor*, a live program that resembled town meeting shows of the 1990s. On the air, ordinary citizens confronted a panel of local government officials for three hours. "Floor participants . . . let fly with statements, criticisms, challenges and, occasionally, questions," wrote Jack Gould in the *New York Times* the next day; "the sight of so many varying personalities speaking with such earnestness was intellectually absorbing and visually interesting." Cooney won a local Emmy award for the program. But even her Emmy did not diminish her frustration with the limited audience for educational TV.[3]

Given Cooney's success in adult television, Lewis Freedman must not have been the only one surprised to learn that she was interested in producing a children's show, but her interest testifies to the same ambition and idealism that took her to Channel 13 in the first place. Unlike Morrisett, she had no children of her own. She later recalled that the project presented an opportunity to join with Morrisett in a TV experiment and to escape the frustration of making documentaries for such minuscule audiences. This new program held out the possibility of changing television, helping millions of children, and reaching a much larger audience. Years later, when *Sesame Street* premiered and journalist Les Brown called her "St. Joan," he may have perceived Cooney's sense of mission.[4]

Morrisett matched Cooney's television experience with his own in psychology and experimental preschool programs. He began his career with a Ph.D. in cognitive psychology but left university teaching for work at the Carnegie foundation. During the 1960s, the foundation's two presidents, John Gardner and Alan Pifer, had emphasized, respectively, education and social reform. Morrisett became vice president in 1964 and worked with both men. Under their leadership, Carnegie made grants to Carl Bereiter for his school and to Jerome Bruner, William Kessen, and Jerome Kagan for their developmental and cognitive research. Another experimental school that Carnegie supported was run by Herbert L. Sprigle, who, ironically, later became an important critic of *Sesame Street*. The foundation funded Maya Pines's study of the "revolution" in cognitive early education as well. In it, she contrasted traditional preschool systems with many theorists and educators, and even with teaching machines. During *Sesame Street*'s earliest planning, when Cooney was working on her study, Morrisett put her in touch with many of these people and those in the world of child development and education research. He understood the preschool moment and the opportunity it presented for an experimental children's program, as his editorial in *Science* had indicated. But he also wanted better shows for children like his daughter Sarah to watch, shows that could cultivate in their viewers a taste for better programming in the hopes that they would then demand better programming from the commercial broadcasters.[5]

Some of the most basic things about *Sesame Street* originated with Cooney's and Morrisett's attitudes toward television and their ambitions for their project. She was more intent on its being as popular as it could be and that it reach and teach as many children as possible. While he shared these hopes, Morrisett could also imagine the show as a social scientific experiment in children's education by TV. In those very early days, no one working on the project had worked out fully how it would change children's TV or even whether it would at all. They focused instead on formulating its educational philosophy and finding the money to pay for it.

In the first year after that fateful dinner party, Cooney studied the feasibility of producing a television show rooted in child development science and proposed that Channel 13 produce such a program. She, Morrisett, and the Carnegie foundation presumed that, upon completion of the study, she would return to the station, write a proposal to its management, and Channel 13 would produce the program. If successful, it could then be distributed to other educational stations. During the summer of 1966, she visited experts in children's development, education, and media across the United States and Canada. The experts confirmed that a television show might prepare preschoolers, and she argued in her study that TV possessed great untapped potential. She supported this argument with her own ideas about how to translate the experts' developmental insights and curricular goals into televisual instruction. She completed the feasibility study in November 1966 and submitted her proposal to the station the following March. For her station's management, she added details of concern to them, such as distribution, and removed some of the educational logic included in the first study.

From this early period, Cooney argued that educational television had to recognize—and accept—the expectations that commercial TV cultivated in even its youngest viewers. Television was already reaching almost all of America's preschoolers, whom Cooney identified as the medium's most regular viewers. To reach and hold this large audience, the proposed show would have to take into consideration their expectations and their viewing circumstances. "Indeed, because of the constant competition presented by entertainment programs on television, educational material must be just as lively, fast-moving and dramatically presented as standard TV fare, if [the show] hopes to win a sizeable audience." To win those viewers over to it, the program had to be "highly visual, slickly and expensively produced." Like television advertisements, she wrote, it should utilize "frequent repetition, clever visual presentation, brevity and clarity." She anticipated that making the program as much like existing TV fare as possible—a proposition that many supporters of educational programming found dubious—would be "risking the criticism of educational purists."[6]

Balancing popular appeal and educational value was essential to stem the potential criticism of educators and parents, and the experts backed up Cooney's assertion that television could teach. When she completed her research for the feasibility study, she could cite many "leading educators" and child development specialists who approved of the idea of a TV program. She wrote that "almost no one doubted that television could play a potent role in preschool education."[7] Her list of experts included influential developmentalists like Jerome Bruner, Jeanne Chall, Jerome Kagan, and Barbara Biber as well as psychologists, preschool educators, and Head Start leaders.[8]

Defining what made the show "educational" required that Cooney make curricular choices, and she again risked creating opposition to the project. She boldly set the program in opposition to "traditional," Progressive-style preschools, like those that the Bank Street College of Education championed. When she wrote a later, final proposal for the program, she ironically invoked Newton Minow's image for television and called the dominant form of preschool an "educational wasteland." Even in her earlier, more cautious, feasibility study, she wrote, "educators were virtually ignoring the intellect of preschool children" in favor of an emphasis on the "child's sense of well-being and emotional adjustment." She suggested instead that "television's potential for fostering the intellectual and cultural development of young children be fully tested and evaluated" because "emotional, physical and intellectual needs are doubtless interdependent from infancy on."[9]

Cooney elaborated further with lists of goals for intellectual development. She drew on these five basic ones from the Educational Testing Service:

1. Basic Language Skills
2. Concepts of Space and Time (shapes, forms, spatial perspective, the notion of time)
3. Beginning of Logical Concepts (logical classification, concepts of relationships)

4. Beginning Mathematical Concepts (conservation of quantity, one-to-one correspondence, number relations)
5. The Growth of Reasoning Skills (cause and effect, reasoning by association and inference)[10]

These five points included many of the elements of what became the instructional goals of *Sesame Street* two years later. In her study, Cooney also cited four "general signs of development" and fifteen "abilities" from the experimental preschool of Carl Bereiter and Siegfried Engelmann. In the seven sections that followed these objectives, she proposed format ideas for the show, all of which related to either the basic ETS goals or the four general signs. Though the program would teach through popular forms like puppetry and animation, its curriculum would put it squarely in the cognitive preschool camp, and its entertainment would be tied to specific teaching goals.[11]

Though Cooney described the style of the program and its curriculum in universal terms, without reference to the special needs of poor children, she did address their needs in a section at the end of her study. A similar section appeared in the middle of the later 1968 proposal.[12] She proposed no special curriculum or distinctive content to help disadvantaged youngsters in particular. Instead, she proposed outreach efforts to insure that poor children watched the show along with supplementary activities to reinforce the lessons it taught. For example, she included a suggestion from Henry Chauncey, founder and president of Educational Testing Service. He recommended that "volunteer-mothers" host daily "'classes' of six or seven children" in their own homes to watch the show and follow up with an activity like a craft or science project. When Cooney had consulted the experts, she found them evenly divided between those who believed that deprived children simply lagged behind their middle-class peers and those who had concluded that they would never develop the needed skills without intervention. Given the scientific uncertainties of the time and the notoriety that such judgments later gained, she wisely avoided joining the fray. As it was, Bereiter "objected" that the program "was being conceived at too advanced a level for disadvantaged children . . . and that its aims were too general."[13]

Cooney's own position on how the program should be changed to appeal to a diverse audience of preschoolers more clearly emerged in her discussion of a little-known educational show then on the air. With funding from the United States Office of Education (OE), WETA, the educational station in Washington, D.C., produced *Roundabout* especially for African-American preschoolers. An African-American man, Milton Rooks, was the host of the program, on which he taught some science and math. He also introduced viewers to people children might typically meet in their neighborhoods, such as barbers and policemen. The show included unrehearsed children expressing themselves creatively through music, dance, and puppetry. After watching the program, Cooney commented in her study that, though it was "well produced," the series probably had not "won a large 'at-home' audience." In the "overcrowded" homes in which most poor children lived, she wrote, the television is "on from early morning until late at night and is simply one more thing contributing to the din and confusion characteristic of most impoverished homes." There was little chance, she imagined, that such a family would "quiet down and permit a preschool child to concentrate on a children's program." Perhaps, to her way of thinking, the sort of program she envisioned—one using "clever visual presentation," for example—stood a better chance of competing with the "din and confusion." But she gave no further indication that the show she proposed would need to be crafted especially to reach an audience of minority or disadvantaged youngsters. Her original study made no effort to address what was later called the "achievement gap" between middle-class and poor children. A later promise that *Sesame Street* could close this gap became a major source of criticism for the show.[14]

When Cooney completed her feasibility study in the fall of 1966, she expected to go back to Channel 13 and bring the show to the air. For the station she wrote a proposal that it produce the show with a budget of four million dollars and distribute it through National Educational Television (NET). Cooney would direct a semi-autonomous production unit within Channel 13. The proposal closely followed the language and logic of the feasibility study. Not only did the station's president reject the proposal, he also questioned Cooney's expertise. She soon quit and returned to the Carnegie foundation as a full-time consultant in May 1967.[15]

Once she left Channel 13, finding or creating an organization to produce the show became a problem to be added to the more immediate one: money. While Cooney was trying to persuade the station to take on the project, Carnegie searched in vain for financial backers. The foundation would not pay the entire cost and could not find partners willing to share it. Several potential backers, including the Ford Foundation and the National Endowment for the Humanities, turned the idea down. Barbara Finberg, an executive associate at Carnegie, worked with Cooney planning the project and made several visits to Washington in search of funding from the Office of Education. OE officials told Finberg and Cooney that funding would have to come through grants to individual states, which would then pass the funds through to the television project. The Carnegie foundation concluded that this arrangement would have been unworkable.[16]

Morrisett stepped in and used his acquaintanceship with the commissioner of OE, Harold Howe II, to try to interest him in the project. Howe took an immediate liking to the proposed preschool show.[17] When he received Cooney's study from Morrisett, he arranged a meeting with several of his subordinates, representatives of several federal agencies, and Cooney, Morrisett, and Finberg. Despite resistance from his associate commissioners, Howe committed his agency to funding half the project's cost. Some could come from OE research funds at his discretion; some would come from other agencies that he could persuade to contribute. Along with these others, OE's support moved the focus of the project more clearly to serving the needs of poor children than Cooney had originally envisioned. While serving as commissioner of education from 1966 to 1969, Howe concentrated on school desegregation and aid to schools with large numbers of impoverished students. He told the National Congress of Parents and Teachers: "This nation is engaged in a great crusade aimed at giving all citizens equal opportunity to achieve their potential, irrespective of race, religion, or national origin. The schools are central to that crusade." After his meeting with the Carnegie foundation, Howe wrote to the director of Head Start and suggested that its preschools might take advantage of the "good solid block of effective television programs for preschoolers" that the project promised. This shift in the intended audience apparently did not preoccupy Carnegie at the time. Half of the cost was now covered, and they expected that finding the other half would now be easier.[18]

Perhaps Cooney and her colleagues did not focus on the audience shift because Howe's offer of support brought with it a major rival for control of the project. The commissioner assigned his special assistant, Louis Hausman, to guide Carnegie's preparation of a proposal for the project, which Howe could use to convince other federal agencies to help fund the program. To this task, Hausman brought expertise unusual in the education bureaucracy: years of commercial broadcasting experience. In much of his more than two decades with CBS and NBC, he had worked in public relations. In between these two positions, he headed the Television Information Office (TIO), created in the wake of the quiz show scandal to improve the image of commercial TV. During the 1960s, for example, the TIO published a weekly guide on how teachers might use commercial TV programs in the classroom. Hausman wrote in the foreword to the TIO's book about children's programming, *For the Young Viewer*, that the book "is for all those who hold a prime concern with improving children or television—or both." From the beginning, Hausman approved of Carnegie's proposal to use commercial television entertainment for educational purposes, but for him that meant using producers from the industry. A struggle ensued between the Carnegie foundation and Hausman over how the show would be produced.[19]

During the second half of 1967, Hausman made suggestions to Cooney and Morrisett about the project's budget and production organization. There was little disagreement when Hausman recommended that the budget be increased considerably. Apparently Cooney and Morrisett had not shown him the Channel 13 proposal because years later he recalled their initial cost estimates to be between $1 million and $2 million, not the $4 million Cooney had proposed to the station. He advocated a figure between $4 million and $5 million in the summer of 1967, which, by March 1968, he and the others working on the project raised to $8 million.[20]

What was important about these raw figures was the way that Hausman equated cost and popularity. When he was told that Cooney had used per-hour production costs from *Captain Kangaroo*, Hausman argued that these figures were too low to produce a truly popular show. "Captain Kangaroo gets no audience in terms of mass media," he wrote. "It gets the audiences of youngsters of middle-class suburban parents who think their little children should see it."[21] Though the logic of equating cost and appeal may or may not be valid, Cooney had expressed a similar conclusion when she had said "impecunious educational television stations" had produced children's shows "too often marked by a slow and monotonous pace and a lack of professionalism."[22] Although for many parents *Kangaroo* had become a symbol of entertainingly educational television, Hausman articulated an industry view that *Sesame Street* would have to model itself on more popular children's programs if it was to prove that education could attract a large audience.

Along with the budget, Hausman suggested an approach to production: contracting with commercial production companies. At issue was the best means of enlisting the expertise of commercial professionals to make the show comparable to those on the networks. Hausman and Cooney agreed that a generous budget, among other things, would allow the project to hire experienced, proven writers, producers, performers, and technical talent—the people who could produce a popular show. Hausman assumed that the project could tap this talent only by hiring the production companies that employed them. Cooney disagreed.

At issue, however, was more than the best way to enlist proven talent; ultimately, control of the project was also at stake. The production process

Hausman recommended gave OE and any other funders tighter control. He proposed that the project create an advisory committee to choose a production company. The committee "would consist of three or four 'show biz' types plus one or two experts in early childhood education." They would select four or five film or television production companies. These, in turn, would receive guidance from the committee about the content of their pilot episodes and about $100,000 each to produce a pilot. When completed, NET would broadcast these prototype shows, and the popularity of each would be gauged. The Carnegie foundation could further test the pilots in several cities "with large ghetto populations," he suggested. "That's how mass-appeal entertainment TV is produced. There is no reason that a similar method shouldn't be employed in this project." Though not identical to the commercial industry's approach, Hausman's system would not have required the semi-autonomous production unit Cooney had called for in her Channel 13 proposal. His commercial model would have also made all of the content decisions before the premiere broadcast.[23]

Though the Carnegie foundation agreed about the budget, they opposed Hausman's production plan. Cooney remarked years later, "That wouldn't have worked. He didn't know that." While he contended that educational television could not produce a popular program, Cooney and her colleagues doubted that commercial producers could create an educational show. When Morrisett, in search of funding, contacted a possible commercial backer for the project, Westinghouse Broadcasting, Cooney did not believe that the company "had in mind anything close to the kind of quality programming" that she and Carnegie were seeking. Her colleague, Barbara Finberg, cited the decline in the popularity of *Ding Dong School* as proof that commercialism interfered with education. She concluded that parents stopped their children from watching the show because its host had promoted products that her young viewers then asked their parents to buy. Hausman's proposal promised to keep advertising out, but, because commercial television had repeatedly put education at a lower priority than profit, the Carnegie foundation had reason to doubt for-profit producers.[24]

Whether or not he did so to placate Hausman, Morrisett met with the three commercial networks (NBC, CBS, and ABC) and tried to interest them in backing *Sesame Street*. It is unclear whether he shared the skepticism of Cooney and Finberg, but he later recalled hoping that OE's promise to cover half the cost would convince one of the networks to fund the rest. When he met with them, during the latter half of 1967, however, none showed more than "polite interest." NBC considered it but found that the most appropriate time to broadcast it was during hours reserved for its affiliate stations to put on their own programs. In the end, none of the networks offered to broadcast or help finance the show. With Channel 13 out as a producer and the networks uninterested, the Carnegie foundation would have to find a new alternative.[25]

To find another way, Morrisett convened a meeting of television industry professionals in the fall of 1967. He and Hausman agreed on a list of six men, four with commercial broadcasting experience as network executives and program producers and two who worked for NET. At the meeting, Lewis Freedman, Cooney's old boss and one of the two from NET, suggested that the new show could not be produced by any existing organization. The group concurred and recommended the creation of an independent production company affiliated with NET that would provide administrative support but no programming supervision. This semi-independent organization would contract with outside production companies for cartoons and films. A few months later, NET accepted this arrangement. Hausman was mollified because commercial producers would be supplying the content with little interference from the educational broadcasters.[26]

The idea of creating a semi-independent production unit did not provide, however, a complete alternative to Hausman's proposed system. Whatever structure the project devised, it would have to demonstrate that the show actually taught children specific lessons. Hausman's approach would have put a committee of advisers in charge of selecting a commercial producer's pilot and fully testing it in advance of the series' broadcast. Doing so would have left the committee to supervise a production contractor who would attempt to create 130 series episodes that taught as effectively as the pilot had. By contrast, Cooney's and Morrisett's semi-autonomous production company gave the project's management direct, day-to-day control of production. But it left the system with no independent evaluation of the show, which Hausman, on behalf of OE, demanded.

Cooney had implicitly proposed a validation procedure in the Channel 13 proposal that OE apparently never saw. In it she included in the three-year project "an experimental year of production and broadcasting in order to ascertain what techniques of entertaining and educating are most popular and effective with young children and whether such a proposed use of television meets with wide acceptance and interest from educators, parents, children-oriented agencies in local communities and, of course, the children themselves."[27] In short, she asked the backers to fund an entire year of production at the beginning, while Hausman wanted to commit initially only to a series of pilots. With his approach, OE would maintain greater control before the project had spent all of the money, in much the same way that the networks could pay for a pilot and later decline to buy the subsequent series. With Cooney's plan, they would have to design an evaluation system that could assure OE and other backers that the show fulfilled its mission.

In October 1967 Morrisett called together another group of experts to create the language and logic of an experimental system of production. He gathered four psychology professors apparently by first contacting Gerald Lesser, a friend from graduate school. Lesser taught at Harvard and had done extensive research in educational psychology, including how social class and ethnicity interacted with school achievement.[28] But he also had some highly relevant television experience. When NBC produced and aired the children's series *Exploring* in response to Newton Minow's "wasteland" speech, it was Lesser who advised the producers. Of the other three professors at Morrisett's seminar, one was Lesser's partner on a recently published article and another was the chairman of his department. In the years that followed this meeting, Lesser became the *Sesame Street* project's guide through the intricacies of child development science. But he was also the one who most keenly understood that to bring research insights to bear on television production meant creating close working relationships between the scientists and the producers.[29]

The psychologists recommended that evaluation be integrated into the show's production. When Lesser had consulted on *Exploring*, he read scripts, talked to the writers and to young viewers, and advised during the taping of the program. He and the other three psychologists suggested that the production company have its own researchers who would work as closely with the production staff as Lesser had for *Exploring*. This research unit could give the two kinds of assessments that Morrisett had told the experts were necessary. In the studio, they could provide "immediate" information to improve production. Outside it, they could perform tests of the program's effectiveness at holding children's attention, motivating them, and teaching them.[30]

What began to emerge after these two meetings was the conception of the program as an experiment. In Cooney's proposal to Channel 13, she had specified that the project's first year would be an experimental one dedicated to finding out what televisual artistic elements appealed to children and what broadcast schedule worked best. In the final 1968 proposal, an experimental year of testing remained a part of plan. Characterizing the program as more research than as an ongoing television program had certain advantages for OE. Howe could allocate research funds at his discretion, and support of an "experimental" project implied a limited commitment by the agency. Making it less like an ongoing TV series had advantages for Carnegie as well. In a December 1967 memo to Carnegie's president Alan Pifer, Morrisett wrote that the project's "main consideration in an experimental year . . . should be the attraction of *some* audience and the *attempt* to measure *some minimal and narrow* educational goals."[31]

Experimental status also helped smooth over one last broadcasting issue: distribution difficulties. Given that the commercial networks had little interest in the project, NET and the newly emerging public television system presented the most appropriate distributor, especially for an educational show. But NET had several disadvantages for carrying the proposed show. Its acronym was deceptive; it was not a "network" because it did not broadcast simultaneously across the nation through a web of interconnected stations. Instead, multiple videotape copies rotated among many stations that would each broadcast a given show when its copy arrived. This system made national promotion of a program awkward.[32] The system's many stations on the UHF band posed another problem for NET because many televisions, especially those of low-income viewers, could not receive UHF signals. And NET's viewership among the poor was particularly small, making the network a weak vehicle to reach disadvantaged children. They simply were not accustomed to tuning in the local educational channel.[33] In short, it was an open question whether a show broadcast by NET could reach the broad and inclusive audience for which Cooney and Morrisett hoped and that Hausman and OE demanded.

Carnegie's answer, to which Hausman seems to have acquiesced, was that NET's effectiveness would also be a part of the experiment. Before the meeting with the TV professionals, Hausman had suggested asking them whether NET could reach an audience both large and minority, with or without extensive promotion and parent involvement. As with his pilot approach, he suggested studying the potential reach of the show in advance of its premiere. In an informal note to Morrisett, Cooney retorted: "Nobody, including your 'advisers' really knows the answers to these questions. That's what the test period is all about, isn't it?"[34] And this was the approach adopted in the final proposal of February 1968. Among the studies that the proposal included, one would have compared the VHF and UHF educational stations "in securing audience." Carnegie and other backers of the project agreed as the proposal became final that commercial TV stations could carry the show in places that lacked an educational station.[35]

Resolution of the distribution issue completed Cooney and Morrisett's sometimes contentious negotiation with Hausman and situated the project between commercial and noncommercial television. The experimental system gained Hausman's assent because it allowed the project to draw on the commercial industry expertise, in which he put great faith. On the other hand, in line with the resentment many parents and other discontented viewers felt toward commercial TV's ratings system, the project's internal evaluation system presented an alternative means of validation. Distribution through NET also positioned the program outside the commercial industry. These parts of the plan stood to give the show some credibility in the eyes of broadcasters and viewers alike.

Different issues animated educators. With completion of the proposal in early 1968, Howe began talks with other federal agencies, which brought to the fore the issue of the program's audience. He had committed OE to cover half the cost of the show, less any other federal contributions he could gather. To keep his own agency's share down and to broaden the funding base for *Sesame Street*, he needed to find other supporters. The Office of Economic Opportunity—and within it the Office of Child Development, the agency responsible for Head Start—ultimately became the only other major source of federal funds. Before OCD would commit funds to the project, it demanded a clear pledge that the show's producers would direct the program to a poor and minority audience. Dr. Martin Spickler—a child psychologist at the Children's Bureau, one of the agencies Howe first contacted as a possible backer of the project—similarly recommended a focus on impoverished children. OE's Associate Commissioner for Elementary and Secondary Education Nolan Estes also suggested that the show be "aimed at disadvantaged children" instead of the "unrealistically large audience" that the proposal indicated.[36]

Hausman apparently convinced Morrisett that a show directed exclusively at poor and minority children would fail. Black viewers would consider such a show "demeaning," Hausman later explained. "They would consider it patronizing and you would lose the middle class whites." Morrisett has since made the same argument; a show directed more exclusively to minority viewers would be perceived by the public and by its audience as "inherently pejorative." Whether Morrisett perceived the issue this way in 1968 cannot be discerned from the documentary record. This conclusion may have grown from Hausman's demand for the largest possible audience or may have followed the logic of the *Brown v. Board of Education* Supreme Court decision. Segregated schools for minorities, particularly blacks, had usually been inferior, and an educational TV show intended exclusively for minorities might have carried a similar stigma.[37]

Cooney stood between this position and the educators' stand that the curriculum must be directed to the disadvantaged. Her feasibility study implied that all preschool children had similar developmental needs and concentrated on special measures to make sure the disadvantaged got to see the show. Cooney concluded that a poor child might simply reach a given stage later than a middle-class child; at different ages, both could learn from the same TV show. On the other hand, her study remained ambiguous listing goals from ETS and Bereiter. ETS's goals applied to all children; Bereiter's did not. He predicated his goals on research that seemed to show that poor children lacked the more sophisticated language of their middle-class counterparts. Cooney admitted that Bereiter, who so inspired her, doubted that the needs of middle-class and poor children could be served by the same show. Nevertheless, she seemed to hope that, by crafting the curriculum with an eye toward the needs of the poor and by making an effort to ensure that they saw the show, the program could be both universal and targeted to the poor.[38]

In the winter of 1968, the negotiations involving OE, Carnegie, Head Start, and the Ford Foundation, another new backer, resulted in a compromise. Edward Meade, Ford's representative, articulated their agreed "target" audience: "There is agreement on the target, that is, the youngster aged four to five, about a year away from school, and particularly, although not exclusively, that youngster who comes from what might be considered an urban disadvantaged community. To my knowledge, no one disagrees with this focus." Hausman, acting as liaison to OEO, informed the agency of this formulation and "that the prime target is the urban poor." *Sesame Street's* audience would be concentric, the circle of disadvantaged children within the larger circle of all preschoolers. This construct became a source of both strength and trouble in the program's early seasons.[39]

The final organizational and financial arrangements fell into place around the same time as the backers agreed to the audience compromise. NET agreed to accept the new production unit, to be called the Children's Television Workshop (CTW). The Ford Foundation joined OE and the Carnegie foundation as the third major supporter, and several smaller federal agencies completed the group. A list of the financial backers of *Sesame Street's* pre-broadcast research and first season appears in table 1. A few months later the Corporation for Public Broadcasting agreed to finance distribution of the show through a network interconnection to eliminate NET's videotape rotation system.[40]

The completion of the proposal and its circulation within OE and the Department of Health, Education, and Welfare apparently triggered wider

Table 1. Major funding for the *Sesame Street* project's first two years, 1968–1970

Office of Education, Research Bureau	$3,325,000
Office of Economic Opportunity (Head Start)	650,000
National Institute of Child Health and Human Development	15,000
National Endowment for the Humanities	10,000
Corporation for Public Broadcasting	625,900
Carnegie Corporation	1,500,000
Ford Foundation	1,538,000
John and Mary R. Markle Foundation	250,000
Learning Resources Institute	150,000
Total	$8,063,900

Source: Richard M. Polsky, *Getting to Sesame Street: Origins of the Children's Television Workshop* (New York: Praeger Publishers, 1974), 114.

discussion of the project. Associate Commissioner Estes astutely concluded that the project had as much to do with the reform of television as it did with education. He wrote to Hausman: "the authors . . . began with the idea that there are vast numbers of preschool age children around the country and that television is a mass medium and concluded that a television series for these children would be 'a good thing.'" The proposal focused entirely on what happened on the screen, he argued, and not on "making some meaningful changes in children," as a more "comprehensive" educational program would have. He also doubted that television could teach without the intervention of a teacher, an opinion often articulated even after *Sesame Street*'s successful early years. Estes twitted Hausman with a quotation from one of the broadcast veteran's own speeches, years before: "Television can and does help teaching, but it cannot be a teacher."[41]

Others in the Department shared Estes's doubts about TV instruction without a teacher present. William Gorham, HEW's assistant secretary for planning and evaluation, suggested that a separate show be devised and tested "primarily [for] children under adult supervision" because "the chances for success seem to me much greater" than those for a program children watched at home on their own. E. James Lieberman, chief of the Center for Studies of Child and Family Mental Health at the National Institute for Mental Health, wrote to Hausman: "Although we do not see television as a substitute for interpersonal education, we view it as a promising supplement." In responding to Gorham, Hausman hinted at a possible basis for these concerns about children viewing alone: "This series is *primarily* aimed at the child in the home with minimum supervision. Instead of a teacher-child response, the effect will be to create a TV program-child interaction. (You cannot assume that this will be all passive viewing)." The well-established belief that children watched television passively may have been behind the skepticism of Estes, Lieberman, and Gorham. Learning is an activity, they seemed to imply, that a child undertakes only when an adult is also involved.[42]

Hausman initially responded that adult supervision would be a part of the project. He answered Estes that "the target audience will be not only in the home, but also in child-care centers, housing developments, etc. The program will be linked up with these activities and the adults serving them." When executives in the Head Start program expressed similar concerns, he readily encouraged them to develop their own materials to go with the show. But later, during the summer of 1968, the project's curriculum design seminars brought together child development scientists, educators, and others. Despite the enthusiastic support of these experts, Estes—and, perhaps, others within OE—continued to oppose the project. Hausman responded that "a number of distinguished child psychologists and teachers [were] not as certain as" Estes was that "pre-schoolers cannot be taught cognitive skills without interacting with adults."[43]

Cooney could not have agreed with Hausman more; she had advocated the same position in the feasibility study and the final proposal. The feasibility study, indeed, had featured a separate show to enlist parents in their children's learning and had included craft kits and books to enhance the show's lessons after children had watched. In the final proposal, these measures received less attention than the program's use as an adjunct to Head Start. But in both documents, Cooney emphasized television formats designed to counteract passive viewing without resort to crafts or classroom activities. In both, she suggested a story-time format, in which an adult would read to a puppet and a clever child. The host would preface the story with the admonition: "This is not just a story you can follow passively; you must listen closely because the reader is going to ask questions about it." This pedantic-sounding format never made it to the screen in quite this form, but another one from these planning papers became a trademark of the show. In a classification game called "One of These Things Is Not Like the Others," the host called for each viewer to identify the object that did not belong in the group by putting a finger on the television screen. Cooney also called for movement and dance activities that would "involve the child actively in the program." Though none of these offered true interaction between child viewer and televised teacher, they might break through the apparent passivity of young viewers. Even after test results demonstrated that children had learned from *Sesame Street*, educational skeptics continued to doubt TV's ability to teach.[44]

Absent from Cooney and Morrisett's debates with Hausman and the other government officials was the reform of television. What surfaced more subtly in the studies and memos was the hope that TV could cultivate and broaden the minds of children. In her feasibility study and final proposal, Cooney promoted television's potential "for fostering the intellectual and cultural development" of youngsters. Children should grow in their "appreciation" of art and music and in their "knowledge of the world." Morrisett seemed to share her objective that the program expose its young viewers to the rudiments of culture. When he recruited the TV professionals who later recommended an independent production company, he wrote that television could help children "acquire the basic tools for learning and an understanding of their culture."[45]

Morrisett had still greater ambitions for the project. Just before the backers reached their final agreements, he turned to the task of persuading his own foundation to support *Sesame Street*. The project could, he concluded, promote public television's potential, prompt improvement in commercial programming, and help "to change the cultural and educational environment of childhood." Although it is not entirely explicit, the two leaders of the project apparently hoped to nurture in children a taste for "better" television. As he put it a few years later: "To the extent that the child feeds upon a diet of unwholesome television food little designed to educate him, to develop his standards of taste, to improve his esthetic judgment, and to convey to him the greatness and quality of man's cultural achievements—to that extent it must be expected that this child as he grows up, will fail to appreciate, demand, and support the creative and artistic aspirations of those in the television industry who would like to see television establish continually higher standards of creative and artistic achievement for itself."[46] Beyond a few early hints, *Sesame Street*'s planners had not fully elaborated a scheme for changing all of children's television through a single model program.

On March 20, 1968, the Office of Education, Carnegie Corp, and the Ford Foundation held a press conference to announce the creation of the Children's Television Workshop. The joint press release summarized many of the major themes in the development of the project to that point. The text characterized the program as an "experiment," a partnership of "television professionals" and "educators, psychologists, and other child development specialists." It would be an experiment to find out "whether the kind of entertainment that children like on television can be put to educational purposes." The press release tersely encompassed both the show's larger purpose and its concentric audience concept with these words: "to stimulate the intellectual and cultural growth of young children—particularly those from disadvantaged backgrounds." With the creation of CTW, Cooney became its executive director and Gerald Lesser became chairman of its Board of Advisers and Consultants.[47]

In one regard, though, the press release significantly departed from the previous planning. It added that the project "could provide one immediate and practical" way to "close the gap between disadvantaged and middle-class children."[48] Though the statement did not elaborate on this goal, it seems to imply that low-income and minority viewers would learn more from *Sesame Street* than their white middle-class peers. Nowhere in the documentary record of the show's planning, up to this point, does this idea appear. It probably was added at the behest of OE or Head Start at the time the press release was prepared. In any case, this ambitious goal later provided an opening for the strongest criticism made of *Sesame Street*.

Though the press release had been silent on the other ambitious goal, television reform, the press brought the issue up right away. On the front page of the *New York Times*, TV critic Jack Gould wrote that CTW would "test" whether "lively, imaginative television programming" could "woo preschoolers from slick advertising-sponsored fare." Calling the proposed program a "new bloom on the wasteland," *PTA Magazine* picked up Cooney's epithet for established preschool practice and aimed it back at its old target, television. At least for TV's critics, implicit in the idea of experimenting with education on television was improvement of the medium as a whole.

Cooney immediately emerged as a darling of the press, and she focused the discourse on the social reform implications of the project. In an extensive story in the *Christian Science Monitor* by Louise Sweeney, Cooney elaborated on the project at some length. Television is "not a classroom or print-oriented" means of instruction, Cooney told Sweeney, insisting that educators had to accept the medium's existing form in the interest of tapping its power. "This is a medium that must involve you emotionally, not a particularly intellectual medium. . . . If 'Batman' did it—reached all the kids—why can't we?" But she also pointed to a broader potential for social messages to poorer black children: "Ghetto kids like TV as much as other kids. Visually they're very hooked. . . . But they never see themselves on the screen. Television's got to begin reflecting them. . . . There are no black cartoon figures to identify with. Why not a tiny Harry Belafonte type? 'Black is beautiful' is a gorgeous slogan. Why not show blacks in beautiful situations doing beautiful things?" Focusing on the inclusion of those previously invisible or depreciated by TV became a part of an early multicultural "pro-social" approach to children's programming in the early 1970s, and Cooney already recognized the potential. Long before it had a curriculum, a cast, or even a name, the *Sesame Street* project had begun to spark anticipation and hope.[49]

It was a lot easier for Cooney and Morrisett to gain control of the production of the show than it was to control its larger public meanings. Casting the project as an experiment in educational television and obtaining government support for it made it possible to create a nonprofit production company independent of its financial backers. A new style of production—one more closely involving child development expertise in the process—became possible. Embarking on this exploration, over the next eighteen months the newly created workshop built a distinctive partnership of child experts and TV producers and brought *Sesame Street* to the television screen.

What had begun as a foray into educational TV quickly became a much-heralded effort at television reform. Cooney's original proposal almost undertook to use TV to reform preschool curricula, but, after encountering its financial backers and the press, the project had turned that formulation on its head. The "wasteland" again appeared to be on the television, not in the classroom. Cooney wanted to adopt the popular style of commercial television; Hausman urged that popularity—sheer audience size—also be adopted as a measure of success, as opposed to Morrisett's more modest goal, the "attraction of *some* audience." And, while Cooney had sought only to ensure that poor children saw the program in an environment conducive to learning, the government backers—OEO in particular—added the ambition that the show would close the "achievement gap" between children who were disadvantaged and those who were not. To these growing aspirations, the press added the reform of television, an understandable hope, given the simmering discontent with the medium. Should *Sesame Street* fail to live up to these ambitions, skeptics like Estes had already invoked the familiar assessment that passively watched television could never teach. Cooney, Morrisett, Lesser, and their colleagues would have a large budget and significant freedom to try to meet these expectations before the show would reemerge in the public eye in November 1969.

CHAPTER 4

The CTW Model

With the Children's Television Workshop established, Cooney needed to find the people to create a show that could meet the vaunted expectations. Early in her search, one person she turned to was David Connell, the former executive producer of *Captain Kangaroo.* Before she first contacted him, he had read about the *Sesame Street* project in the *New York Times.* Bringing together child development advisers and TV producers to create a show struck him as the wrong way "to do a television program that's going to appeal to kids." Nevertheless, a few months later, she was able to convince him to become *Sesame Street*'s executive producer. "I was out of children's television," he later recalled. "I didn't want to do that anymore." She persuaded him by promising that the show was an experiment that would only last a year or two. He would soon be able to return to the film production company that he and a friend had just started.

Connell's first months on the project, however, renewed his interest in children's TV. When Cooney hired Edward L. Palmer to head the internal research group at the Children's Television Workshop, Connell remembered her telling him, "I want you to make Ed Palmer your best friend." Connell remained a little dubious but became interested in a contraption that Palmer called the "distractor." CTW's head researcher had invented it to test how much children liked a TV program by showing them competing images on a second TV to distract them. Connell recalled: "I asked him to do a test on a *Captain Kangaroo* program, a specific show." He chose an episode in which "the Captain and Mr. Greenjeans explain to kids how the U.S. government works, with bicameral legislatures, reporting bills out of committee, the balance of powers and all that. I knew four-year-olds wouldn't get that." After the tests were completed, Palmer graphed the amount of time the young viewers had their eyes on the screen and set up the graph to scroll below the television set, synchronized to the program the children had watched. When they watched the *Kangaroo* episode along with the graph, Connell remembered, "it was very clear that as soon as [the Captain] started talking about the constitution, the four-year-old attention level went way down. But when he said, 'Now, here's a word from Mattel,' it went way back up again. So I became a real believer in the [distractor] at that point."[1]

Connell's conversion exemplifies the enthusiasm that the project kindled in both TV professionals and child science experts. This enthusiasm made possible the partnership of child science and TV production that is at the heart of what became known as the "CTW Model." *Sesame Street*'s creators began to develop the Model—their system of planning, production, and evaluation—soon after the workshop's founding, but it did not emerge fully until the end of the show's first season. Once the Model was complete, CTW offered it as the ultimate product of the project—a better way to make educational programs for children, a means to ensure that young viewers actually learned. The Model had four parts: the interaction of receptive television producers and child science experts, the creation of a specific and age-appropriate curriculum, research to shape the program directly, and independent measurement of viewers' learning. Gerald Lesser, the project's academic adviser, guided the meetings of the core production department staff and the experts during the summer of 1968 and the creation of the curriculum during the following fall. In the ten months remaining before the premiere, the producers wrote and produced the show in close collaboration with CTW's own researchers, who tested parts of it. The last part of the Model fell into place when an outside testing firm, Educational Testing Services, studied groups of preschool viewers who watched the show during the first season in 1969 and 1970. The Model's distinctive mixture of production and research made more obvious *Sesame Street*'s position on the boundary between education and commercial TV than it had been in the early planning stages.[2]

To appreciate fully the novelty of the CTW Model, the place to start is commercial television's approach to similar problems. No network producer or executive would have needed a curriculum because their purpose seemed clear. With the possible exception of news programming, the ultimate purpose of any commercial television show has always been to entice viewers to watch long enough that they also see the accompanying advertisements. Ironically, this simple goal—to entertain—demanded subtle, intuitive, creative decisions from producers. For example, Quinn Martin—a singularly successful producer of action-adventure shows like *The Fugitive* (ABC, 1963–67)—sought to make his audience "feel something of lived experience." Another producer—Norman Lear, most famous for *All in the Family* (CBS, 1971–79)—said, "An audience is entertained when it's involved, involved to the point of tears or laughter." When interviewed, several other producers confidently expressed a faith in their knowledge of what made an audience laugh, while admitting to occasional failures. These judgments were not easy artistic tasks, and their business exacted a toll on them because success was often so uncertain. The Model gave producers clearly specified educational goals that did not demand the same degree of sheer intuition, but the focus remained on the audience's reactions to the show.[3]

These difficult, intuitive judgments about entertainment gave rise to a self-reliant, closed approach to understanding their audiences. Complex, subjective interactions between viewers and programs like "something of lived experience" or "involvement" demanded art and instinct. The producers' subjective judgments, in turn, did not lend themselves to interaction with an objective style of research that might have led to new insights or to a dynamic consensus about the audience's needs and desires. Television executives shared with producers this same insularity, and programming decisions hinged on conventional wisdom and personal experience, not on testing. The Model's emphasis on consultation between expert and producer and on useful testing of program material created a more open process.

Though it did not effectively study its audience, the industry was not without its means of researching viewer reaction to a program, both before and after it aired. Most familiar were the Nielsen ratings, which simply estimated the total number of people watching each network's prime time shows. TV insiders generally gave the impression that this simple indicator—"circulation"—was the only measure of audience reaction that they took seriously. However novel the Model was, CTW considered the sheer size of its audience important and monitored its Nielsen ratings during *Sesame Street*'s first seasons. On a more intimate level, the distractor quantified the simple benchmark of viewer attention to the show, providing a measure not wholly unlike a Nielsen rating.

The networks also did not have to rely solely on ratings; they had

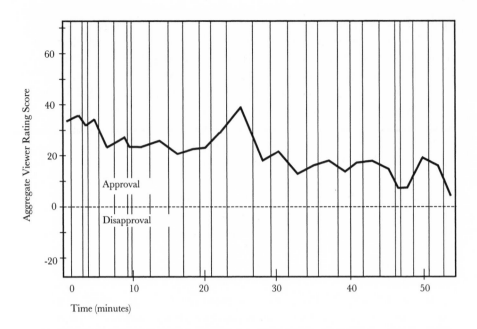

Fig. 2. Audience reaction to a test screening of a television show. The momentary "like,"
"don't like," and "indifferent" scores of the entire test audience were aggregated and graphed
over the duration of the show, from left to right. The vertical bands represent plot segments
of the program. Adapted from "Figure 14.4: Program-analyzer audience profile," in Sydney W.
Head, *Broadcasting in America: A Survey of Television and Radio*, 2nd ed. (Boston: Houghton-
Mifflin, 1972), 316.

other means of testing the potential popularity of a show before it went on
the air. For instance, researchers presented drawings of characters to children when testing children's cartoon programs for their appeal. In a more
sophisticated test regime used with adult shows, viewers watched a program on film in a theater and registered their reactions with hand-held
devices. Researchers then discussed the show with a subset of the audience
afterward. The hand-held device communicated a viewer's momentary
approval at particular points in the program. Quantifying each viewer reaction, these scores could be aggregated to create a score for the entire
audience's reaction at each point. These points could then be graphed as
in figure 2 to give a sense of the trend of audience favor or disfavor over
the length of a show. Other research methods included major opinion
studies and telephone polling after special cable broadcasts. With its com-

mitment to testing, CTW had no greater resources or more elaborate techniques at its disposal than the networks did.

But there were often reasons that industry executives disregarded test results. For the most commonly used method, theater screening, the samples did not replicate accurately the national audience, and executives could easily dismiss results contrary to their plans. They also commonly disregarded as unrepresentative the opinions of audience members who wrote letters to the networks. By integrating testing into the production process and by taking its results seriously, CTW broke through the insularity that separated the commercial industry from its audience.

In general, test results of network shows rarely became an issue because only a minority of programs were ever pre-screened to a sample audience. In fact, the real test audience for any proposed program were the network executives—who had to approve, and whose networks had to finance, any projected TV series. Most programs reached the air because these crucial decision-makers watched a prototype episode, called a "pilot," of the show and approved it. Typically, a new commercial TV program began with an idea contracted by one of the networks to be developed into a pilot. Under network supervision, a production company or film studio produced the finished prototype, which the network executives then used to decide whether or not to fund the production of more episodes. The process in animated children's shows was only different in its details. For these, storyboards and recordings of the voices of the proposed characters served the function that pilot episodes did for prime time shows. For live action children's shows—those with human actors instead of cartoon characters—the process resembled that of prime time programs. Network executives might also consult network censors (standards and practices departments) and, often, advertisers as well. But all of these people, like the executives and producers, operated from nothing more substantial than the industry's conventional wisdom and their own personal understandings of the audience.

Like the program producers, the network executives in control usually relied on their own personal experience and judgment with no research. This personal faculty grew from pre-critical personal taste, the taste of family and friends, the analysis of previously successful shows, and the insights of media peers. Many network executives pursued their own artistic visions early in their careers but, in time, developed a sense of the public's taste as distinct from their own. Their personal tastes continued to differ, often disdainfully, from that which they attributed to the public at large. Like the personal theories of producers, this "second self" admitted little access to other opinions—least of all those of the viewers themselves. In fact, beginning with a subjective purpose—one ill-suited to research input—commercial TV disregarded the audience reactions it could gather and relied on the instincts and experience of its producers, on the one hand, and its executives, on the other. It was uncommon for fresh insights from the audience to impinge directly on this system. The CTW Model and the people who developed it had no greater wisdom than their network counterparts, nor more novel testing techniques. What most differed was the workshop's openness to insights from their audience.

Some of this receptivity may have come with the men Connell hired for the workshop's production staff in the spring of 1968. Like the executive producer, many had worked on *Captain Kangaroo*. Connell brought in Jon Stone as head writer, Samuel Y. Gibbon Jr. as producer, and four others from *Kangaroo*.[4] Connell began as a production assistant with *Kangaroo*; when he left more than ten years later, he had risen to executive producer. Likewise, Stone had begun as a production assistant but had left in the early 1960s. During their years working on that show, *Kangaroo*'s ambivalent relationship to its commercial environment may have influenced them. Robert Keeshan, star of the program and owner of the production company, carefully controlled the show's sponsorship, occasionally rejecting some sponsors. But he never rejected the sponsorship system as a whole, and he appreciated CBS's support in the face of poor ratings. On the other hand, one executive complained that he was rude and self-important. Gibbon remembered Keeshan as "a man with principle in the middle of commercial television." After years with *Kangaroo*, the producers and writers at *Sesame Street* may have been more open to an approach that ran counter to the industry's usual methods than others from commercial television. Thinking about their audience in developmental terms required a receptivity that was critical to the CTW Model.[5]

Jim Henson also came to the workshop with commercial experience and a degree of alienation. He came to the show only after years of performing in commercials and variety shows. He had tried repeatedly to get his own program on the networks and had produced two pilots with only one special called *Hey, Cinderella* ever reaching the air. Once he started working on *Sesame Street*, however, his puppets ceased appearing in commercials. After the premiere, he and Cooney, as the two most publicly prominent creators of the show, spoke on behalf of the Action for Children's Television reform campaign in 1970. A few years later, when Henson finally did get his own series, *The Muppet Show*, he produced it in

London and sold it through syndication, outside the network TV production system.[6]

Other motives probably also made commercial TV veterans among the CTW staff amenable to a fresh approach. Connell's expectation that his commitment would be a brief one might have made him more receptive to an experiment. Others may have felt as Gibbon did, that the social reform ambitions of the project justified new methods. After the assassinations of Martin Luther King Jr. and Robert F. Kennedy, "it felt to most of us," Gibbon later recalled, "as though the country was in real danger of crumbling, . . . I remember that my wife Carol and I went to a memorial service for King in Central Park, and to see tear-stained faces of all colors, people holding hands . . . was overwhelming. The notion that maybe it was time to do something useful was pretty overpowering."[7]

Even with a receptive production staff, the workshop needed to find potential partners among educators and child development psychologists. In the spring of 1968, Cooney and Lesser began planning a series of seminars that would bring together producers and experts. Though the final proposal had not called for these meetings—the advisory board was simply to write the goals list—Lesser convinced Cooney to substitute a series of seminars for the board's work. Based on his experience consulting for *Exploring*, he had concluded that simply taking a curriculum and handing it to the producers and writers would not work. They needed an education in child development, and the experts who would teach them needed a practical sense of what was possible on television. Lesser carefully chose experts who were receptive to using television for education. During the seminars, he worked to prevent fruitless debates on fine theoretical points, and the producers came to insist that the experts speak in a language they could understand. CTW held these meetings in New York City and Cambridge, Massachusetts, between June and August 1968.[8]

Initially, the seminar process demanded a leap of faith by the production staff. Along with his original skepticism about "this huge list of advisers," Connell also admitted later, in an unfinished memoir, that, when he attended the first seminar, he "really felt intimidated by all of the participants, ranging from eminent psychologists, expert teachers, children's book authors, advertising pros and miscellaneous other luminaries."[9] In short, he began from the perspective that academics could not devise popular television and that TV producers could not hold their own intellectually with the experts. What he and his colleagues found was that some of the experts—first, Harvard University psychologist Sheldon White, and later others—could contribute useful production ideas and thereby become partners in the practical work of television.[10] Connell's notes from the seminars, by their sheer volume, demonstrate his engagement.[11] Like the others, his understanding of child development grew and, with it, his receptivity to the workshop's own research that followed in subsequent years. By the end of 1968, a small group of advisers had emerged—one more informal than the board of advisers called for by the proposal.[12]

The encounter of expert and producer during the seminars generated a universe of possible curricular goals and many production ideas. In fact, it is futile to search the seminar reports for indications of *Sesame Street*'s underlying theoretical orientation. Primarily, the reports listed specific ideas and general suggestions, too numerous and diverse to summarize effectively here. An example suffices to suggest the nature of the ideas that emerged. During the second seminar, which dealt with language and reading, White suggested: "Have a character, such as a Mr. Fluster, get things wrong. This would give both the idea that it is permissible to make mistakes and also the chance for the child viewer to be one up on the model."[13] At the fifth seminar, on perception, according to White's report of the discussion, Connell brought up the Mr. Fluster idea again, and the group considered how the character's "systematic disorders in the way he viewed the world . . . [would provide an opportunity for] the kids to analyze."[14] Ultimately, the eight-foot-tall, yellow Big Bird puppet character developed from this idea. Lesser later used the following example to describe Big Bird: "Viewing children attend to Big Bird's effort [to learn the difference between the letters E and F] until the letters are completed (they are alert to Big Bird's tendency to make mistakes, which they enjoy correcting)."[15] What White had done was imagine a character whose bumbling gave children the opportunity to think, respond, and learn. He had translated child development theory into stereotypic televisual action. Not all of the experts in the seminars were as skilled as White—or as enthusiastic. But as the seminars progressed, the producers themselves became better at this creative process. Lesser remembers Henson, for example, having a particular gift for creating scenes that might teach.[16]

The seminars opened the production staffers to developmental and educational ideas about their audience. At the most basic level, Lesser understood that to make a curriculum connect with production, the producers had to "understand both the intent and the meaning of the goals." CTW Assistant Director Robert Davidson, who organized the seminars, later recognized that "educating the staff" was a major purpose of the seminars. Gibbon later explained that he and his fellow producers got "a crash graduate course in human development and early childhood education."

Though Connell initially came to the seminars with some anxiety, he became comfortable with the experts and with their educational ideas. By the end of the seminars in August 1968, the producers had found authorities, like psychologists White and Chester Pierce, on whom they could later call for advice. CTW took a receptive group of writers and producers and prepared them to collaborate closely, first with these experts and then with the internal research department.[17]

The summer seminars began the process of writing a curriculum for *Sesame Street*. From the goals proposed at those meetings, the workshop wrote the show's first curriculum during the remaining months of 1968. In September, Morrisett, White, and Samuel Ball of Educational Testing Service (ETS) met with the workshop staff to put together a preliminary list of objectives. CTW had chosen ETS to do the independent evaluation of the show once it went on the air, and Ball assisted in the selection of goals to ensure that they would be testable. Before the meeting, the production and research departments, as well as several individuals, distilled lists of possible objectives from the seminars and circulated these lists among themselves. Once the meeting began, they soon found that they could not agree on a set of criteria by which to select the goals. Jane O'Connor—the curriculum specialist in the production department and one of only two African-American staff members—suggested a practical solution: find the common objectives from all the lists.[18]

The group then voted on goals and achieved consensus on five core cognitive skill areas. The "Numbers" area included rote counting, enumeration, and number recognition. Under "Alphabet" was a similar set of skills, including an awareness that letters made up words. CTW's planners could not agree on what they meant by "Relational Terms," but these came to include an understanding of size (big, little, etc.), position (over, under, etc.), and other concepts. "Classification and Ordering" of objects and "Reasoning Skills" formed the remaining two consensus categories. The five almost correspond to the five basic goals for intellectual development that Cooney had cited from ETS in her 1966 feasibility study. During *Sesame Street*'s first three seasons, roughly 60 percent of the show's air time was spent teaching these five skill areas. These cognitive rudiments make up a central and consistent part of its educational agenda.[19]

The planners considered many other kinds of goals, and their discussions further testify to the importance of the five basic areas. The group de-emphasized "body parts and functions" and "emotions" by including them under the larger rubric of "labeling and identification" and only teaching the words for them. What this decision meant in practice became more clear with emotions. Instead of presenting dramatic skits that might evoke emotional responses in young viewers, actors would "display stereotyped emotions" and label these. Looking glum, an actor or puppet might say "sad." The underlying concern was to avoid unpredictably scaring or saddening youngsters when parents and caretakers might not be immediately available to the children. A few years later CTW did extensive research and planning before adding "affective" goals to the curriculum. Despite their efforts, one disastrous episode aired in 1976 when the actress Margaret Hamilton appeared on *Sesame Street* as the Wicked Witch of the West from *The Wizard of Oz.* Though she did not scare Big Bird, she terrified many children watching at home, and their parents wrote to complain. Anticipating such reactions, the workshop staff initially avoided goals that seemed likely to pose problems.[20]

Planners also considered teaching about social concerns like "justice [and] fair-play." These issues could not be treated on TV as they would have been in a preschool. Instead, White suggested presenting "alternative points of view" and showing that "these have legitimacy and validity." He proposed a bold series of comic skits addressing prejudice. In these a black man and a white man would have confronted one another in situations of "mischief, cooperation, competition, comparison." Inspired by James Baldwin's play *Blues for Mister Charlie,* White hoped that through these skits *Sesame Street* could "convey the bitter tinge" of American race relations. However effectively these scenes might have encouraged "stout self-respect" in young black viewers, they also promised to provoke controversy in pursuit of curricular goals that had never been central to the project. Determined to follow an integrationist vision, the workshop had no interest in treating racial identity and children's self-esteem on the show. However, in the show's first seasons, critics forced CTW to address these issues.

During the curricular planning, the workshop's staff opted to follow O'Connor's suggestion to "show indirectly that color didn't matter." In the months before the premiere, CTW also created a puppet character, Oscar the Grouch, to dramatize this aspect of the curriculum. His manners and tastes set him apart from his neighbors, allowing the show to treat racial and ethnic diversity by analogy to personal differences. The workshop had not conceived Oscar as a stand-in for urban minorities with his rude and aggressive behavior and his preference for his trash-strewn home. But during the program's early seasons, some black viewers perceived him as a surrogate for poor, urban African Americans. These isolated difficulties with more complex affective and social topics underscore CTW's determination to hew close to its central mission: to experiment with cognitive instruction through television.[21]

The written curriculum became a central feature of the Model. Just as they did during the seminars, the staff and advisers carefully considered television's limits as a teaching medium. Building on the knowledge and awareness that the seminars had instilled in the producers, the goals document dictated the show's content. It also specified the particular skills on which evaluators would test young viewers to determine the program's effectiveness. In a larger sense, the curriculum linked child development expertise to the producers' creative guidelines. Figure 3 is an outline of the first season goals. Over the 1970s and early 1980s, CTW revised it nearly every year, and planning research guided methodical expansion of the curriculum. After the show's first season, when foreign broadcasters asked for permission and help to produce their own versions of *Sesame Street*, the workshop prescribed that the development process begin with writing a curriculum.[22]

During 1968, the two remaining elements of the Model developed from two competing ideas about testing. Hausman and the project's backers demanded independent confirmation of the show's educational effectiveness before any episode was broadcast. They relinquished control only on the promise of independent testing. Lesser and his three fellow psychologists suggested instead that internal researchers work closely with producers in the studio. As a part of this partnership, these experimenters could also test in the laboratory how well the program taught child viewers. Cooney's final proposal called for research helpful to producers and for testing independent of them. The backers would get the latter results, however, only after an experimental year of broadcasts. Once CTW began to collaborate with the Educational Testing Service, "formative research" and "summative research" became the names for these two respective approaches to evaluation.

These two kinds of validation had to meet two incompatible needs. First, they had to provide information to assist the producers in shaping the skits, films, and cartoons to teach effectively. This requirement closely tied research to production. Second, evaluation also had to be independent because the backers needed credible proof that *Sesame Street* actually educated children. In advising the workshop, ETS echoed the Office of Education's Harold Howe that "the social scientists should maintain considerable objectivity" and not "be 'captured' by" the producers.[23] By splitting evaluation into formative research, done by CTW's own, internal unit, and

I. Symbolic Representation
   A. Letters
   B. Numbers 1–10
   C. Geometric Forms (circle, square, triangle, rectangle)

II. Cognitive Organization
   A. Perceptual Discrimination and Orientation
      1. Visual Discrimination
      2. Auditory Discrimination
   B. Relational Concepts
   C. Classification
   D. Ordering

III. Reasoning and Problem Solving
   A. Problem Sensitivity ("What's wrong here?")
   B. Inferences and Causality
      1. Inferring Antecedent Events
      2. Inferring Consequent Events
      3. Ordering on the Basis of Causality
   C. Generating and Evaluating Explanations and Solutions

IV. The Child and His World
   A. Self
   B. Social Units
      1. Roles
      2. Social Groups and Institutions
   C. Social Interactions
      1. Differing Perspectives
      2. Cooperation
   D. The Man-made Environment
   E. The Natural Environment

Fig. 3. CTW's curricular goals for the first season of *Sesame Street*. Adapted from "CTW Goals Outline," September 16, 1969, "Research for Program Development, 1968–69" file, Box 33, CTW Archives. Courtesy of Sesame Workshop.

summative research, performed by ETS, the workshop resolved this conflict in priorities. Throughout the production cycle, Edward Palmer's researchers would test newly produced material and advise their counterparts in production. ETS would work independently to create larger, more complete studies of the show's effectiveness during its first broadcast season.

Formative research addressed two aspects of teaching through television, as CTW conceived it. TV instruction consisted of holding children's attention and delivering a comprehensible lesson.[24] Established testing principles could govern the assessment of comprehension, but it was the distractor that credibly measured attention. The distractor's inventor, Edward Palmer, came to the workshop in the summer of 1968 from the education department of the state of Oregon. An academic psychologist who had taught at Florida State University before turning to full-time research, he had not set out to study television and children until he took over a project from an ailing colleague. In the process of completing this research in Oregon, he created the distractor to measure children's attention moment by moment.[25]

Researchers used the following routine to measure attention. They seated a single child in a room with two "television sets"—one a real TV and the other a slide projector mounted in a box made to look like a television. While the show being tested played on the television, the projector showed a sequence of images that researchers believed would be attractive to children. The competing slide images changed every eight seconds and served as a meter for the researcher, breaking a one-hour episode into roughly 450 observations. The researcher watched the child's eyes, noted when they left the television screen, and recorded a number score from zero to three. The score quantified the degree of attention the child paid to the program during each slide's eight-second duration. From the resulting data, researchers could aggregate the attention scores of many children and calculate averages that described the appeal of a particular excerpt or of an entire episode. From these figures they could also draw conclusions about which televisual forms and content would hold children's attention, and the entire line of study opened new insights about the way children watched TV. The distractor became a mainstay of the workshop's research on the effectiveness of its own programs (and other programs), as it remained for decades.[26]

If the curriculum made the purpose of the program explicit and scientific, the distractor made the entertainment value of excerpts quantifiable in a way that the production staff would accept. Had they not first attended

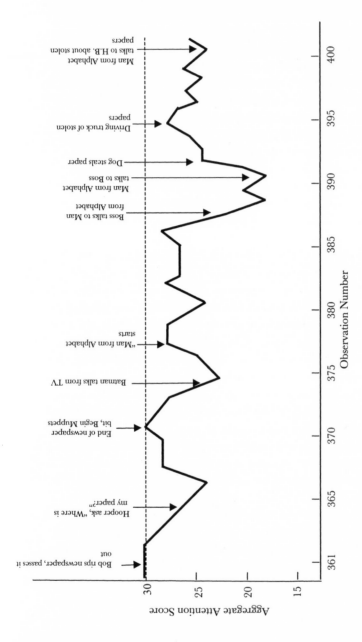

Fig. 4. Distractor graph from summer 1969 screening of test episode number 1. For each observation (8 seconds of program time), a researcher scored each child's attention level from 0 (ignoring the TV) to 3 (total attention to the set). With ten children's scores combined and all watching with rapt attention, the maximum aggregate score a program segment could reach would have been 30. At an aggregate score of 15, the children still are watching half of the time. This sample indicates, for example, that the "Man from Alphabet" segment (obs. 377 to 400+) held attention less well than the previous segments (obs. 360 to 377). Adapted from page 10, distractor graph in Appendix, Memo, Research to Production, "Report of Research on Five Test Shows," September 24, 1969, Box 33, CTW Archives. Courtesy of Sesame Workshop.

the seminars, the list of learning goals might have seemed alien to Connell and the others. Similarly, the distractor won over industry veterans to the new production system, just as the test of Captain Kangaroo's explanation of American government had convinced Connell. Not only did the device confirm and elaborate on producers' own instincts, it presented its findings in a form resembling the results of test screenings for commercial TV programs (see figure 4; compare with figure 2). Data generated by the distractor later helped to persuade producers to abandon program segments that scored poorly and, more generally, to create a body of conventional wisdom that affected many production details. Deliberation among CTW executives, producers, writers, and researchers did not need to pit each person's subjective concept of what appealed to an audience against those of the others. Instead, objective data of apparent and intuitive validity advanced the discussion in potentially productive directions.

From Palmer's assumptions about child viewers, the distractor emerged, and it was these premises that made it possible to move from the testing of individual excerpts to a science of children and television. Beginning from a developmental orientation, Palmer found that children learned over time to understand television, to "read" it. As they did so, they began to recognize programming directed to them. The distractor's chronological sampling technique arose naturally from Palmer's observation that children watch TV moment to moment, sampling it for material they can understand. Age-appropriate television was programming that children comprehended and recognized as intelligible. Extending the concept a little further, CTW conceived of an excerpt's appeal in terms of a child's persistent attention in the face of distraction. An appealing cartoon or film held a child's eyes on the TV set despite the regular appearance of fresh alternatives. Palmer and CTW assumed that the observable, quantifiable action of looking was the outward manifestation of recognition and appeal, giving their approach a distinctly behaviorist cast.[27]

Though the distractor was the workshop's most novel research tool, formative research and development included other elements, such as measurements of viewer comprehension, typified by tests of letter recognition. Before showing a child a cartoon about the letter "J," a researcher would lay out on a table a set of cards with different letters on them and ask the youngster to pick out the one with the letter "J." After the child watched the cartoon, the researcher would repeat the test with the cards. Tests like this one and more complex ones demanded of children as few language skills as possible, allowing them to answer questions nonverbally—by pointing to pictures, for example. Further indications of children's understanding came through recording their remarks while watching parts of the show and interviewing them afterward. Like the concept of attention, CTW's concept of learning constructed this process behaviorally in terms of explicit actions with minimal consideration of the mental processes that connected watching the show with demonstrated learning. At the time, the reigning theory of children's intellectual development, that of Swiss psychologist Jean Piaget, postulated abstract mental processes that could only be inferred from observing learning behavior. *Sesame Street*'s researchers and producers were relentlessly practical and had no use for such abstractions. Years later, it would fall to academic researchers to pick up where years of the workshop's observations and insights left off and create the theories that explained why children watched and learned from television as they did.[28]

In addition to communicating their findings about attention and comprehension, the research department offered additional guidance to the producers and writers of the show. CTW's own child development experts specified what children could be expected to know already and be ready to learn in terms of the skills that the curriculum dictated. For example, a November 1968 memo outlined the specific relational concepts—up, down, over, through, and so on—that children understood, at what age they mastered them, and what percentage of them had done so. The seminars also supplied similar guidance, making the production staff more familiar with their audience's abilities.[29] Another aid to the production department was the "writer's notebook," a compilation of programming ideas to teach specific curriculum elements. These suggestions came initially from the seminars and later from researchers and others. Lesser recommended that they be based on "situations familiar to young children." Under the rubric of formative research, the workshop not only tested its own work in advance of broadcast but also linked child science and the curriculum to the production process.[30]

Summative research, the fourth element of the CTW Model, gave the project an evaluation independent of the workshop. The Educational Testing Service provided it, although not without some close involvement in the early planning stages. ETS's Samuel Ball attended two of the seminars and the September 1968 goals planning meeting to assure that, given the objectives chosen, the viewers' gains could be accurately tested. Despite its potentially adversarial nature, the relationship between the two companies remained cordial during the years they worked together. ETS brought a degree of prestige that enhanced the credibility of its findings, balancing the potential bias inherent in the close contractual relationship it had with the workshop.[31]

ETS brought to its evaluation a degree of methodological rigor, as well. Its researchers administered pre-tests and post-tests to carefully selected samples of children across the country. For their first season evaluation, they tested 943 children in Boston, Philadelphia, Phoenix, and Durham, North Carolina. They divided the children between groups encouraged to watch the show at home or in school and those not so encouraged. The tests before and after covered eight areas of the curriculum, primarily those that were easier to test, such as letters, numbers, shapes, and classification. ETS adapted standard tests and created new ones. Its researchers interviewed mothers and observed children not only to assess the curriculum's effectiveness but also to understand viewing patterns and viewers' reactions. Beyond regional differences, ETS considered race, gender, social class, and language spoken at home. Though the initial season's evaluation received criticism for its design and generalizability, the press gave it a positive reception.

ETS's report had two benefits for the workshop. It opened CTW's producers to the learning outcomes of ordinary child viewers more scientifically than anything routinely done by the commercial TV industry or by CTW itself. ETS's more rigorous evaluation also worked to promote *Sesame Street*. When the workshop publicized the study just before its second season, it used the research, as the networks would use ratings or favorable reviews, to tout the show.[32]

The first such review came in February 1969, ten months before the show's premiere. Stuart Little of *Saturday Review* enthusiastically introduced readers to the elements of the CTW Model, although without using that moniker. He described the program's funding, philosophy, and staff, and so the distractor made its first appearance in the press. In a concluding paragraph, he conveyed Carnegie foundation president Alan Pifer's assessment that the show's "big challenge" was to "set high standards for children's television." Even with "program format and content . . . still to be determined," Little expressed the hope for reform that was already being vested in the program.[33]

The Model positioned *Sesame Street* on the boundary between commercial TV and education. Bringing together producers and experts had injected developmental and educational insights into the creation of actual television material. And the workshop and the process itself insisted on experts who believed that television could teach. The Model made this partnership work by reducing education to a practical problem to be solved by practical people—TV producers and child experts who stuck to the practical task of television production. When considering the learning process, both groups constructed it in terms of outward behavior, which made it easier to measure and to arrive at consensus about the show's fruits. A written curriculum gave the show an educational thrust, but educational effectiveness did not become the only measure of success. *Sesame Street* and the Model retained commercial TV's concern for ratings of audience size. Through the finer measurement of attention, however, producers could move beyond speculations based on crude counts of viewers to more closely consider why the audience was watching at one time but not at another. Summative research reports provided a public side to the evaluation of the show roughly analogous to the critical reviews of an entertainment show. This independent endorsement of *Sesame Street* not only promoted the show to the public but also supplied its financial backers with proof that the program had succeeded. While the producers moved on to writing the show, selecting cartoons and films, and taping skits in the studio, the Model continued to develop. The systematic method and the television show grew simultaneously; with them came deeper insights into children and television.

This montage by *Mad Magazine* artist Jack Davis features *Sesame Street*'s cartoon and human characters at the expense of the later stars of the show, the Muppets. *Left to right* are the four human residents of the Street, Mr. Hooper, Gordon, Susan, and Bob. Cartoon characters—Wanda the Witch (*upper left*), the Fishing Boy (*bottom center*), and Alice Braithwaite Goodyshoes (*bottom, left of lamppost*)—also receive more attention than they would ever again. Even elements from some of the films are included: the skywriting airplane (*top center*) and the cow from "Hey, Cow" with Big Bird perched on her back. CTW Archives. Courtesy of Jack Davis and Sesame Workshop.

Ernie and Bert and the word "No." *Sesame Street*'s first two puppet characters, Ernie and his friend Bert. Ernie played the role of a trickster or comedian, and Bert played an authority figure or straight man. The ambiguities in their relationship held a wealth of comic possibilities. CTW Archives. Courtesy of Sesame Workshop.

Children learn to count at a Head Start classroom in Guilford, Maryland. Some curricula in these federally funded preschools included academic skills, as *Sesame Street* did, in addition to socialization in more traditional preschools. *Baltimore News American* Photograph Collection, Special Collections, University of Maryland Libraries.

Joan Ganz Cooney (*right*), founder and president of CTW, discusses *Sesame Street* with a young girl. The show's popularity arose in part from its creators' sensitivity to the show's audience. Charlotte Brooks, photographer, *Look* Magazine Collection, Library of Congress, Prints and Photographs Division, Reproduction no. LC-L9-69-5095-I#20/20A.

In her office, Cooney (*center*) watches two children watch a *Sesame Street* letter "commercial." Attending to the nuances of youngsters' reactions to the show added to its producers' understanding of their audience. Charlotte Brooks, photographer, *Look* Magazine Collection, Library of Congress, Prints and Photographs Division, Reproduction no. LC-L9-69-5095-1#34/34A.

CTW research director Edward Palmer uses the Distractor to test a *Sesame Street* cartoon's ability to hold the attention of two children. The children are watching the "J Commercial" on the television while a competing image is projected in a box made to look like a TV. CTW Archives. Courtesy of Sesame Workshop.

Cooney (*top*), executive producer David Connell (*center right*), and Matt Robinson (*bottom*) review storyboards for new cartoons in March 1969, six months before the premiere. Connell's aesthetic and sense of humor shaped much of the artistic vision of *Sesame Street*. Charlotte Brooks, photographer, *Look* Magazine Collection, Library of Congress, Prints and Photographs Division, Reproduction no. LC-L9-69-5095-E#9A/10.

Jim Henson (*left*) began his career during the late 1950s as an entertainer on local TV in Washington, D.C., while he was still in college. His puppets developed significantly in the twelve years between this photo and the premiere of *Sesame Street*, but Kermit the Frog (*center*), later a star on the show, is already a member of the Muppet troupe. Though Kermit became Henson's alter ego, the puppet here is being worked by Henson's future wife, Jane Nebel. *Baltimore News American* Photograph Collection, Special Collections, University of Maryland Libraries.

Loretta Long (*left*), who played Susan, rehearses with Carroll Spinney, the man inside the puppet character Big Bird. Spinney created both of the original Street Muppets despite the vast differences in personality between the innocent preschooler Bird and the abrasive, seemingly adult, Oscar the Grouch. Charlotte Brooks, photographer, *Look* Magazine Collection, Library of Congress, Prints and Photographs Division, Reproduction no. LC-L9-70-5503-V#9/9A.

Oscar the Grouch shows folk singer Judy Collins how obnoxious his taste in music can be. Oscar's conflicts with the other residents on Sesame Street were CTW's way of addressing conflicts arising from racial and ethnic diversity. CTW Archives. Courtesy of Sesame Workshop.

Jim Henson (*left*) entertains a young girl held by writer and producer Jon Stone (*right*). Even when children could see the puppeteer, they acted as through the puppets, in this case Kermit the Frog, were living creatures. Charlotte Brooks, photographer, *Look* Magazine Collection, Library of Congress, Prints and Photographs Division, Reproduction no. LC-L9-70-5503-J#14A/15

Children, here on the front stoop of 123 Sesame Street, seem to tease Oscar the Grouch and ignore Carroll Spinney, the puppeteer. In its early years, *Sesame Street* had a fresh quality, due in part to Connell's insistence that no child actors be used. Lively and rambunctious, these children could be a handful for more than just Oscar. Charlotte Brooks, photographer, *Look* Magazine Collection, Library of Congress, Prints and Photographs Division, Reproduction no. LC-L9-70-5503-DD#15A.

Jim Henson, Jerry Nelson, Caroly Wilcox, and Frank Oz (*from left to right*) hold Muppets aloft. Wilcox occasionally performed minor Muppet characters, but no woman puppeteer created a major Muppet in the early years. When the National Organization for Women complained about the lack of credible female Muppets, Henson responded that women might not be not strong enough to hold the puppets over the long hours of taping. Charlotte Brooks, photographer, *Look* Magazine Collection, Library of Congress, Prints and Photographs Division, Reproduction no. LC-L9-70-5503-O#11/11A.

Early newspaper advertisements featured cartoon characters—Fishing Boy (*left*) and Wanda the Witch (*upper right*)—not the Muppets, as later viewers would expect. CTW Archives. Courtesy of Sesame Workshop

CHAPTER 5

"The Itty Bitty
Little Kiddy Show"

In the fall of 1968, while CTW's research staff was putting the finishing touches on the show's curriculum, the producers began creating what children would see on their TV screens. By February 1969, Executive Producer David Connell had received from cartoon and film contractors their first finished pieces, and he asked the head writer, Jon Stone, to create a promotional film for the show. The Children's Television Workshop needed a half-hour introduction to *Sesame Street* that could be shown to the NET station representatives. But there was a problem: the show still did not have a title—a situation that had become a joke within the workshop. When Stone wrote the script for the film, he made the lack of a title the central gag.[1] To do so, he wrote a set of satirical Muppet skits that he interspersed between the explanatory parts of the film. In these skits, a committee of puppets sat around a conference table considering aspects of the show that might suggest an appropriate title. With each facet, the group incrementally added new words to the title. They began with "The Little Kiddy Show" to indicate the show's audience and added "city" and "nitty gritty" to evoke its urban realism. By the final scene of the film, the puppets had arrived at a complete title: "The Itty Bitty Farm and City Witty Ditty Nitty Gritty Dog and Kitty Pretty Little Kiddy Show." One of the Muppets, Rowlf—a figure familiar to later viewers of *The Muppet Show*—acted as host of the film and expressed frustration at the group's incompetence. The film ended with the quorum of Muppets failing to produce a real title for CTW's program.[2]

The humans at the workshop were not doing much better than the Muppet committee; it took them two more months to agree on a title. Members of the staff submitted lists of possible titles. Among the advertising executives and writers working as consultants were Barbara Demaray and Virginia Schone. Demaray proffered her favorite candidate, "1–2–3 Avenue B." According to Cooney, the staff thought that this one was "too New York." Schone, who had left Madison Avenue to work in a preschool, had heard children on the playground saying, "Open Sesame." These words also appear on the lists of possible titles preserved in the archives, and Schone may have combined them with Demaray's title. No one liked Schone's suggested title. "But nobody came up with anything else, so it won by default," Connell later recalled. Once they settled on the title, the producers returned to the studio and appended to the promotional film a closing Muppet scene in which Kermit—Jim Henson's oldest puppet and his alter ego—suggests "Sesame Street." While the producers were adopting a realistic, urban setting, the title of the show evoked a magical place. CTW and its consultants apparently never confronted or contemplated this incongruity.[3]

Between August 1968 and November 1969, the workshop created much more than a title, a promotional film, and a set. While it was devising the CTW Model, the producers created a format and style for the show, mapped the curriculum to the planned episodes, contracted for cartoons and films, and wrote and taped puppet and studio segments. When cartoons and films came in, the workshop's researchers tested them and, later, when enough material became available, tested entire prototype episodes. Five such episodes reached the air on an educational station in Philadelphia during July 1969. While production and research continued, Cooney and an assistant persuaded educational television stations to broadcast the program at times when preschoolers would be able to watch.

But more than a television program emerged from those first months and the show's first seasons. *Sesame Street* made clear that TV could be educational, nonviolent, and child-centered. To illustrate these broad generalizations and explore *Sesame Street*'s more striking insights into TV, I have sampled and closely studied a few episodes from the program's first ten seasons. Based on this sample, I can answer questions about *Sesame Street*'s style and format, such as, how often did the producers reuse segments? Watching these early shows, I also began to notice subtler aspects of the program, such as the way that the workshop used children's voiceover narration to adopt a child's viewpoint.[4] Edward Palmer and his research staff discovered that a kind of interactive relationship developed between viewers at home and performers on the screen when segments were written and performed in particular ways. The workshop also speculated that the show could help spark supportive relationships between its viewers and their families. These insights revealed that new techniques might eliminate some of the effects on children for which television was most criticized. The result was a program that demonstrated how television could fulfill its social potential.

Connell and his colleagues in production began to design the show during the 1968 summer seminars; one of their first decisions was to adopt a magazine format. Instead of a single continuous episode-length plot, like that of a situation comedy or drama program, *Sesame Street* would consist of a series of largely unrelated segments, like a variety show. The bulk of local children's programs before 1968 had a variety format, alternating studio scenes with cartoons or puppet skits. Similarly, on network TV, any given episode of *Captain Kangaroo* worked its way through a series of short scenes. When conceiving *Sesame Street's* format, Connell recalled that "once we had gotten confident in the research . . . , we felt very strongly that we should do a magazine format, so that if a segment didn't work you could delete it without affecting the rest of the show." This led to a sequence of segments, each designed to fulfill a particular learning goal, each standing on its own and essentially unrelated to the others in the episode.[5]

Sesame Street's style, on the other hand, came from a less likely source. In the winter of 1968, when CTW began its work, *Rowan and Martin's Laugh-In* (NBC, 1968–73) was quickly becoming a hit, and it remained the top-rated prime-time program for the next two seasons.[6] "*Laugh-In* crystallized a kind of contemporary, fast-paced, unstructured comedy 'happening,'" as TV encyclopedists Tim Brooks and Earle Marsh put it; the program became a common point of reference in popular culture. Americans appropriated lines from the show as popular expressions, such as "You bet your bippy," "Sock it to me," and "Here come de judge."[7] Cooney noticed that many children watched *Laugh-In*: "We can't get the inner city kids if we don't reflect what's going on out there," she recalled thinking. She insisted that CTW's show be "hip and fast and funny." Connell also remembered *Laugh-In*, with its frenetic editing, inspiring *Sesame Street's* style and format.[8]

Besides emulating *Laugh-In*, the magazine format also accommodated both the curriculum and the show's demanding production schedule. Plans called for daily episodes, five days a week for six months, a total of 130 per season. CBS executive Michael Dann had recommended Connell to Cooney because he was a "volume producer." Dann felt that Connell could handle the organizational challenge of producing a daily program. To balance the treatment of the entire curriculum across an full season, Connell assigned particular curriculum elements to each episode. For example, he specified one or two letters and one or two numbers to be covered in each episode, covering more important letters in more episodes than less important ones. He included in each episode segments covering each area of the curriculum.[9] While any single episode covered only a fragment of the curriculum, the program covered all parts of it over the course of a season.[10]

The workshop's producers decided to build the show with four types of segments: animated cartoons, short films, puppet skits, and studio skits, the genres they thought were most appealing to children. By planning to videotape the skits in the studio with Henson's Muppets and with the show's human cast, CTW's production staff would handle this part of the production themselves. As for the cartoons and films, independent production contractors would supply these, necessitating greater lead time than the studio segments. Enough time was necessary for animators and film-makers to propose segments, for CTW to approve and fund them, for the contractors then to produce them, and for the research department then to test them. As the seminars came to a close in August 1968, Connell knew that he had to begin soliciting proposed cartoons and films from potential suppliers. By the end of the first season, CTW had commissioned work from thirty-two animators and film producers.[11]

During 1968 and 1969 the development of each segment genre illustrates the CTW Model in action and the show's clear connection to the planning that preceded production. As Cooney had wanted, the show's creators drew heavily on popular culture, learned practical lessons from testing, and kept their audience firmly in mind. Connell's first trip to the west coast in early August 1968, before the last seminar, began the workshop's quest for effective cartoons. During the next fourteen months he went back and forth among New York, Los Angeles, and San Francisco, commissioning animators to produce short cartoons that taught letters, numbers, counting, and words. In December 1968, he brought storyboards, scripts, and ideas for cartoons back for approval by several of CTW's executives and advisers. They approved most of them, and the first finished ones became available in January 1969.[12]

Of the ones they approved, "The Story of J" became the first and prototypical cartoon designed to familiarize children with a single letter. During the planning phase before the creation of CTW, George Dessart, a programming executive from WCBS in New York, had suggested to Cooney that advertising agencies might each donate a commercial for a letter of the alphabet.[13] Though the workshop did not get its cartoons this way, it did turn to animators with the open-ended directive: "Do storyboards on letters of the alphabet."[14] When "The Story of J" arrived, the producers were relieved. Connell later recalled: "All of sudden it worked. We could see somebody understood how to do this." The workshop did adopt Dessart's evocative name for these short cartoons and called this first one the "J commercial." It became a part of the promotional film and exemplified the program's teaching style in early press accounts and in Gerald Lesser's later explanation of *Sesame Street*.[15]

Calling a cartoon like "The Story of J" a "commercial" aptly captures the CTW teaching style. In this sixty-two-second cartoon, a man's voice, booming, God-like, offscreen—offers to tell two boys a story about the letter "J." When they accept his offer, another man's voice chants in verse to the syncopated beat of brushes on a snare drum. The voice-over, accompanied only by percussion, seems vaguely to reflect the Beat poetry style, and the cartoon appears self-consciously "hip." The "story" that the voiceover relates is a nonsensical one—like a children's nursery rhyme—about a carefree man arrested and punished for something trivial. Many of the words in the rhyme begin with the letter "J," and it even includes *Laugh-In*'s familiar tag line, "Here comes the judge!" (see figure 5). Like a television advertisement, it tells a short story that illustrates the product, the letter "J," as people use it. It closes with a glib moral that again reinforces use of the product, and upbeat music accompanies the text and action, as it would in any commercial that might catch a child's ear. If a viewer retained only a snippet of the story, he or she would remember several words that illustrated the sound of the letter that looks "like a fish hook." Short cartoons like "The Story of J" made up 37 percent of the segments in my episode sample.[16]

The research department extensively studied the J commercial with children from local New York City day care centers. In his early article about the show, Stuart Little cited three conclusions that the staff drew from the commercial's testing: "Children can learn their letters and numbers" from cartoons, interruptions like commercials attract children's attention to the TV rather than degrade it, and "the four-year-old can endure enormous amounts of repetition." Typical of the way that CTW's formative research specifically answered questions for the production staff was a study at a day care center. Palmer's researchers found that repetition within a single episode imparted familiarity better than single iterations

Video	Audio
Picture of two small boys sitting and talking	*1st Boy:* What's happening, man?
	2nd Boy: I don't know.
Letter "J" appears from top of screen	*1st Boy:* What's that?
	2nd Boy: I don't know.
"J" enlarges & boys huddle together	*1st Boy:* It looks like a fish hook.
	Man (Voiceover): It's not a fish hook! It's a "J."
	Boys (Together): A what?
	Man (Voiceover): The letter "J." Like to hear a story about the letter "J," boys?
"J" moves to the left	*Boys (Together):* Yeah!
Little man walks over to "J"	*Music up, Voice over:*
and lies in hook, sees bug on toe	Once upon a time a guy named Joe
Gets off "J," puts bug in jar	Noticed a June bug on his toe
Judge enters from right	Put it in a jar and started to go
	But here comes the judge and said, "No, no, no."
Joe jumps	But Joe said, "why?" and started to jump
Joe dances on tree stump	And danced a Jig on an old tree stump
Joe jogs to left of screen	And jogged along to the city dump
Joe puts bug in tire pump	Where he jammed the June bug in a tire pump.
Judge appears & hits Joe on head with gavel	And the judge caught up and started to wail,
	Said to Joe, "Justice will prevail."
Joe in courtroom	And the Jury met and set the bail
Joe behind bars	And Joe got an hour in the city jail.
Cut back to 2 boys sitting, then lying down looking up at "J"	*1st Boy:* So that's the letter "J."
	2nd Boy: It still looks like a fish hook.
Boys sit up	*1st Boy:* You know what else we learned?
Words starting with "J" appear as they are spoken	*2nd Boy:* Yeah. Don't jive a judge by jamming a june bug.

Fig. 5. Text of "The Story of J" or the J commercial. Adapted from "'J'-Commercial," two-column script, n.d., file: "Scripts and Storyboards: 'J,' 1969," Box 37, CTW Archives. Courtesy of Sesame Workshop.

on consecutive days. Because children at the center were absent and missed the show some days, the workshop could be more certain that they would see the commercial several times if they ran it several times during a single episode. The more general conclusion, later reinforced by the ETS's evaluation, was that sheer volume of exposure to *Sesame Street*, among other things, determined instructional effectiveness.[17]

In at least one way, this early research illustrated how the workshop's empirical, untheoretical approach could leave puzzling questions unanswered. The study on the J commercial reported that, when first shown the cartoon, 15 of 19 children "watched the film intently but in a zombie like fashion."[18] By "zombie" viewing, the workshop's researchers meant that a child seemed so absorbed in the program that he or she sat motionless, manifesting "either intense concentration or stupor."[19] Ironically, CTW's adoption of the pejorative word "zombie" cast a negative light on the very attentiveness that their research and artistic efforts sought. Many of their later research studies document child viewers who, in response to particular segments, danced, sang, or talked back to the screen.[20] Despite their meticulous documentation of these reactions, CTW's researchers' could not resolve their implicit question: Was "zombie" viewing the outward manifestation of learning or of passivity? Critics of television had long accused the medium of hypnotizing children into a thoughtless, inert state. If *Sesame Street* had this effect on children, it could hardly be educational. On the other hand, if one theorized that children actively worked to decode television and that this activity commanded great concentration, "zombie" viewing might be a positive sign. Although CTW's research system created outward, behavioral information that researcher and producer alike could accept, it could not resolve a question like this one without some resort to theory.[21]

During the spring of 1969, while animators created cartoons under the production department's supervision, other contractors produced films. In the *Sesame Street* context, "film" meant segments that depicted human actors or real animals instead of animated characters; it did not designate the physical medium on which contractors submitted their work to CTW. Connell collaborated closely with one contractor on a series of films featuring "The Man from Alphabet," a bumbling super-spy. Starring *Laugh-In*'s Gary Owens, these films were each a complete story, roughly five minutes in length, in which "Man" solved a case. Connell and the contractor apparently modeled these films on the spy spoof *Get Smart* (NBC/CBS, 1965–70).[22] Only with the help of an African-American boy, H. B.—the only intelligent character in the series—could Man catch the two criminals, Digby Dropout and Dunce, who appeared in every film and were as inept as he was. H. B. found the clues needed to capture the crooks in his "Alphabet Book." In the course of the comedic action, these segments familiarized viewers with letters and taught them other skills, like telling time. Judging from his appointment book, Connell devoted significant time and attention to the series.[23]

In spite of his and the contractor's efforts, when the research department tested the films, it found that they confused children, did not appeal to them, and failed to teach them. Palmer and an assistant tested the films with four-year-olds at a New York City day care center, using the distractor and other techniques. They closely observed the children's behavior and noted when they laughed, imitated the characters, and remarked on the action. Questioning the youngsters, the researchers found that Man's combination of bumbling and solving the mystery puzzled them, though they could tell that Man was the "good guy." H. B. and the Alphabet Book simply added to the confusion without adding any real instruction. The distractor results made it clear that the "Man" segments, when included in complete episodes, held children's attention less than almost any of the show's other elements. Possibly explaining the failure to hold the children's attention was the films' use of comedy. Palmer wrote that the "humor is probably peculiar to an exceedingly small adult audience, consisting predominantly of *males*, and even more predominantly of males in the entertainment business. I don't believe it will have all that much appeal to people in control of the set." To make matters worse, he added, "The amount of truly effective educational content, relative to our goals, is virtually nil." However, the workshop learned two important lessons: children become bored when adults talk, but they laugh and pay attention to slapstick comedy.[24]

The "Man from Alphabet" experience was a remarkable instance of the Model at work. Palmer's study and the test episode broadcasts in Philadelphia eliminated the "Man" series from the workshop's library of effective segments, despite all of the effort Connell had put into them. CTW dropped them without ever including them in a *Sesame Street* broadcast. Unlike commercial television's approach, CTW allowed children's closely studied reactions to override the artistic judgment of producers and management. Films made up 17 percent of the segments in the episode sample. Much more popular with young viewers were the films that showed animals in action. Later, other film series starring human characters, like the Mad Painter, did succeed on the show.[25]

Besides cartoons and films, *Sesame Street* would have puppet segments.

Jon Stone, the head writer, recommended a friend of his named Jim Henson, who had a troupe called the Muppets. The two men had worked together on several projects, including Henson's first network show—a special called *Hey, Cinderella*. Stone and the producers told Cooney that Henson's puppet company was the only one that had the "hip" quality CTW was seeking. Henson resisted initially but became more interested after attending the third summer seminar. Like many others, he joined the project to contribute to a noble social goal, and his puppets were crucial to *Sesame Street*'s popularity. But working on *Sesame Street* was a decisive breakthrough for Henson's career as well, bringing him the national recognition for which he had long struggled.[26]

Henson Associates and CTW carefully balanced their partnership, each with its self-interest in mind. Henson's company remained a contractor, like those who made cartoons and films. His initial reluctance arose because he wanted to continue to entertain adults, as he had in his earlier advertisements and variety show appearances. He did not want to be identified as a children's entertainer, as most puppeteers were. For *Sesame Street*, his company would design Muppet characters but would reserve at least one established character, Rowlf the Dog, who appeared in the promotional film, for later commercial ventures of his own. Only Kermit the Frog, his trademark character, crossed over between *Sesame Street* and his later productions. Thomas Kennedy, CTW's vice president of finance, later remarked that Henson "was clearly heading to make a lot of money." In addition to his altruism and the prominence and revenue *Sesame Street* brought, the opportunity to produce animated and live-action films for the show also attracted Henson. The arrangement worked well for the workshop, as well because it retained control of *Sesame Street*'s characters and thus of their personalities. Exclusivity avoided controversies like the one that involved Kermit when he introduced advertising spots on *Hey, Cinderella* for the R. J. Reynolds tobacco company. After he had already become a recognized character on *Sesame Street*, his association with a sponsor, especially a tobacco company, provoked criticism. The relationship between CTW and Henson's company was not untroubled. But, by fashioning their relationship carefully, they avoided problems and, as of this writing, the partnership continues.[27]

Their collaborative production of the puppet segments also divided the labor between the two companies. CTW wrote the scripts, and Stone directed production of the skits. Henson's designers built the puppets, and his performers brought them "to life," inventing voices and personalities to fit the workshop's needs. During production, Henson and his puppeteers improvised on the scripts and shaped them to the troupe's distinctive style. The characters that emerged typically had evocative, individual traits.[28]

Bert and Ernie, *Sesame Street*'s first Muppets, exemplify the kinds of characters that Henson developed and help to explain the appeal that the program has had for viewers of different ages. Bert and Ernie have been likened to Neil Simon's famous "odd couple"; their friendship survives in spite of their clashing personalities. For example, on one occasion, Ernie, the carefree trickster, plays a joke on his friend and roommate, Bert. In another instance, Ernie displays child-like naïveté and tries to save ice cubes in a box under an electric blanket. Bert, sober and earnest, plays straight man to Ernie and takes an interest in remarkably boring things, like collecting bottle caps. Their ages are indeterminate and liminal. Much of their behavior seems that of school-age children, but they live without parents, maintaining a household on their own. Christopher Finch, author of two official Muppet books, plausibly characterized Bert as "the stodgy adult figure" and Ernie as "the cocky kid." But their interactions seem more those of peers than mentoring adult and young protégé. In short, a child might find their antics simply funny, while a grown-up might see humor in them as adults, children, or comedians.[29]

In the first test episode there are only two Ernie and Bert skits, but they typify the early role of the Muppets on *Sesame Street*. In their first scene, they teach viewers about the number two by pointing to two eyes, two ears, etc. Ernie adds "two noses," a comment that Bert hastens to correct. Ernie responds by removing Bert's nose (apparently affixed with a temporary adhesive) and sticking it on the end of his own, giving himself two noses. In their second skit, they have a disagreement over what to watch on TV. Ernie wants to watch "Batman," and Bert wants to watch another program. As they argue, Batman himself, from the screen, interrupts them to suggest that they take turns. Watch Bert's show today, he suggests, because they watched "Batman" yesterday and can watch it again tomorrow. Typical of many of the Bert and Ernie segments, this second one centers on a mundane domestic disagreement and teaches a lesson about "cooperation," one of the few social goals in the original curriculum. Skits involving these two puppets ranged over many of the curricular goals during the ten years of episodes that I surveyed, and Muppet segments, in general, made up 20 percent of those in the sample.[30]

Research on the test episodes and subsequent findings justified the growing importance of the Muppets during the first few seasons. In the distractor tests, Bert, Ernie, and the nameless "Anything Muppets" that also appeared, scored well but not the best. An animal film, for example, held children's attention better, but Palmer's report did point to the puppets as one of the stronger parts of the test episodes. Thereafter, CTW added more Muppets during the first and subsequent seasons, not only because their popularity increased but also because they taught effectively. Children readily recognized them. As stereotypic characters, their bright, distinctive appearance and simple, striking personalities made it easy for young viewers to know what to expect. They held children's attention without leaving the youngsters to puzzle over their identities. Grown-ups also enjoyed the Muppets' humor because it was written to appeal to different ages and because Henson had always entertained adults. Keeping older viewers watching alongside the preschoolers could prompt educational conversations at home.[31]

With cartoons, films, and puppet skits in production, the only remaining design decisions involved the studio skits. The production staff began with a conception that they abandoned, perhaps in part due to testing but, more likely, on aesthetic grounds. Connell asked Clark Gesner, a colleague from *Captain Kangaroo* and the author of *You're a Good Man, Charlie Brown*, to create a pilot for the studio skits with a few of his own animated and film segments interspersed. The studio segments involved two children whose inner thoughts were dramatized. For example, when J. J. becomes angry with Sheila, he imagines hitting her over the head, but dramatizing this fantasy confused young viewers about whether it had "happened" or not. Preschool-age children could not distinguish between what was "real" and what was "imagined" within the frame of a TV drama and found other aspects of the studio skits confusing. But Stone's objections probably outweighed those of the researchers. Gesner's conception of the studio setting "was the *exact antithesis* of where my mind was going," Stone later recalled. "It was very clean and high tech, plastic looking. . . . I wanted something really funky and down to earth." Though CTW kept the cartoons and films Gesner produced, Stone's vision prevailed, and his concept became that emblematic place, Sesame Street.[32]

He conceived of it as "down to earth . . . a real inner city street" where "real people" lived.[33] He designed the studio set to resemble a poor neighborhood in New York City with a brownstone apartment building and a corner grocery store. Initially, the workshop considered casting teachers in the roles of the neighborhood's inhabitants but rejected the idea. The production department cast two actors and two singers to play a married African-American couple, Susan and Gordon, and their white neighbors Bob and Mr. Hooper. Mr. Hooper owned and ran a grocery store on Sesame Street. Bob and Gordon worked as teachers, and Susan was a full-time housewife. The characters that they played seemed more real because all four performers were new to TV viewers. As is so often the case in television, an unfamiliar actor fuses with his or her character in the minds of viewers. On the street, in front of the buildings, the four neighbors met, chatted, solved problems and taught the "neighborhood children." In keeping with using little-known performers as the adult stars, the producers recruited from local schools and day care centers children who were not actors to appear as children in the street skits. These studio segments made up 25 percent of the segments in the episode sample.[34]

Choosing to set the show in a low-income, urban neighborhood grew out of the workshop's desire to help poorer African-American children identify with the place they saw on their television screens. As Stone later explained, his idea for the street set "was that inner city disadvantaged kids are so often housebound, stuck home all alone while their mothers work, and God knows where the fathers are." Stone continued, "They look out the window and that's where the big kids are playing and the noise is going on. The street outside is where it's really happening[;] that's where the action is."[35] Poor children would identify the Street scenes with a part of their own lives, the CTW staff reasoned, and they would see "real" people there whom they could emulate. The boys and girls who appeared on *Sesame Street*, who played on the Street, were African-American, white, Latino, and Asian in what seem carefully composed combinations. Judging by the episode sample, never is only one gender or ethnicity represented among the children, though there are proportionally more minority youngsters than in the American population as a whole.[36]

Initially, the workshop conceived the most important character, Gordon, as a sort of father figure for the low-income African-American children in the audience. In the first season, he sometimes opened the episode, speaking directly to the audience and explaining the opening scene. His direct address somewhat resembled Fred Rogers's fatherly tone on *Mister Rogers' Neighborhood*, and, among the four adult Street characters, he acted as the first among equals, the unofficial host.[37] In his family, he was the breadwinner, a steadfast husband whose wife did not have to work. Reflecting on this characterization years later, Stone called it "real middle class modeling." Gordon was "a strong competent male image to inner city children who often do not have a stable masculine figure in their lives," Cooney wrote early in the show's first season. Researchers, such as Daniel Patrick Moynihan, had blamed absent African-American fathers, in part, for the failure of their children in school. When Gordon taught youngsters on the show or helped Big Bird, for example, CTW hoped that poor children watching would share in an affirming experience that was missing from their real lives. Though the workshop directed the other types of segments to children in general, it designed the Street skits for the impoverished African-American children who were at the center of the show's concentric audience.[38]

Along with the set and cast, CTW initially tried to maintain the realism of the Street segments by excluding the puppet characters, who lived underground instead. CTW's academic advisers recommended that the realistic and the fantastic be clearly separated. In the test episodes, the Muppets—primarily Bert and Ernie—apparently lived in a basement and did not appear with the human characters on the Street. Cartoons, films, and Muppet segments helped set off the Street segments as less fantastic. Connell later remembered questioning the experts' advice: "Tell me, define for me what is fantasy and what is reality for a four-year-old watching a television set." Despite his doubts, the producers kept the division of the realistic and fantastic until the test episodes revealed problems.[39]

In July 1969, the production department took examples of the four types of segments and created five complete prototype episodes to test the program as a whole. With these, the research department measured how well the show as a whole would teach the core curriculum items and tried out the summative research techniques to be used during the first season. To provide realistic broadcast conditions, a Philadelphia educational channel, WHUY (a UHF station, operated by the NET affiliate WHYY), broadcast the episodes. CTW's researchers used tests developed by the Educational Testing Service and administered them before and after the week of broadcasts. The pre-tests confirmed that middle-class children began ahead of poor ones, and poor children in day care centers ahead of those who were not in such centers. The post-tests showed that children in all three categories made gains. Researchers found that children learned from the show while watching it at home, despite problems of distractions and broadcast reception. Learning took place most extensively in the curriculum areas that received the most air time and varied treatment—using several different cartoons or using the combination of animated, puppet, and studio segments.[40]

Information about attention as well as comprehension came from the test episodes. As a whole, the hour-long show held four-year-olds' attention as well as virtually anything on TV and better than *Captain Kangaroo*, *Mister Rogers' Neighborhood*, *Roundabout*, or *The Friendly Giant*—all leading examples of educational children's programs. Palmer's researchers found that it also surpassed cartoon shows, including *Yogi Bear, Huckle-*

berry Hound, and *Roger Ramjet.* Among the four kinds of *Sesame Street* segments, cartoons and puppet skits particularly appealed to the children. Adding more detailed insights, the distractor's graph of the moment-to-moment attention scores could be synchronized like a seismograph and viewed in tandem with the program itself. As notations on the copy of the graph in the research report show, when the action stopped and adults began talking, children stopped watching. When Susan sang or cartoons appeared or animals frolicked, children looked back to the television set. Animated segments with simpler plots taught more effectively than those with more complicated ones. These early tests reassured the workshop that its new program could teach and entertain and that its research system was generating useful information.[41]

With growing faith in its own internal research, CTW began to rely less on outside experts. This trend began to emerge in the wake of the test broadcasts. In August 1969, the workshop convened a meeting of the advisory board to review the test results but ultimately ignored most of the board's advice. A central conclusion from the distractor testing was that the Street segments bored children. After viewing the episodes, the experts offered a variety of critiques. Paul Taff, NET's children's programming director, and others offered ways to strengthen the Street skits. Making the Street an idealized place of child empowerment was one suggestion. Psychologist Chester Pierce recommended that "the ghetto [be made] a vital, vibrant place where [the child] is in control." Psychiatrist Leon Eisenberg asserted, "The show seems unrelated to the problems that confront the inner-city child"; he proposed that the producers write segments in which "the kids participate in a rent strike, for example." Though the records do not reveal anything further of his logic, Eisenberg was one of the first to note that *Sesame Street*'s urban realism was superficial. Instead, CTW had envisioned a fantastic place, urban in appearance but divorced from the systemic problems of impoverished neighborhoods. Instead of rent strikes and the like, conflicts had been displaced into an interpersonal realm among the residents. Child development psychologist Jerome Kagan encouraged CTW to situate conflict within the community and suggested that the show include "short morality skits on tolerance for deviates."[42]

Increasingly confident in their own resources, the workshop's staff chose to ignore much of the experts' advice about the Street segments. Despite Eisenberg's call for a more "real" setting, the producers wanted to "jazz up the street" and offered to "mix reality and fantasy" by adding puppets.[43] The importance of expert advice began to pale in the face of a successful partnership of internal researchers and producers.[44] Connell recalled that this drift began with earlier meetings and started "because I felt we knew pretty much what these kids were like and what we were supposed to do." While they considered the experts' recommendations and followed Kagan's, the producers avoided politically controversial ideas. They relied on their own artistic instincts and the workshop's own research.[45]

They decided to add more of Henson's Muppets. They conflated the fantastic and the realistic by adding the puppets Big Bird and Oscar the Grouch to the Street cast. Big Bird was born of Sheldon White's idea for a Mr. Fluster character and of Henson and Stone's plans for a giant bird puppet. Joining a human cast of adults, Big Bird was like a child, a bumbling, three-year-old struggling to learn. More effectively than the Man from Alphabet, he stood for the learner whom children could emulate or surpass. Oscar filled the role of Kagan's "deviate," whose conflicts with others on the Street taught "tolerance" for "differing perspectives," as the curriculum dictated. He also could represent a cranky neighbor or an aggressive sibling.[46] Like Bert and Ernie and unlike Big Bird, Oscar's status as an adult or a child remained unclear. More important than Big Bird's and Oscar's possible ages, though, were their relationships to each other and to the human cast. Big Bird served as the student of the teacher-like adults, Oscar as their prickly opponent. As Lesser put it years later, because puppets "can portray more exaggerated and therefore clearer roles and functions than human figures," their interplay is easier for children to follow.[47] As the realistic ghetto street became less so, pedagogical concerns had overshadowed elements meant to address the minority audience, but CTW had also balanced its experts' advice with its own televisual art.

While the workshop was designing the program, Cooney and assistant director Robert Davidson were attempting to ensure that the maximum number of preschoolers would see the show. To do so, they had to persuade as many educational television stations as possible to carry it and to broadcast it at the best possible times. Ideally, CTW wanted stations to air each daily episode twice, once in the morning at 9:00 a.m. and again sometime in the afternoon. There were a number of reasons for the workshop's keen interest in the 9 o'clock time slot: the large number of preschoolers watching, their control of the set with siblings at school, scheduling convenience for day care centers, and the dearth of preschool programming at that time of day.[48] CTW also wanted to avoid competing with *Captain Kangaroo* at 8:00 a.m. because they considered it the only other good program on the air for preschoolers.[49] Stations readily agreed to the afternoon times, but resisted a morning air time because it conflicted with many stations' existing instructional programs for classroom use in public schools. Consequently, the workshop's strong preference for a 9 o'clock broadcast brought it into conflict with local school authorities. Ultimately, 196 stations carried the show in its first season, a quarter of which did not air it in a morning time slot. At least sixteen commercial stations carried it in areas where there was no educational station or where the local NET affiliate refused to carry it. In its first Nielsen ratings in the fall of 1969, *Sesame Street* could be received in 67.6 percent of American households with televisions.[50]

A closer look at *Sesame Street* and the way its viewers interacted with it reveals several ways in which it became an ideal program to respond to longtime criticisms of children's TV. Most fundamentally, the program seemed educational to adult viewers, unlike much of commercial TV. For example, when CTW's polling firm quoted verbatim comments from mothers in three "ghetto communities" in 1970, twenty-eight of thirty-one lauded the show's educational value. One typical comment went: "It is very educational for the children. It helps mothers to teach their children." Much of the press similarly lauded the show's educational value. For example, *Nation's Schools* concluded that "If Kids Act Smarter, 'Sesame Street' May Be the Reason."[51]

Reinforcing this popular impression was the minimal number of segments that the workshop included for non-educational purposes. Though CTW attributed a curricular goal to every segment, it left a category called "miscellaneous" for segments that were merely entertainment. In my sample, 6 percent of the segments belong in this category. These included appearances by popular music groups and transitional segments to smooth the program's flow. For example, in a 1976 episode, Stevie Wonder, an African-American singer and songwriter, plays with his band on the Street, and children listen and dance. The workshop intended musical segments like Wonder's to hold the interest of older siblings and parents. Some of the transitional segments introduce the ones that follow; others close the episode. For example, at the end of every episode, a member of the cast— human or puppet—delivers the familiar line *"Sesame Street* was brought to you today by the letter ___ and the number ___" filling in the letter and number taught that day. Before this line is delivered, there is usually some closing banter or action to conclude the episode.[52]

The show also provided an alternative to violent programming. Around the time of *Sesame Street*'s premiere, the National Commission on the Causes and Prevention of Violence (Eisenhower Commission) had called for the elimination of all "non-comic violence." By the end of the show's first season, a writer in *PTA Magazine* lauded *Sesame Street* as "a child's world without violence, without fear."[53] The episode sample reveals little or no violence, though there is mundane conflict of the sort that ordinary courtesy and compromise might resolve.

What violence the show included clearly worked as slapstick punctuation at the end of cartoon segments. For example, in one segment, a comic figure heckles an instructor character, who is trying to deliver a few examples of words that begin with the letter "H." The heckler peppers the instructor with other "H" words and demonstrates many of them, distracting the teacher from the orderly lesson. When the instructor becomes weary of the distractions, he draws a circle around the feet of the comic, who then falls through a hole that opens beneath him. As the comic drops from sight his "Help!"—also an "H" word—can be heard to echo as though he were falling a great distance. In two other segments, cartoon instructors are eaten by fearsome animals in one clean bite to mark the end of the segment.[54] Most famously, a set of number segments made by Henson each closes with a "baker" standing at the top of a short flight of stairs with an armload of desserts. The number of desserts matches the number that the segment taught. He intones, for example, "Ten chocolate layer cakes." Then, the desserts begin to topple from his arms, as he tries to regain his grasp, loses his footing, and falls down the stairs. When the closing music plays, he is lying in a heap with the cakes scattered everywhere. Some critics of the show complained that this punctuating slapstick was too violent.[55]

More typical of *Sesame Street* was the way violence was avoided. In one cartoon segment, two small monkeys are watching television. The soundtrack of a western indicates the kind of program they are watching until one of them changes the channel to a classical music concert show. As the two change the channel back and forth, their argument over what they will watch escalates until each has puffed himself up into a large gorilla. Before they come to blows, however, they agree that, if the classical music fan agrees to watch the western today, they will both watch the music show tomorrow. Both settle down to watch calmly again, returning to the size of monkeys. Given that such disputes over program choice appeared more than once, the workshop may have been suggesting that older siblings defer their own programs until later and allow preschoolers to watch *Sesame Street* today. Typical of the way the program addressed both more and less naïve viewers, CTW designed the program to be not only evidently educational and nonviolent but also attuned to the audience's viewing circumstances.[56]

Sesame Street went beyond these virtues to present the world from a child's perspective. It envisioned, for its young viewers, an idealized world of learning and play. The workshop did not articulate this vision as an objective *per se*, but it evolved out of its research. Most clearly, though, it is apparent in the show itself.

Based on an important insight from its research, CTW crafted *Sesame Street* to take on a child's perspective when it used children's voices to describe the action on the screen. Early studies led Palmer and the researchers to conclude that children "have enormous difficulty constructing a mental image of a scene from a spoken description." Consequently, children became bored with "full-face" talk, particularly by adults. Instead, CTW decided that *Sesame Street* should portray dramatic action instead of describing it through character dialogue.[57]

Voiceover commentary could then accompany the actions shown. In my episode sample the voiceovers come from a mixture of adults and children. But many of these adult voices did not bring with them a tone of authority that would have intruded on this idealized world. Authoritative male voices are often used ironically, and other adult voices come from women or friendly Street cast members. For example, comedienne Anne Meara humorously comments on two silent film segments, in which the protagonist tries to solve a problem. Based on the sample's 179 examples, voiceover commentary more often emulated the authority of the classroom teacher than that of the news anchorman or documentary narrator.[58]

More relevant to the show's relationship to the child viewer, though, were the sixty-three film segments in which children provided the voiceover commentary.[59] In these, the children comment, explain, and discuss the action as the viewer watches it on screen. Film contractors or CTW producers seem to have recorded the children while they watched the films. The youngsters comment, explain the action, and even warn the characters onscreen. For example, in one film a man is in a small room with two doors in the back wall. After having entered through one, he notices the other, which is labeled "Danger." Despite a group of voiceover children repeatedly and vehemently warning him not to enter, he opens the door anyway, and an explosion ensues.[60] In another film, a more typical example, a group of children, in voiceover, explains the steps in automobile manufacture. When one sees a large assembly line drive chain, he says, "Oooh, weird. What's that, a great big chain?" Another answers, "It makes the car go around because the men can't lift it by themselves." Seeing the engines pass by, the children exclaim, "The engines!" but one, seeing an exposed flywheel, mistakes it for a wheel. The others repeat: "The engines!" The children comment on each step until, at the end, a train carries the cars away "to people, to all the places, New York, Virginia. . . ." In other segments, child voiceovers remark on the "unsung beauty of manhole covers," count twenty penguins, and stop and restart the action of birds in a film.[61]

By using voiceovers like these, the workshop seemed to hope that young viewers would identify with eager learners like themselves who speak like themselves. These segments offered models of inquiring children, discussing their world and mastering it through language. These real voices—evidently unscripted—presented idealized learners for viewers at home to emulate. And by using real children—perhaps of preschool age or a little older—CTW could avoid the problems of presenting language too advanced for their particular audience of poor children, or language too detached from those children's ethnicity and culture. Lesser wrote that "since modeling effects are strengthened through children's identification with the character they are watching, we decided to introduce varieties of speech forms on the program, including some spoken dialect and a considerable amount of informal 'street' language."[62] Though he was not writing specifically of the voiceover children, the same identification effect might have operated. Most importantly, though, the voiceovers presented the action on the screen from a child's perspective.

Besides looking at the world through children's eyes, the show took a child's view toward learning and play. Cooney wrote in her 1966 feasibility study that "children receive pleasure from achievement and mastery and do not differentiate between work and play." She added in the 1968 proposal that "the line dividing 'work' from 'play' may well be a barrier erected by the adult mind." When the show made it to the air, it erased this adult boundary.[63]

Examples in all four types of segments obscured the line between the work of learning and the joy of play. In one cartoon, a boy teaches a younger girl the difference between up and down. Repeatedly, he says "up" as they run up some stairs together, and "down" as they run down. When he asks at the end what she has learned, out of breath, she replies that down is easier. In a studio segment, Gordon plays a game with two girls. After he places an object in a box, the girls must reach into the box and guess what the object is by touch alone. Playing the "touch box" game, the children find that it is unexpectedly hard to recognize familiar objects without seeing them. Learning and play with the Muppets often took the form of friendly interaction in which children taught the puppets. In one such segment, the Count, the ebullient and harmless vampire Muppet, learns to count in Spanish from a young girl. In a film, a group of children go on a "blind walk." Blindfolded, they try to identify particular objects on a city street, like a parking meter, by feeling them. By putting children on the screen who are learning and having fun, the show put forward models of inquisitiveness for all its young viewers to emulate.[64]

Sesame Street also showed that television could encourage a more active posture in its young viewers—one that addressed existing concerns about passivity. Fears that TV fostered inert viewing by children took several forms. Signs of this popular apprehension surfaced as early as 1952 in the research of social scientists like Paul Witty and Wilbur Schramm, who wrote that children seemed to "prefer the 'edited' life on television to real life."[65] Teachers feared their students had come to expect entertainment and were becoming bored in school.[66] Many other adults, like Nolan Estes of the United States Office of Education, insisted that television could not teach because it led children to view passively. Undermining this common perception, CTW discovered that children responded verbally to certain kinds of segments and that segments could be crafted to promote interaction.

Critical to this discovery was the workshop's embrace, from the beginning, of segment repetition. Showing the same pieces over and over again was "an effective teaching technique," Cooney wrote in her first study, and she planned to borrow it from the standard practice of television advertising campaigns.[67] It remained a major feature of the show throughout the first ten seasons. Judging from the episode sample, more than one in six segments was a repeat of an earlier one; the vast bulk of these were cartoons.[68] Repetition of segments had financial advantages; expensive cartoon segments could be used repeatedly, better justifying their high cost.[69] And the research department established early on that repetition did not bother young viewers.[70] Repeatedly watching the same segment or type of segment over and over made it possible for young viewers to become thoroughly familiar with it.

CTW's experience with an often repeated alphabet recitation segment revealed to the researchers the interactive possibilities. During the first season, the producers asked James Earl Jones, an African-American actor, to come into the studio and recite the alphabet in front of the camera. He did so with long pauses between each letter, and, when the producers readied the film for use, they superimposed each letter in a corner of the screen just before Jones said it. When the research department tested the film, they discovered an intriguing phenomenon. Children watching the segment had time to repeat each letter after Jones did due to his long pauses. Youngsters who had seen the film a few times began to be able to say each letter along with Jones and then, on later viewings, to anticipate the next letter before he spoke it. For the ones who could beat him to the next letter, Jones confirmed that they were right or corrected them. Observing what CTW dubbed the "James Earl Jones Effect," the staff realized that they had found a way to make television interactive. The letter superimposed next to Jones on the screen prompted the children, they responded by saying it, and the actor then gave the correct response.[71]

The "One of these things . . ." segments illustrate a simpler but also more common example of TV teacher-child viewer interaction. Cooney had invented this format herself and included it in the 1968 proposal. Designed to teach sorting and visual discrimination, these segments always presented four things, one in each of four cells of a two-by-two matrix. Three of the things would be identical or have some common characteristic that they did not share with the fourth. The segments always began with the same lyrics:

> *One of these things is not like the others;*
> *One of these things just doesn't belong.*
> *Can you tell which thing is not like the others*
> *By the time I finish my song?*

> *Did you guess which thing is not like the others?*
> *Did you guess real hard, with all of your might?*
> *If you guessed this thing is not like the others,*
> *Then you're absolutely right!*[72]

As it was sung by one of the cast members, the child viewers had time to examine the four objects and decide which one did not match the others. When the song concluded with a distinct cadence, it prompted the child to make a selection. The host would then point out and explain the correct answer, usually with reference to the common characteristic of the three matching objects.

There were many variations on this format. The matrix itself began as a board on an easel in the Street studio and later became a split screen with films of children in each cell. For each variation the lyrics of the song changed, but the melody never did. Seventeen segments that follow the format appear in the episode sample.[73] Though not as cleverly interactive as the Jones segment, the "One of These" games posed a question, gave children time to answer, and reinforced the correct response. Repeating the format while varying the details, Palmer concluded, gave a child the chance to become "quite proficient in grasping and coping with its nuances . . . [and] developing [a] facility (wiseness) in the given format."[74]

In time, CTW even admitted that the question, "which thing is not like the others," could have more than one correct answer. In one segment from the ninth season, the grocer character, Mr. Hooper, uses boxes of detergent and food from his store to play the game with Big Bird, and shows him the correct answer: The box of custard mix is smaller than the other three. Bird then replies that there is another possible answer: The detergent is the only one that is not food. He cajoles Hooper to admit that there is more than one possible right answer.[75] Repetition, in a sense, made the many variations of this format possible. It also made an almost interactive style of television possible, and these segments vindicated Hausman's retort to Estes that all viewing did not necessarily have to be passive. Not all of *Sesame Street* elicited such active viewing, but it did demonstrate that television could teach in new and unexpected ways.[76]

Just as critics doubted that *Sesame Street* could solve the problem of passive viewing, most observers questioned whether any television program— certainly one so focused on rudimentary literacy—could help preschoolers develop the self-esteem that they needed most. The Bank Street College of Education prescribed the development of confidence as a goal for the preschools that followed the Progressive or traditional approach. Likewise, Edward Zigler, one of Head Start's founders, considered "achievement motivation" more important than specific cognitive skills. In retrospect, he thought that the federal preschool programs had been too influenced by available standardized tests, and he concluded that the demand for "results" had denied poor children the benefits of the "social and emotional orientation of traditional middle-class nursery schools." Despite *Sesame Street*'s creators having a clear allegiance to more experimental and cognitive approaches, such as those of Carl Bereiter, they had to consider the belief of many preschool educators that self-confidence was more important. As Cooney and the others planned the show's curriculum, they speculated about ways that the show might simultaneously teach cognitive skills, nurture self-esteem, and stimulate inquisitiveness.[77]

The incremental construction of CTW's informal self-esteem theory began with an insight about the power of a cognitively oriented program to stimulate children's interest in learning. In the 1968 proposal, Cooney pointed out that there had been no adverse emotional effects on children from a strongly cognitive curriculum in the two schools she had visited. She wrote that "learning itself" and "a sense of achievement and mastery over the environment" promoted a child's adjustment to school. A growing sense of competence might whet a child's appetite for learning, she implied, and all preschoolers, regardless of social classes or race, might experience this excitement.[78]

Lesser arrived at an informal theory by adding to Cooney's idea a parent-child interaction described in the psychological literature. But these interactions also added a social class aspect to the theory. In the midst of the preschool moment, researchers sought the source of the initial disadvantage of poor children in school and found evidence of a variety of "deficits" in their environments and families, as compared to their middle-class peers. One such study stressed the differences in motherly nurture between the poor and the middle class. Psychologists Robert D. Hess and Virginia C. Shipman concluded that an authoritarian parenting style, often associated with the poor, did not evoke the kinds of discussions that a "cognitive-rational" style, more typical of middle-class parents, did. By discussing the "sequence of events, a long-term payoff, or a principle which states the rationale behind a rule or demand," non-authoritarian mothers initiated conversations that ultimately developed their children's verbal skills better than prescribing behavioral norms or demanding blind obedience.[79]

In explaining the basis of Lesser's thinking, Palmer described an idea related to Hess's and Shipman's findings, the notion of the (largely middle-class) "educating mother" who motivates her children by associating learning with love and intimacy. Describing a possible exchange over breakfast between such a mother and her son, Palmer illustrated "that middle-class stereotype": "Oh, Johnny, look! Three pats of butter. Can you count the butter on your pancakes?" "Those exchanges between children and parents in . . . middle-income homes would have had an educative intent," he continued. "I think that [it] was clear that that wasn't found as prevalently in low-income—which [in 1968] also meant largely minority—communities." When he recalled this research many years later, Palmer hastened to add that he recognized the "racist overtones" of such research at the time because to most Americans, "low-income" was synonymous with "black."[80]

Lesser combined elements of Cooney's idea with the parent-child interactions Hess and Shipman had found. In a 1972 article, Lesser began by conceding that a sense of competence "remains a profound mystery" and did not "proceed in a neat succession of discrete steps." But he speculated that when children learn letters, numbers, and geometric shapes and show off their new skills to someone who cares about them, they receive, in turn, "attention and admiration." These emotional rewards could convince children of their competence and "stimulate" an "appetite for learning."[81] In keeping with his landmark study with Susan Stodolsky, Lesser did not adopt the cultural deprivation research out of which Hess and Shipman's work came. Nothing in his theory made reference to "educative mothers" or deficits or minority children. But the reinforcement of learning through love and intimacy played a central role, as did Cooney's sense of competence. Lesser's concept embraced all preschoolers universally while using means to build inquisitiveness that at least some would have considered middle-class.[82]

The workshop never tested this theory, but it did promote the show with anecdotes that support it. Two testimonials from a public relations department compilation, for example, hint that some of this interaction did take place. "In New Jersey, a regular viewer of the program, who was three years old, burst into his parents' bedroom in the middle of the night clutching his pillow. His parents, fearing that some accident had occurred, listened intently as the youngster exclaimed: 'Mommy! Daddy! My pillow— it's a rectangle." A mother from New Rochelle, New York, wrote: "The other day I noticed my 18 month-old daughter sitting with an abacus-type toy. She was separating the beads and saying 'four,' 'sept,' 'sis,'—I suddenly realized she was trying to count. We have not attempted to teach her counting as yet ourselves."[83] Unspoken in these short vignettes are the parent's supportive responses, but the delight expressed in the letters implies that parents rewarded learning from *Sesame Street* in ways no television show could and in ways Lesser's theory anticipated.

If these idyllic bonding experiences between parent and child did commonly occur, *Sesame Street* could boast of eliminating one divisive influence that television had had when it encouraged children's consumer desires. Advertisers had encouraged children to press their parents to buy particular products. Television critic Jack Gould had complained that "hard-hitting salesmanship . . . even to blatant coercion of unsuspecting small children to persuade mother to buy [a specific] product" disrupted *Ding Dong School*'s teaching. So notorious had this practice become by the time of *Sesame Street*'s premiere that a standard text on advertising to children strongly advised: "Don't urge children to 'ask Mommy to buy.'" Instead of stoking a hunger for toys, candy, and sugared cereal, the workshop hoped to nurture inquisitiveness and self-esteem. In time, it found commercial sources of funds necessary when the early ones dried up, and this shift led to an extensive product line, the culmination of this tendency being the likes of Hokey Pokey Elmo.[84]

By the time *Sesame Street* premiered, Assistant Director Robert Davidson recalls, the staff knew that its new show was no mere experiment. Though the deeper insights about interactivity and self-esteem remained inchoate, they expected that after all the testing, the show would teach and entertain. And anticipation among the general public had built up enough that the program quickly made a splash. What they could not have imagined was the way in which it became an object of controversy and an exemplar for a major reform campaign. In November 1969, *Sesame Street* moved out of the studio and into American culture, where it became a lightning rod for all sorts of ideas about children and television.

CHAPTER 6

"Hope for a
More Substantive Future"

Just two weeks before *Sesame Street* premiered on November 10, 1969, Lillian Ambrosino of the mothers' group Action for Children's Television (ACT) appeared before Senator John O. Pastore's committee. The senators were considering whether the Senate should confirm Dean Burch to be chairman of the Federal Communications Commission. ACT demanded that Burch commit himself to reducing commercialism in children's television. If "television is so important in the life of the child," Ambrosino asked, "why can't it begin to be regarded as a positive force?" A thirty-six-year-old mother of three, she received a warm welcome from the powerful committee chairman, who called her "a very, very alert young girl."[1] A few weeks after *Sesame Street*'s premiere, ACT returned to Pastore's committee with its proposal for eliminating commercialism. The committee was considering the chairman's bill to make it harder for citizens to challenge FCC renewals of TV station licenses. When Evelyn Sarson, another of the group's founders, accused Pastore of protecting broadcasters from citizens' criticisms, the chairman rejoined, "I am not beholden to that industry."[2] His defensiveness was understandable. His bill flew in the face of a growing number of media reform groups that, like ACT, pressed for greater regulation of television. In fact, from the late 1960s to the early 1980s, the industry confronted a myriad of social groups trying to change television programming. It is into this public ferment that *Sesame*

Street entered and became exhibit A in the case against children's programming on commercial TV.

As a model for what children's television could be, *Sesame Street* could not help but be defined, at least in part, by the larger public debates. ACT filed a petition with the FCC that children's TV be decommercialized through regulation. Critics of TV in the press immediately seized on *Sesame Street* as self-evident proof of how well such a proposal might work. The public's enthusiastic reception for the show strengthened the critics' position. Though the workshop had planned it as a model, they had focused on its production, distribution, and promotion. They had not considered exactly how the show would promote a particular reform agenda, and they had taken no part in fashioning ACT's proposal. Nevertheless, Cooney and others at CTW joined in the ACT campaign.

Two other public debates also defined *Sesame Street*. Educators, researchers, and other observers evaluated how well the program achieved its explicit purpose: to help all unschooled pre-kindergarten children—particularly low-income, African-American, urban youngsters—prepare to enter school. With its Model and its expertise, the workshop could effectively influence the way that the public perceived *Sesame Street*'s educational value. More difficult to shape was consideration of the show's value for promoting the social reform goals of various activist communities. Not only African Americans, but also Hispanic and feminist advocacy groups, pressured CTW to change the show to serve particular parts of the program's young audience better. What had been a secondary goal of promoting racial tolerance became much more important for some and became a third public debate that defined *Sesame Street*'s meaning. This chapter and the next treat the way that these three public debates about the show played out between CTW's promotional campaign in 1969 and the mid-1970s.

In the mid-1960s, more intensely than they had in more than thirty years, American citizens pressed their government to regulate the broadcasting industry. The civil rights movement had succeeded in overturning the legal basis for segregation in the South in part because television coverage had engendered the sympathy of Northern whites. In 1964, the United Church of Christ's Office of Communication and local Jackson, Mississippi, activists challenged the license renewal for WLBT, the city's NBC affiliate. A prominent member of the racist White Citizens Council managed the station, and, in its broadcasts, black America and Jackson's African-American population—45 percent of its residents—were invisible. The petitioners argued that the station did not serve the public interest, as required in the 1934 law under which all stations operated. At first, the commission refused even to recognize any right to petition against WLBT's renewal, but in 1966 the federal appeals court set a new precedent, ordering the commission to hear the petitioners' complaint. After its hearings, the commission still upheld the station's license, but the court overruled it upon appeal. In 1969 WLBT lost its right to operate. Coming as it did, during an era of citizen protest against not only racial discrimination but also the Vietnam War and soon many other injustices, the court's decisions set off a wave of petition efforts. African-American, feminist, Hispanic, gay, senior, and culturally conservative groups began to lobby the FCC to regulate the content of programming and to pressure the networks to censor programming.

ACT was one such group. Founded by four Boston mothers—Ambrosino, Sarson, Peggy Charren, and Judith Chalfen—ACT began as a local Boston organization. All four women had worked outside the home, and Sarson and Ambrosino were both married to executives at WGBH, the Boston educational TV station. They mounted their first campaign when the Boston station WHDH cut *Captain Kangaroo*'s hour-long show to a half-hour in order to accommodate another program. The FCC later refused to renew the station owner's license, and a new owner took it over. In response to this decision, the earlier WLBT one, and a number of such petitions, Senator Pastore proposed the protection bill for which Sarson later chided him. By the time that *Sesame Street* premiered, the debate about how the broadcasting industry served the needs of the public had become quite intense.

Before *Sesame Street* reached the air, the show's producers promoted it with an extensive campaign. Their central message was that it was the "first time that television has been used for some kind of socially useful purpose."[3] Unlike WLBT, the show would include African Americans, and the promotional campaign reached out to black and white alike—to both the inner and outer circles of the concentric audience. White, middle-class readers of the print media could be reached easily; getting word to poorer African-American viewers required greater efforts. Because the workshop had created a program that was entertaining and educational, it reached out to the broadcasting industry and to educators. Just as one of the networks would have done with one of their new shows, CTW planned extensive promotion. To carry it out, the workshop hired a full time press agent, Robert A. Hatch and his firm, Carl Byoir and Associates. It also accepted help from one of the networks and several local stations. National Educational Television (NET), CTW's parent organization, also carried a press conference for the show, broadcast live nationwide. This balanced, broad campaign partially explains why *Sesame Street* became so popular so rapidly and how its message and its Model reached the public so effectively. Professional promotion set the stage for its place in the reform of children's television.[4]

At the first national airing of *Sesame Street*, the televised news conference and the accompanying press release presented the workshop's message and the CTW Model. Given that *Public Broadcasting Laboratory* was the only NET program distributed over a network, CTW's live, simultaneous national news conference was almost unprecedented. On May 6, 1969, Cooney, Connell, and Palmer introduced the program, showed Stone's promotional film, and answered journalists' questions before the viewers of 180 educational stations across the country. The film gave a tantalizing glimpse of the show's distinctive style. "It was a tightly scripted, highly visually oriented presentation with show business properties," Hatch later remarked.[5] The press release called the show an "experiment primarily designed to establish whether entertainment techniques that preschool children are known to enjoy on television can be put to meaningful educational purposes." As it had promised at the March 1968 press conference, the workshop restated the hope that, backed by the federal government and foundations, it could reach children who would otherwise not receive any preschool instruction. While raising high-flown expectations, the press statement spoke also of practical means, the CTW Model, the format, and the cast. Building anticipation, the promotional campaign combined a peek at the show with an articulation of high purposes and solid prospects.[6]

Among the major newspapers and popular magazines that covered the broadcast, two types of reactions emerged. Many of the resulting articles echoed *Newsweek*'s attention to the show's style: "Can these genuinely funny bits and lively one-minute 'commercials' actually be educational TV?" The film's segments "showed Sesame Street to be a very slick product indeed," the magazine added. On the other hand, the same quality that delighted most of the journalists provoked TV columnist Terrance O'Flaherty to accuse CTW of "lowering teaching standards so perilously close to vulgarity from which their audience seeks to escape through education." Whatever the critical response, the press conference received serious consideration from the press, again bringing the project to the attention of many readers.[7]

Reaction in the broadcasting industry trade press was surprisingly positive, given the campaign's claim that television had never before been put to a "socially useful purpose." *Variety* was impressed with the idea of teaching children with some of advertisers' "most potent tricks," adding that the workshop's "four-man research staff [had] learned . . . to talk to [CTW's] creative people. (If true, that alone beats a lot of ad agencies.)" The show business daily, however, also sneered that NET "despised commercialism" and suffered from an "everlasting dollar famine." Unlike the aloof educational broadcasters, in *Variety*'s view, CTW had embraced what it found useful in the commercial industry and had even surpassed the industry in some respects. Whether the reaction of commercial broadcasters can be gleaned from *Variety* is impossible to tell, but clearly *Sesame Street* had already garnered some respect in that quarter and achieved a position between the opposing network and educational camps.[8]

Help offered to the workshop's promotional campaign represented further signs of goodwill from the networks and some stations. Most significantly, NBC broadcast a half-hour pilot episode on the evening of Saturday, November 8. When the network and Xerox had both expressed interest in helping the project, the workshop put together the preview show. Like the promotional film, it presented typical cartoons interspersed with an explanation of its format and purpose by the puppets Ernie and Bert. It closed with words from Commissioner of Education James E. Allen, Harold Howe's successor. In keeping with CTW's central message, Allen said, "*Sesame Street* represents both an historic first step forward by the medium of TV and an equally significant innovation in mass education."[9]

Besides the pilot, the networks and several stations joined in the promotional campaign on the eve of its premiere. Stations owned and operated by CBS carried spot advertisements announcing the program, as did local stations like Channels 41 and 46, two Spanish-language stations in New York. ABC and CBS reported on the show's premiere during their national evening newscasts. As Allen put it in his remarks during the pilot, this free promotion departed from the norm that "networks never preview programs scheduled by other networks." This free publicity undoubtedly reached some who had not read about the project in the months since the March 1968 press conference, and many viewers probably noted the extraordinary nature of this attention, adding to the sense of expectation.[10]

CTW's promotional campaign reached beyond the general reading public and TV viewers to educators and poor urban African Americans. Dubious that television could ultimately help prepare children for school, teachers, principals, and administrators were understandably wary of what Allen called an "innovation in mass education." *PTA Magazine* called *Sesame Street* "something new and different" and approvingly reported on the project's use of experts and curriculum. But the show's inclusion of animation—"the children's choice" of format—aroused fears of "teaching indirectly the substandard diction and insolent manners of many children's shows, especially cartoons." According to the magazine, modeling violence and "unreason, or inanity" seemed another likely risk when combining popular entertainment and education. The writer also remained skeptical that the program could appeal to both the "disadvantaged" and the "privileged." Despite these reservations, the article may have made some teachers and parents who had not seen the pilot aware of the show.[11]

In another effort to publicize the show to educators, Cooney spoke to an association of elementary and preschool teachers at the National Education Association convention in July 1969. After explaining the project's use of research, its curriculum, cast, and format, she tried to allay fears that popular entertainment would bring violence with it. Nonetheless, "slapstick humor in our animation is virtually necessary," she insisted, "because of our need to compete [with commercial programs] for the child's attention." Even without egregious violence, a truly educational show could not substitute for preschool, Cooney hastened to add. CTW repeated her message in a "Memo to Pre–First Grade Teachers." If the workshop had accurately anticipated teachers' worst fears about TV aspiring to educate, *Sesame Street* had to overcome significant skepticism regarding its educational effectiveness and popular style.[12]

Whatever their doubts, public school teachers in southern California pledged to encourage their students to watch the show. Richard D. Batchelder, president of the California Teachers Association, Southern Section, had chaired the National Education Association's debate on universal preschool three years earlier. In a spring 1969 editorial, he began with the same argument that Cooney and advocates of public preschool had long articulated: children develop half their intellectual capacity before reaching first grade and should have appropriate stimulation to maximize their growth. Along with the union's efforts to persuade state legislators to allow public schools to create preschool programs, it promised to help *Sesame Street* by organizing viewing groups and gathering research results. Just as Cooney had, Batchelder emphasized that the TV experiment could not replace classroom instruction; consequently, the teachers' union pledged to support both preschools and the show. If there were doubts on the part of educators, there were also signs that they might embrace *Sesame Street* as a useful adjunct. Poised between popular culture and education, the show initially seems to have elicited less ambivalence from broadcasters than from educators.[13]

Like its efforts to reach the general public and educators, CTW's efforts to publicize the show to low-income urban African Americans began with simply making them aware that it would be on the air. Unlike the attention to teachers, the workshop anticipated no objections and occupied itself instead with the difficulties of simply getting children to see the program—a long-anticipated problem. Hatch tried to enlist the African-American print media by hiring an African-American public relations man, James E. Booker, who wrote and placed articles in African-American newspapers.[14] But too few newsstands existed in poor neighborhoods, they concluded, for African-American and Hispanic residents to become aware of the show through the print media.[15] Some might hear about it through the free promotion on commercial stations, but Hatch and others soon decided to try grassroots approaches.

At the local level, the question became which groups could and would help most. Booker made contacts with African-American civil rights and other organizations and promoted the project to the Urban League, the Delta Sigma Theta sorority, and the National Council of Negro Women. The last of these proved the most helpful in the show's earliest days because the Council, along with the National Council of Jewish Women, worked to activate local groups and to ensure that children watched. They set up "vest pocket viewing groups" in churches, apartment buildings, and community centers and supported black mothers who volunteered to lead the groups.[16]

The women's efforts helped to reach families who did not read the print press or watch educational TV stations. Initially, CTW requested that NET stations reach out to poor and minority viewers, with widely varying results. Many early efforts foundered on the ignorance of white, middle-class station management. KERA in Dallas, Texas, was an exception because it had hired Charlie Smith, an experienced African-American community activist. Under his direction, volunteers placed television sets in day care centers and taught additional lessons to complement the show's instruction. Just weeks before the premiere, the workshop hired Evelyn Paine Davis, a fundraising executive from the Urban League, to direct its national outreach. Under Davis, volunteers in New York City distributed leaflets at public events like parades and football games, and the local electric utility provided mobile trucks for showing a promotional film in poor neighborhoods. Most effective, however, were simple meetings with teachers and parents to tell them about the show. When it became clear that these efforts would be insufficient, CTW created its Community Education Services (CES) division. As head of CES, Davis opened a national network of local offices, which offered enrichment services to day care centers and viewing groups.[17]

Enlisting local Head Start schools became another way to reach poor African-American children. The federal program's August 1969 newsletter simply described *Sesame Street* to the staff of its centers. Next, Head Start Acting Director Jule Sugarman wrote to the local schools to encourage them to use the show as a resource and to inform parents about it. Echoing the workshop, Sugarman reassured the centers that *Sesame Street* "is not a substitute for the classroom experience."[18] CTW followed these contacts up with a presentation at the national Head Start and Child Development Conference a few days before the premiere.[19] These efforts indicate some resistance within Head Start to using the show. Although it is impossible to be certain of the extent or source of teachers' objections, they may have arisen from sentiments like those expressed in *PTA Magazine*. Possibly some perceived a conflict between the strongly cognitive emphasis of the show and the existing curricula of Head Start programs around the country.

Whatever the misgivings of preschool educators, when *Sesame Street* premiered in November 1969, it rapidly became popular in the households of preschoolers. As measured by conventional TV ratings, however, its viewership seemed small. Paul Klein, vice president for audience research at NBC, was renowned throughout the broadcasting industry as the leader in his field, and he offered his expertise to the workshop's staff. Before the show went on the air, he convinced them to subscribe to the Nielsen ratings service. Nielsen calculated the size of the program's audience for each episode, reporting figures to CTW each week. From the individual daily figures, Nielsen reported the average rating and a cumulative rating, which indicated the percentage of people who watched the show at least once during the week. Because *Sesame Street* appeared not as a single episode once a week like a prime-time program but as daily episodes on each of the five weekdays, cumulative ratings were an important measure. Nielsen's first report arrived in late 1969 and showed that, on average, 2.8 percent of households watched the program each day with a weekly cumulative audience of 3.8 percent.[20]

The program's defenders could argue that these ratings understated the significance of *Sesame Street*'s tiny audience. Although only a small percentage of all viewers watched it, roughly a quarter of all preschoolers were watching *Sesame Street* in its first months. Ninety percent of the households that tuned in had children under the age of six. Aimed only at families with preschoolers, the show effectively reached the vast majority of its narrow audience segment. The problems of UHF reception also limited its ratings. Most of NET's stations were UHF, and only two-thirds of all American households with televisions could even receive a station that broadcast the show.[21]

Sesame Street's ratings grew steadily for its first five seasons, and, though they never approached those of a prime-time hit, they indicated the show's importance for its viewers and its network. The audience share figures climbed until *Sesame Street* reached a weekly *cumulative* audience of 8.2 percent in February 1973. By contrast, *All in the Family,* the top-rated evening program that year, attracted 33.3 percent of all viewers *on average* across the entire season. Nevertheless, Ralph T. Clausen, Nielsen's representative to CTW, pointed out that the show had reached the same average audience as a typical Saturday morning children's show. He added that its audience loyalty—the regularity with which its viewers tuned in the show—achieved high levels, like those of a daytime soap opera. He remarked two years later that *Sesame Street* "has had the highest ratings of any PBS program we have rated."[22]

The ratings only hint at *Sesame Street's* impact on its viewers, whose letters stand as more vivid testimonials. An examination of the viewer mail preserved in the CTW archives reveals diverse expressions of delight, respect, anger, and concern, as well as many anecdotes that attest to a breadth of viewing experiences. Not only did letters stream into the workshop, but even its federal and foundation backers also received "cartons of mail from parents across the country telling . . . about the favorable responses of their children." One mother related that her two-year-old could point out triangles overhead in a store. A teacher of "ghetto children" in Los Angeles related the story that her students had begun to raise their hands in their eagerness to demonstrate that they had learned to count to ten and recite the alphabet. It was "the most thrilling experience of [my] entire teaching career to see these children from under-privileged families being so enthusiastic." In great numbers, friends petitioned CTW for a visit from Big Bird to a dying boy in his hospital room. Toward the end of the first season, the workshop had begun to hear a second time from parents whose children initially had been upset by the show but had "passed through the phase" and become "loyal, devoted fan[s]." CTW began to tally up the mail and created a summary that showed letters of "praise" outnumbering those of "protest" by more than six to one. Judging by the mail, *Sesame Street* had excited and moved people—preschoolers, parents, teachers, poor and middle-class—in unexpected ways.[23]

There were also many who wrote in outrage or dismay, and CTW naturally paid closer attention to these dissenting voices than it did to approving ones. Some critics of the show found the puppet character Cookie Monster dubious. He ravenously ate cookies whenever given the chance, and some parents thought his behavior modeled poor nutrition for children. One father wrote: "Your show has us really upset! . . . [Our two-year-old son] has picked up the ignorant habits of your cookie monster." Characters used too much slang and bad grammar on the show, others complained, and particular segments or episodes aroused fears in children. One mother banned any further watching of the program after her four-year-old son adopted Oscar the Grouch's rude manners, telling his parents, "'Get out of here,' 'Leave me alone,' 'Scram!' etc." His mother grumbled, "He is a duplicate of Oscar the Grouch." Those opposed to the feminist movement wrote to object when Maria, a human character in the Street cast, tried out to work on a road construction gang: "I will not subject my children nor myself to programs trying to abolish the 'traditional' roles of men and women—we are not equal, and anyone can see that at a glance." Following a false rumor that the show would treat sympathetically the subject of birth control, a deluge of letters and cards came from the anti-abortion movement. Acting as a magnet for almost any concern regarding children, the program took on an unanticipated prominence. Whatever the complaint or approval, the public was paying attention to *Sesame Street* and taking it seriously.[24]

The viewing public was not alone. Media organizations also honored *Sesame Street*'s accomplishments. During its first season, CTW won three Emmy awards. In the children's programming area, the show won the best program Emmy, and the writing and music awards went to the staff responsible for each. The show also won seventeen other awards, including a George Foster Peabody Broadcasting Award and a Prix Jeunesse International Award. The promotional campaign won a Silver Anvil from the Public Relations Society of America, and the cartoons won a Clio from the American Commercials Festival "for applying commercial techniques to education with 'consummate skill and success.'" Cooney herself won two of the seventeen awards. As of 1998 *Sesame Street* had won more than one hundred awards, including seventy-one Emmys. Approval came from many organizations, but was most intense during the show's first season when its popularity and prestige most seemed to foreshadow changes in children's television.[25]

In the press, superlatives abounded. A few weeks before the premiere, *TV Guide* called *Sesame Street* "indisputably the most prestigious, exhaustively researched effort ever undertaken to teach preschoolers (3 to 5) at home through TV." During the show's first week, *Saturday Review* called it the "most completely researched and thoroughly publicized show in television history." After its first six weeks on the air, *Newsweek* called *Sesame Street* the "most promising and highly praised children's show this season." Among the popular magazines that offered positive reviews were *Time, Newsweek, Look, Life, Good Housekeeping, Ebony,* and *Saturday Review.* Several published more than one article during the show's first season. Sharing the magazines' enthusiasm were the nation's newspapers from every region, publishing more than one hundred articles and editorials between October and December 1969. More specialized magazines like *Today's Health, Nation's Schools, PTA Magazine,* and *Publishers Weekly* joined those with general readerships to carry CTW's message to diverse audiences.[26]

Several elements of that message commonly appeared in most, if not all, of the coverage. Most journalists remarked on the commercial style of the program despite its NET distribution and implicitly located the show between the two opposing forms of American TV. The show's curriculum—the fact that it set out to teach specific lessons—usually also attracted comment, which functioned to cement the program's image as a serious educational effort. CTW's search for techniques that would hold children's attention, a third element, underlined the show's scientific qualities. Articulating its concentric audience construct, journalists related its educational efforts for all preschoolers to its antipoverty efforts for the impoverished ones. The workshop's outreach to the poor, a fifth common point in these articles, highlighted the show's social reform ambitions. By relaying the workshop's core message of educational entertainment and social action, journalists lent the project credibility and enhanced its public momentum.

Before *Sesame Street* had been on the air for two months, as its prominence grew, ACT's leaders filed their petition with the FCC. After presenting their proposal to Senator Pastore, they contacted the three networks, but only Michael Dann, CBS's vice president of programming, would meet with them. Perhaps because they anticipated rejection, they also suggested that each network name an executive with exclusive responsibility for children's TV. In response, all three networks did so, but none—including CBS—responded to ACT's more radical proposals to stop treating young viewers as "potential customers."[27] The activists had won their first victory on the national level, but had made little progress enlisting support from the most powerful people who might be able to bring about the changes they sought.

Sesame Street's connection to the ACT petition was hardly accidental. Cooney spoke at its symposia, testified at hearings, and joined ACT's board. Early in 1970, Ambrosino wrote to CTW's Palmer with a research question. Along with his answer, Palmer wrote back "to reiterate our interest in your efforts and to express once again our willingness to explore ways in which we may be able to cooperate with you." Television's critics picked up on the connection and made the show an example of what would be possible if the FCC forced the industry to reform. Fundamentally, the logic of ACT's plan shared important features with the workshop's approach.[28]

Basically, ACT reasserted the linkage between commercialism and program content. Unlike Senator Thomas Dodd almost ten years earlier, powerful men, like Pastore and Dann, could not—or said that they could not—see how television's finances had anything to do with its content; the networks controlled programming, and the advertisers only bought access to viewers. ACT's leaders, too, had started from this point of view but soon concluded that advertising was at the root of poor programming. Peggy Charren, who became ACT's president and spokeswoman, later explained, "The fewer the commercials, the less reason to put on the rotten programs." Children's programs reached for the cheapest way to maintain the attention of the largest number of youngsters. Poor programming was the direct result of the commercial imperative to hold all eyes on the set long enough to see the advertisements, Charren and her colleagues concluded. Soon after they filed with the FCC, the *Christian Science Monitor* editorialized that ACT and its supporters among teachers and TV professionals "have simply concluded that the airwaves are a national resource, and that this resource could have a far more helpful effect on their children than it is. Non-commercial TV's 'Sesame Street' is proving how constructive TV can be." ACT had found a way to link the two major critiques of TV— exploitative programming and commercialism—and *Sesame Street* demonstrated that noncommercial production could solve both problems.[29]

Like *Sesame Street*'s Model, this anticommercial critique grew from developmental roots. The organization's leaders began with the observation that children's television did not primarily nurture its viewers' emotional and intellectual growth. Instead, it served the needs of sponsoring advertisers. They added that children, particularly the youngest viewers, did not understand the purpose of sales messages, could not evaluate their claims, and could not distinguish them from the programs. In July 1971, during the FCC's deliberations on the petition, a credible study confirmed that children younger than seven years old did not generally understand advertising's purpose. Cooney vividly articulated their argument that advertising to "the young" was "like shooting fish in a barrel. It is grotesquely unfair. The target audience is, after all, illiterate, uneducated, unemployed and hopelessly dependent on welfare from others."[30]

ACT's petition included three major proposals. First, children's programs would carry no commercials or sponsorship of any kind. Advocates conceded that finding money to produce programs would probably require government funding. Some, like Cooney, suggested that corporate image advertising or sponsor name announcements at the beginning or end of a program might be a compromise or partial replacement for lost spot advertising revenue. Second, no products or brand names would be mentioned and no program host would deliver sales pitches. *Sesame Street* epitomized programming free of commercials. Not only did it appear in most places over the Public Broadcasting Service, but, on commercial stations that carried it elsewhere, CTW prohibited any advertisements during the show's broadcast.

The third part of ACT's proposals would have required developmental sensitivity in the scheduling of programs. The FCC would require each station to broadcast fourteen hours of children's programming per week. Specifying that programs be age-appropriate, the commission would require a mixture of programs for three different age groups and would end the practice of broadcasting the same shows for viewers from two to twelve years of age. The workshop had carefully directed *Sesame Street* to the youngest viewers in this range, two- to five-year-olds. Its five to fifteen hours of programming per week (depending on a given station's repeat schedule) appeared at times which would be optimal for its preschool-age viewers.[31]

The FCC published ACT's petition for comment on February 12, 1970, but it did not issue a formal response for four and a half years, in October 1974. During that time many Americans commented on *Sesame Street*'s relationship to reform—both to ACT's agenda and others. It is with these many points of view that the idea of reform by example betrays its inherent uncertainty. Important critics of commercial television adopted the show as a straightforward illustration for reform. Les Brown in *Variety* saw in *Sesame Street* "hope for a more substantive future." The show "answered the long-standing criticism of the medium—namely that it takes of a viewer's time without giving anything in return." In his first review of the show, he made no mention of ACT's petition because it had not been filed yet.[32]

A little later, two others made the connection between the petition and the program explicit. John Leonard, a freelance critic, and Norman Morris, a CBS news writer, also began as *Sesame Street* skeptics. Writing in the *New York Times Magazine* during the summer of 1968, Leonard doubted that the program could lessen the difference in school readiness between poor and middle-class children. Lacking the contextual knowledge necessary to make the best use of the show, the disadvantaged would lag behind their well-to-do counterparts, he predicted. Though impressed with Cooney and her plans, he questioned that television could teach at all. Morris wrote in the *Atlantic Monthly* three months before the premiere that the problem of children's television did not need a new solution like *Sesame Street*. It simply needed more of the fatherly variety of educational TV found in *Captain Kangaroo* and *Mister Rogers' Neighborhood.* On these programs, the host established "a *relationship* with the child at home." Robert Keeshan and Fred Rogers could entertain, educate, nurture children's development, and calm them. Leonard's and Morris's respective critiques became major lines of attack on *Sesame Street* made by others in subsequent years.[33]

However, once the show aired, both men became supporters who strongly connected it to the demands for reform. Leonard called *Sesame Street* "a program of intelligence, sophistication, good humor and noble intent, to be enjoyed by preschoolers, schoolchildren and parents alike." After praising it, he turned his fire on the industry's commercialism: "If [*Sesame Street*] proves only that by spending as much money on every minute of children's programming as advertising agencies spend on every minute of commercials we can reduce airwaves pollution, it proves something very important; the trolls and mercenaries who feed garbage to our children do so because they have respect neither for themselves nor for children." Morris similarly called *Sesame Street* "the ruination of classic television trash for kids." It "has shown commercial TV officials," he continued, "that a program does not have to be devoid of genuine content to draw large audiences." That both men had so astutely pointed to effective criticisms of *Sesame Street* but then turned so thoroughly into supporters illustrates the linkage between the show and the reform campaign. This is not to say that they and similar critics embraced *Sesame Street* only for its polemical value but that support for the petition and praise for the show became, for many critics of television, tightly bound together.[34]

Some observers did not focus on the show as a means to change children's TV but instead considered its effectiveness for its explicit educational mission. At the beginning of the second season, in November 1970, ETS announced the results of its study, and these reinforced the positive press. The researchers found that the more a child watched, the more he or she learned, regardless of social class, ethnicity, and age. Those who watched with a parent gained more than those who did not. Younger children gained more than older ones. Goals to which the show allocated more time showed more improvement in children's scores. Newspapers and magazines that had covered the show extensively in its first year also covered the second season's opening, and none questioned the validity of the ETS results. *Time* magazine put Big Bird on its cover with a banner reading, "Sesame Street: TV's Gift to Children."[35]

As *Sesame Street's* first viewers reached school, teachers and others testified that they were more psychologically ready for the classroom and more advanced in the basic literacy that the show taught. Writing about teenage girls who volunteered to teach poor children in viewing centers during the summer after the first season, *Seventeen* magazine expressed the hope that *Sesame Street* was "helping to reverse the pattern of discouragement and defeat that, until now, has doomed the ghetto child before he has even started." Children were arriving at school already convinced that learning was "exciting and fun," according to Robert Gilstrap of the American Association of Elementary, Kindergarten, and Nursery Educators. When *Nation's Schools*, a journal for public school administrators, did a survey of hundreds of kindergarten and first grade teachers, it found that three of four teachers agreed that "the show has made a difference in the amount of demonstrated mastery of rudimentary skills by children who watched it." Unlike most journalists, some teachers tempered their enthusiasm and worried that children would become restless or that the show would create expectations that teachers could not meet.[36]

Among others, critics of commercial television faulted *Sesame Street's* educational approaches. Several commentators objected to the program's embrace of commercial television techniques, while an educator objected to its curriculum. On the whole, however, *Sesame Street's* most effective detractors did not enter the public discussion until after 1971. Leonard and Morris articulated the most common early reaction to the show: that it demonstrated the potential for television's redemption.[37]

Besides reform and education, a third way to define *Sesame Street* involved racial tolerance, related to what would later be called multiculturalism. Les Brown, like others, began to look forward to long-term effects of this "sweet show," hoping that it might even bring "racial peace and harmony" when its young viewers grew up. Though the workshop had certainly attempted to project a functioning, interracial community as a secondary concern, the hopes that this vision raised eclipsed, in some minds, the primary mission of school preparation. Jim Fiebig, a newspaper columnist in Bremerton, Washington, expressed similar hopes that his three-year-old would learn to see past skin color to the human being beneath. *Sesame Street*, he hoped, would nurture racial tolerance in all its young viewers. To another author, the program created "a positive appreciation by having attractive adults and children of various skin colors and backgrounds taking part in all the scenes." With these words, Dr. Benjamin Spock, the most popular authority on early childhood development, added his voice to the acclaim.[38] The workshop and its entire project emerged from a liberal, integrationist perspective, and, to many, its implicit social messages about race outshone its educational objectives.

In its earliest seasons, *Sesame Street* provoked comments from not only journalists and teachers; the FCC and the broadcasters responded to it as well. During the first eighteen months after the FCC accepted ACT's petition for comment, it received one hundred thousand letters from citizens, the vast majority of them prompted by the National Citizens Committee for Broadcasting (NCCB), ACT, and other reform groups. These groups made several submissions, as did the networks, stations, advertisers, and professional organizations like the American Dental Association. In support of the petition, the NCCB submitted a study of children's programming abroad. Independent of that organization, Cooney concurred in her testimony that no other "free enterprise country" permitted its children to be used to advance business interests. An FCC staff economist studied the economic impact of the petition's provisions on the industry, and ACT rebutted the FCC's report with its own analysis.[39]

President Richard Nixon's newly appointed FCC chairman, Dean Burch—whose confirmation hearing first brought ACT to Washington—gave reformers reason for hope. Burch had managed Barry Goldwater's 1964 presidential campaign and served as Republican Party chairman. It is surprising that he responded favorably to suggestions from his Democratic predecessor, Newton Minow. According to an account Minow wrote years later, Burch wanted a job in Washington through which he "could do good in the world." Minow convinced him that the FCC was such a place and that children's programming was a fruitful area on which to focus. Burch's appointment just before submission of the ACT petition brought him back into contact with an old friend. He and Cooney had been close friends at the University of Arizona, and their correspondence during the reform debate testifies to their rekindled friendship. Beyond these personal aspects, Burch voted with two of Lyndon Johnson's appointees to begin the formal rulemaking process, although, at the time, he called ACT's proposals "radical." Early in the four-year deliberations, he proposed that the networks share responsibility for the production of an hour of educational programming each week—an idea that Minow had pushed in the early 1960s. When the industry ignored his idea, he became impatient and remarked, "The good ladies of ACT have gone to the core issue. They are asking, in effect, whether a commercially based broadcasting system is capable of serving up quality programming for an audience so sensitive and malleable as children. Or, by contrast, is there some sense in which 'commercialism' and good educational vibrations are fundamentally inconsistent?'"[40]

Nicholas Johnson, one of the commissioners who voted with Burch, also gave reformers reason to hope. Johnson had been a thorn in the sides of broadcasters since he had come to the FCC in 1967 and had enraged them by suggesting in print ways that citizens might challenge station licenses through the FCC. In an article directed to educators, he connected *Sesame Street* to ACT's objectives. He called the show a "new beginning . . . of what we hope will be the end of commercial television's shameless hucksterism of American youth." *Sesame Street* showed, he said, that TV could teach positive social values, like "friendliness, self-esteem, a sense of belonging, and fairness," and could "entice interest in numbers and letters of the alphabet, not junk cereals and worthless toys."[41]

There were even signs from the television industry that they might emulate *Sesame Street* or respond to ACT's pressures. During the show's second season, the networks added several programs that either imparted information or taught social lessons. *Hot Dog* (NBC, 1970–71), for example, showed its viewers how things were made, such as tubes of toothpaste, and why things happened, such as snoring. *Hot Dog* shared with *Sesame Street* the effort to familiarize children with the "man-made environment," in the words of CTW's curriculum. Related more by format was *Curiosity Shop* (ABC, 1971–73), which combined cartoons, films, puppets, and live action in a fast-paced style. Chuck Jones, the creator of Bugs Bunny and many other cartoons, designed *Curiosity Shop* to address in each episode a single topic such as "tools" or "flight." CTW writer and producer Jon Stone called it "an absolute cosmetic imitation of *Sesame Street.*"[42]

By far the most successful of the shows, one that kindled hope for improvement, was Bill Cosby's *Fat Albert and the Cosby Kids* (CBS, 1972–81). Though its pilot aired two days after *Sesame Street*'s premiere, the series did not begin on CBS until the 1972–73 season, while the FCC was still considering ACT's petition. Cosby drew on his own childhood and stand-up routines to present a comedy of social and emotional growth among a group of African-American boys. Like many other shows of its generation, it remained mostly within the popular cartoon genre and taught social lessons through a narrative form. Though instructionally and formally quite distinct from *Sesame Street,* its producers had relied on panels of expert reviewers, just as CTW and others in the industry did. *Hot Dog, Curiosity Shop,* and *Fat Albert* were not the only "brownie-points shows," as

Broadcasting magazine snidely called them. During *Sesame Street*'s first few seasons, the industry responded with other programs, such as *ABC After-school Specials* (ABC, 1972–88), *Make a Wish* (ABC, 1971–76), *Schoolhouse Rock* (ABC, 1973–85, 1993–96), *Take a Giant Step* (NBC, 1971–73), and *You Are There* (CBS, 1971–73).[43]

Beyond what appeared on the small screen, the networks, producers, and advertisers responded in diverse ways. NBC planned *Watch Your Child*, a new preschool program "to be different and not competitive with 'Sesame Street,' being conceived as a program that adults and children would watch together." But it would be broadcast every weekday at the same time, in a "strip," as *Sesame Street* was. Early in the reform debate, however, CBS's new vice president of children's programming, Allen Ducovny, explained that his network's producers saw themselves as entertainers and not educators. Another network executive described the new shows as "appeasement gestures, and expensive ones at that . . . [created] to placate those who don't think we're living up to our responsibilities in the area of children's programming." Larry Harmon, the independent producer of *Bozo's Big Top*, suggested looking for new combinations of education and entertainment, limiting the amount and type of advertising, and broadcasting shows in weekday strips. Otherwise, the federal government might begin "legislating advertising, or fun, or both, off children's tv shows." On the other hand, advertisers, through an industry association, called for the networks to "reduce the use of violence as an attention-getting device" and to "encourage intensive and careful research" on the "impact" of violence on consumers. The industry's response left ambiguous the prospects for change.[44]

In spite of these gestures, commercial producers clearly were not copying the workshop's formula. Though the use of expertise was touted, their reliance on it never rose to the level of the CTW Model. The most high-profile instance came when CBS hired two academics to consult generally on "its entire output for 'consistent planning.'" Both men knew the relationship of experts to production to be limited to respectful, albeit "vigorous," review far short of the Model's research-production partnership. Nor did any of the new shows publicize an explicit curriculum. Despite *Sesame Street*'s impact, commercial producers did not adopt its methods.[45]

The workshop's program demonstrated how a reform model might operate in the context of a public debate. It rose with the tide of public discontent about children's television and was designed to fix many of the things about that genre of TV that its critics found most objectionable. Its production system became a part of its message: make television a more worthy medium by giving educational experts more influence than advertisers. It naturally became the icon for the most important initiative for reform, the ACT petition. But it also yielded many possible understandings of its meaning. For some, it turned television into a rudimentary preschool for children who would otherwise receive no early education. Others focused, instead, on the presence of girls and boys, men and women of various races and ethnic groups carefully balanced and mixed to create a vision of a multicultural America. By the end of *Sesame Street*'s second season, it was unclear whether noncommercial production, television education, or multiculturalism was the most important message.

With this uncertainty, the FCC and the industry could respond to the program and the reformers with many possible regulatory measures, advertising policies, and new programs. Though the commission, under Burch's leadership, was divided, it kept consideration of the petition open for years, giving the activists time to make their case and the industry opportunities to avoid regulation. The networks responded with new programs, as they had done under pressure from Minow in the early 1960s, but they seemed otherwise resistant to change, particularly in their reliance on advertising revenue. Enmeshed in the public debate, *Sesame Street*'s meaning could not help but be shaped by these forces beyond the workshop and its exemplary production system and program. Cooney and her colleagues could create an example for others to follow, but they could not control the lessons taken from it by those who produced and critiqued television.

CHAPTER 7

"The Verdict on
SESAME STREET"

T he debate in the Federal Communications Commission about the
Action for Children's Television reform proposal reached its climax
in October 1972. At ACT's third annual symposium, Cooney spoke
passionately to her comrades in the reform movement. Paying for a program through commercials might work financially, she said. But "the indi-
rect costs for a commercial program are incalculable but enormous. They
range from our children's bad teeth to a warped value system; and the possible *psychic damage* that is done to hundreds of thousands of our youngsters who are urged to buy and to own what their parents cannot possibly
afford to get them." Children stood helpless before the advertising on-
slaught, she argued. "The first thing that we must decide is whether or not
we are going to put the interest of our children first." That is what was at
stake in ACT's proposal to remove all commercials from children's programming, she said. And they, the reformers, had to reach the executives
who made up the "middle ground of corporate America and win them to
the position that the hard sell of products to children is wrong." Theirs
was a work of persuasion, and *Sesame Street* was their best argument.[1]

In the early 1970s, not only would the debate about ACT's proposal
be settled, but so too would Americans consider whether *Sesame Street* truly
served the noble ends to which it was dedicated. What appeared on the
screen and the way it was made—the CTW Model—demonstrated that a

noncommercial approach could be popular and beneficial. Convincing the television and advertising industries to relinquish profits, however, would be difficult. At the climax of the ensuing debate, executives argued to retain control of a profitable part of their businesses by redefining *Sesame Street* as irrelevant. They did not have the last word on it, though, because educators, psychologists, researchers, and journalists also contested the show's educational value. And citizens' groups pressured CTW, just as they pressured the networks to represent children and adults on the screen in a way that advanced social reform. *Sesame Street* met the challenges of these latter two debates more effectively. It became an example—though an ambiguous one—of how television could teach and it communicated a vision—though an idealized one—of how diverse Americans could live together.

However powerfully *Sesame Street*'s popularity stood as evidence for the Model's efficacy, commercial TV made only a limited effort to emulate CTW's method. Though network producers during the early 1970s frequently employed consultants and attempted educational shows, most of these programs did poorly in the ratings and quickly failed. They could be put into several rough categories with a few examples to illustrate how little the networks followed the Model. One category included series that educated by simply imparting information, four of which have already been mentioned. All of them did poorly in the ratings. As the producer of *Hot Dog* (NBC, 1970–71) mordantly observed, "The day we got a Peabody Award we were cancelled." *Curiosity Shop* (ABC, 1971–73), *Take a Giant Step* (NBC, 1971–73), and *You Are There* (CBS, 1971–73) each lasted only two seasons. An exception was *Make a Wish* (ABC, 1971–76), which lasted for five seasons and also won a Peabody Award. Like *Sesame Street* it used cartoons, films, and puppets, and, like *Curiosity Shop*, it was organized around topics. But it may also have survived longer because it aired on Sunday mornings and did not have to compete in "children's prime time"—Saturday mornings. None of these shows approached education as systematically as *Sesame Street* did; for example, none used a curriculum or evaluated what children learned.[2]

More ambitiously educational shows made up another category but did no better than informational programs. *Korg: 70,000 B.C.* (ABC, 1974–75) portrayed the harsh life of a Neanderthal family. Despite its realism, dramatic format, and use of expert advice, it received poor ratings. A similar fate awaited *The Archies* (CBS, 1968–76, NBC, 1977–78) cartoon series, which had been the most popular children's show in its second season, 1969–70. CBS programming executive Fred Silverman had introduced it as an alternative to violent superhero cartoons and took particular pride in its wholesome comedy. In anticipation of the United States bicentennial, CBS retitled it *The U.S. of Archie* (CBS, 1974–76), and the teenage characters traveled back into American history to aid Harriet Tubman on the underground railroad, for example. Young viewers abandoned the show in great numbers. Though these shows might have had rough curricula, they lacked any alternative measure of success to replace ratings.

"Pro-social" programs made up yet another category, which often took on a vague definition. In 1974, *Television/Radio Age*, a magazine directed at advertising agencies and their clients, proclaimed that "'pro-social' is the number-one buzzword" in a year in which the networks strove to rise in "public esteem," increasing their revenue all the while, of course. The industry's objectives were diverse and loosely defined the term *pro-social*: reducing the amount of violence, using less animation, and "getting more social significance."[3] Given these nebulous purposes, some shows were more clearly educational or informational; others posed issues of social behavior and relationships for viewers. Two of the latter sort were fairly successful. In *Shazam!* (CBS, 1974–77, 1980) teenage Billy Batson could transform himself into Captain Marvel, a comic book hero with great strength, but he rarely did so because he found he could rely on reasoning and common sense to solve people's mundane problems. "Every story had a moral," remarked one of the producers, "Captain Marvel didn't usually come in until the last minute-and-a-half, and really only to add advice and air fair warning."[4] The show ran for three and a half seasons. A longer-running series of programs—like *Make a Wish*, broadcast outside Saturday morning—was *ABC Afterschool Specials* (ABC, 1972–88). Appearing in the late afternoon a dozen or so times a season, these dramatic and documentary films won so many Emmy awards that, by 1985, they were challenging *Sesame Street*'s position of critical eminence. ABC originated these in 1972 after a seminar with three hundred experts, and in its first few seasons the series included installments that treated divorce, peer relationships, and gender equality. One episode that treated sex and childbirth attracted an audience of twenty-five million, the largest for any daytime special. Pro-social programs became the networks' favorite variety of educational shows, but they never lent themselves to formal evaluation.[5]

One remaining type of program differed not only in content and ambition but also formally from the others. "Inserts" were not shows but advertisement-length films that could be sprinkled among the Saturday morning entertainment shows. In 1968, Paul Klein, who had advised the workshop on ratings, first created a set of these entitled *Pop Ups* (NBC, 1970–71), which taught miniature reading lessons similar in style to

Sesame Street's "commercials." Both Cooney and *New York Times* critic Jack Gould likened them to CTW's cartoons. Most insert series, however, hewed to an informational, rather than instructional, curriculum. An advertising executive named David McCall created another series of inserts, the popular and durable *Schoolhouse Rock* (ABC, 1973–85, 1993–96), which typically explained how a bill moves through Congress or how the human body works. They relied on music and repetition for appeal and effectiveness. In general, adding inserts functioned as an expedient means to inject education into the Saturday morning schedule without disrupting profitable programs that easily held children's attention. Some observers have questioned just how effectively inserts teach and have contrasted them to *Sesame Street*'s more systematic approach.[6]

Despite the success of a few critically acclaimed shows in marginal time slots, the networks began abandoning these experiments by the mid-1970s. William Hogan, NBC's director of children's programs, explained: "Our thinking is that the networks are in the business of entertainment, not education. Entertainment, though, has an education value to it. . . . It educates feelings. It's a tangential sort of thing." His counterpart at CBS, Jerry Golog, added: "'We don't believe that, in a competitive atmosphere, a show that combines entertainment and education will work. On Saturday morning, the networks own 90–98 per cent of the viewers, with *Sesame Street* all over the dial." The networks concluded that, after a week of school, children craved diversion. None of the programs survived for long on Saturday morning. The *Schoolhouse Rock* inserts and an occasional program represented the only efforts made for years afterward to educate during prime-time hours for youngsters.[7]

Little rigorous thought about education had animated the four types of programming. Though the networks called on experts and adopted elements of *Sesame Street*'s form, their emulation of CTW's example had distinct limits. In no case did producers attempt a systematic approach like the workshop's, integrating research and production, using a curriculum, and formally evaluating their shows. Most of the networks' educational programs did poorly in the ratings, except those in marginal Sunday or weekday afternoon time slots. When they could not find ways of making education attractive and profitable enough to compete with entertainment, network executives rationalized a return to better established programming formulas.

Similarly, their answer to the threat of FCC regulation brought compromise measures and more rationalization. Besides these attempts at educational programming, broadcasters also had to offer some sort of reforms to forestall federal action. They refused to recognize the connection that ACT alleged between advertising finance and poor programming. They ignored ACT's proposed requirements for a minimum amount of children's programming and for age-specific shows. But they could not simply disregard the petition; they had to make some changes in response to the groundswell of public displeasure. Though they refused to eliminate advertising, they reduced the amount of it during children's programming and modified its character. These measures made it seem that the industry had addressed ACT's proposals. For its part, the FCC, unwilling to regulate TV content, could claim that it had persuaded commercial television to restrain commercialism without federal censorship. Once the changes in advertising were in place, executives of the networks, stations, advertisers, and advertising agencies reinterpreted the meaning of *Sesame Street*, weakening it as a model for commercial programming change.

During the first year after ACT filed its petition, FCC Chairman Dean Burch called upon the television industry to make changes of its own accord. At the beginning of the debate, one observer remarked that "no one believes that the FCC seriously contemplates any such revolutionary step [as a ban on advertising]. The commission may wish to prod the networks into more children's programing."[8] Nevertheless, Burch coaxed the networks in a couple of speeches during 1970, crediting, for example, "the good ladies of ACT" for asking whether commercialism and education were not "fundamentally inconsistent." In September he proposed joint responsibility for the production of one hour per week of educational programming and concluded the speech by saying, "'The thrust of my speech is not to threaten the broadcaster with the possibility of governmental action. Rather, it is to urge that he take up the challenge—really, the opportunity." After almost a year of fruitless admonitions, the chairman voted with Nicholas Johnson and one other commissioner to enter a formal rule-making and investigation process.[9]

Though the industry did not present a united front, its response was often every bit as emotional as many of the reformers' rhetoric. Westinghouse's Group W, a station chain that did some of its own production, asked the commission itself to consider doing a study of children's programming and advertising. In a May 1971 speech, ABC president James Duffy asked other executives, "Have we, in our competitive zeal, been morally delinquent?" and proposed that ratings for Saturday mornings be eliminated in favor of studies of child viewers. Soon after ACT filed its petition, however,

TV and advertising representatives presented a series of arguments, ranging from conciliatory to alarmist. Beginning with an admission that programming might be improved, the candy manufacturers association, for example, suggested that advertising might be made more "appropriate" to children. ACT had hit "the panic button," these advertisers suggested, when it made its radical proposal. The National Association of Broadcasters (NAB) contended that decommercialization would rob its members of the money needed to improve programming, would lower the quality, and, ultimately, would make it impossible to produce children's programs at all. Given that children watched many programs—not just Saturday morning cartoons—the NAB feared that other parts of the programming schedule also would be made off-limits to advertising. ACT's proposal could begin a process of eliminating all advertising and could then bankrupt the industry, the association warned.[10]

Under the auspices of the NAB, broadcasters moved to reduce the amount of advertising. Given the public discontent over commercialism, it is surprising that until ACT brought pressure to bear, whereas the networks sold nine and a half minutes per hour during adult shows in prime time, they sold fully *sixteen* minutes of advertising on children's programs. As the industry's primary response to ACT's petition, ABC, CBS, and NBC negotiated an agreement to cut that figure to eleven per hour in January 1972. Children would still see more commercials than adults. Later that year an FCC economist, Alan Pearce, concluded that "the networks will suffer no appreciable loss of revenue in the short to medium term. . . . Most major advertisers will remain in children's television for the simple reason that they have no other place where they can advertise as cheaply and as effectively." He predicted that the networks could raise their rates to make up for the decrease in minutes.[11]

The second tactic to smooth the way to FCC inaction came from the advertisers, who responded not only to ACT's proposed reforms but also to a study of children and TV commercials. ACT had petitioned to ban sales pitches by program hosts and had recommended that programs be designed to meet the needs of different age groups. A series of studies by Scott Ward, a Harvard business professor, showed that the sales intent of advertising was not understood by preschoolers and that children, as they matured, became more cynical about commercials. Underlying both ACT's demands and the new findings was the idea that children's developmental progress determined their comprehension of TV. The Association of National Advertisers created a code to make an allowance for young consumers' innocence. To lessen the deceptiveness of commercials, the code limited fantastic depictions of toys and called for more realistic portrayals. It also acceded to ACT's proposed ban on sales pitches.[12]

While the broadcasting and advertising industries came to these compromises, the FCC did some studies of its own. A children's television task force under Elizabeth Roberts, a journalist, produced some studies critical of commercial TV, but Pearce's economic research had much greater public and regulatory impact. The commissioners asked their economist to evaluate the financial effects on the industry if ACT's specific limits on advertising and minimums on programming hours were to go into effect. His report justified the industry's position that a reduction in advertising minutes was economically viable, while more radical solutions were not. The elimination of advertising, Pearce concluded, would force the networks to subsidize Saturday morning programming with much higher advertising rates during prime time. The substitution of institutional commercials or underwriting messages—similar in style to sponsorship in the 1950s—could replace only a small fraction of the lost revenue. Pearce also argued that broadcasting more age-specific programming would require coordination among the networks so that shows for smaller preschool audiences did not have to compete against those for larger audiences of school-age children. By asking the economist to consider only the financial consequences on the industry, the commissioners had foreordained the conclusions. Cutting out advertising without alternative sources of funds could not help but reduce network revenues. Neglecting to balance these costs with benefits to children could only produce a study that reinforced the industry's opposition to the reforms.[13]

ACT countered with a study of its own and brought the *Sesame Street* example into play. Media economist William Melody produced a more comprehensive analysis of the entire business of children's television. Only by removing children's programming from the "existing economic structure and incentives of the industry" could it be improved, he asserted, in keeping with ACT's central argument. "The differences between children's television on public and commercial television are primarily attributable to the objectives of children's television on each system. Such programs as *Sesame Street*... are all directed toward the single objective of enriching the lives of the child viewer." CTW had shown, he contended, that a program funded at a level commensurate with the networks' shows could educate and gather a significant audience without commercials. In his book, ACT proposed that government and foundation grants along with corporate image advertising take the place of the lost funds from spot commercials. The FCC held a series of panel discussions in October 1972 and "final arguments" in January 1973. Although Melody's book did not reach the public until after these hearings, he appeared before the FCC to make the same points.[14]

Given the developments before these hearings, the FCC's ratification of the broadcasting and advertising industries' self-regulatory actions was a foregone conclusion. The panel discussions and final testimony provided the industries' representatives and the commissioners with an opportunity to confront and deflect the reformers' arguments. *Sesame Street* was not the only grounds for debate, but it came up frequently, especially during the panel discussions. During these hearings, on three consecutive days in October 1972, the commissioners listened to representative groups of executives from networks, stations, advertisers, and ad agencies, as well as activists, public TV producers, and child development experts. Of the five panels, the first included David Connell, CTW's vice president of production, and the fourth, Cooney. Over the three days of discussions, those representing the industries applauded *Sesame Street*, co-opted it, conflated it with their own failed education efforts, and characterized it as unpopular. Though their profuse attention to the show was one more tribute to its importance, the ease with which defenders of the status quo could discard it as a model testifies to a central failure of media reform by example.

All participants in the debate affirmed *Sesame Street*'s quality and superiority. Michael Eisner, ABC's vice president of daytime programming, called it "a very good program." CBS Vice President Fred Silverman said that *Sesame Street* proved that TV "can be entertaining and informative at the same time." Both men later became major figures in the entertainment industry. As for the advertisers, Robert Thurston of Quaker Oats called the show "a brilliant combination of fast-moving exciting television that holds audiences and teaches at the same time." It demonstrated, he added, that "educational-informational" programming "does work." Robert E. O'Brien, an advertising agency executive, applauded *Sesame Street*'s ability to "maintain the child's attention in helping him absorb and use the skills being taught." By merely recognizing the show as being both informative and entertaining and as simply holding attention, these industry spokesmen could cast the show in terms of their own programs. Their programs always sought to be entertaining, occasionally adopted a nonfiction format, and always worked to hold attention. They could ignore *Sesame Street*'s many differences with their programming system, and the commissioners—except Nicholas Johnson—never challenged them.[15]

Owing to *Sesame Street*'s use of cartoons, though, the industry's defenders did not have to work as hard to co-opt it for their defense. ACT and other critics of commercial children's programming frequently complained that cartoons uniformly lacked any educational value and were filled with violent action. They hoped that greater use of "live action" programming—filmed or videotaped performances by human actors—would decrease violence and increase educational content. Responding to this argument, the networks had programmed shows like *Korg, Shazam!,* and *Make a Wish.* The first of the five panel discussions concerned "content diversification," during which the participants veered off the subject so much that they came to no real conclusions. However, Silverman, for example, contended that "a good percentage of the total program time on 'Sesame Street' is animated. I think animation is a medium, like [live] action programming, to reach children." (My episode sample found that 37 percent of all *Sesame Street* segments were cartoons.) Naturally, Connell, who also appeared on the same panel, agreed that animation was a "highly effective technique" but added that confining production to either cartoons or live material limited diversity. *Sesame Street* might have been an effective model for mixed material, but the chaotic discussion moved to financial considerations. In any case, the show had not served ACT's anti-cartoon agenda.[16]

Likewise, diluting the show's unique model, the same panel eventually moved to consider what made for a "quality" children's show. They hardly approached an answer to this obviously difficult question, but no one noted the workshop's use of an explicit curriculum and of an evaluation process to judge effectiveness. When Connell raised the issue of research to determine merely what children liked, the dialogue swerved away from quality to appeal, turning attention then to a still cruder measure of appeal—ratings. The discussion counterposed the show to ACT's argument against cartoons and then bypassed how it might have modeled a better way to assess quality. As the participants jumped from one subject to another, the muddled panel discussions functioned better as a forum for potshots at opponents' arguments than as a place for a carefully reasoned reform debate. Lost in the fog was the logic that made *Sesame Street* so successful.[17]

Having averted consideration of the show's most distinctive features, industry defenders could insist that they too had produced similar programs but that they had been unpopular. *Garfield Goose and His Friends* "is every bit as educational, every bit as helpful and entertaining, every bit as clean," said Ward Quaal, president of Chicago independent station WGN.[18] He offered this example in support of his contention that "the networks have done a lot of things along these lines and have accomplished exactly" what *Sesame Street* had. In addition to the fact that *Garfield Goose* was not a network program, it also did not approach the educational value of *Sesame*

Street or the rigor of the CTW Model. It was instead typical of shows hosted by, as one TV historian put it, "an army of make-believe captains, sure-shooting cowboys, neighborly uncles, and cornball comedians, each holding youngsters' attention with a mixed bag of participatory games, moralistic lessons, and cheap films." In WGN's case, they added puppet skits to the mix.[19]

Another station executive similarly ignored *Sesame Street*'s virtues to equate it to locally produced shows, even ones that flopped in the ratings. George Koehler, general manager of Triangle Broadcasting in Philadelphia, claimed that his stations had produced and broadcast good programs that attracted a small audience and that the station then cancelled them. In his view, finding a successful program occurred randomly, so there was no difference between public broadcasting and its commercial counterpart. *Sesame Street* could just as easily have popped up on one of the networks, he contended. None of the commissioners—except Johnson—ever challenged these self-serving arguments.[20]

What at least one commissioner did challenge were any claims that *Sesame Street* attracted a large audience, making the industry's case for it. On the first day of the panel hearings, Thurston of Quaker Oats began the attack on the show's ratings, but later in the week, one of the producers of *Mister Rogers' Neighborhood*, Elliot Daley, testified that his show and CTW's both drew a majority of preschool viewers when broadcast. Commissioner Benjamin Hooks aggressively questioned these claims. He was the FCC's first African-American member and had at various times been a minister, judge, bank vice president, and civil rights leader before coming to the commission. Expressing skepticism of Head Start and of any television program that claimed to help prepare minority children for school, he also insisted that children would not choose to watch educational shows. On at least four occasions in the panel hearings, he made the point that children want entertainment, that children will not watch anything else unless parents make them, and that, as a result, only ratings— which indicate kids' real preferences—are a valid measure of success. Two days later, on the last day of the panel hearings, ABC executive Fred Pierce asserted that only 2 percent of the Saturday morning audience watched *Sesame Street*. Cooney retorted that the episodes in that time slot had already been broadcast once or twice on an earlier day during the same week.[21]

Utterly alone, without the support of any of the commissioners, Cooney resisted the characterization of her program as a ratings failure. When Pierce quoted the show's low rating, he did concede that 66 percent of preschoolers were watching the show. And Cooney used this fact to point out that the commercial system, in seeking the largest possible audience at all times, worked against a developmentally targeted show. Directing a program to preschoolers alone discouraged older children from viewing, and the resultant lower rating would yield too little advertising revenue, she explained. This same logic lay behind ACT's recommendations that programs be targeted to three distinct age groups of children and that commercial motives be eliminated. The discussion worked to the benefit of ACT's petition, but it did nothing to advance *Sesame Street*'s status as a model for emulation by the networks. The commissioners and industry executives persisted in their contention that the program attracted a small audience. Whatever its popularity and critical acclaim, the broadcasters could insist it was no better than their intermittent attempts at educational shows, which received poor ratings.[22]

Industry representatives had one last argument that—at least for them—decisively proved *Sesame Street*'s irrelevance as a reform model. On the first day of the panel hearings, Harry Francis, the programming director of a station group, said that his company did not have the resources that the workshop had, and several others echoed his complaint in the ensuing days. The argument was not new. Soon after ACT filed its petition, NAB asserted that its members lacked the lavish government funding that CTW enjoyed: "Commercial television is blessed with no such largesse. It must buy and sell in the marketplace, and for commercial television to be required to present without sponsorship, children's programming at costs even approximating those relevant to 'Sesame Street' . . . is patently unrealistic." On the third and final day, Cooney appeared on the fourth panel regarding "alternative methods" of finance. She took the occasion to contradict the claims of Francis and the others; *Sesame Street* had cost no more to produce, she insisted, than commercial programs did.[23]

Settling this dispute requires data that producers and networks usually do not release, but a closer look at available cost figures sheds some light on the question. In the press, journalists and industry representatives sometimes cited cost figures, as they did, for example, at the beginning of the petition debate. When arguing that the removal of advertising would make it impossible to produce programs, NAB cited a per-episode cost of $215,000 for *The Wonderful World of Disney*, a show usually considered among the most expensive. More typical were costs of $22,000 per hour of *Curiosity Shop* and $15,000 per hour of *Take a Giant Step*, both Saturday morning programs and both cited by Pearce in his report to the FCC. These figures take into account the cost of each new episode, its length (half-hour episode costs are doubled to arrive at a per-hour figure), and repeat broadcasts of a given episode. For a typical Saturday morning show, Pearce concluded, "the program cost to bear in mind . . . is an average of $10,000 or $11,000 per half hour per showing." Based on the cost of animation, this figure took into consideration the more common cartoon programs, as well as these two examples of educational shows. He also provided a figure of $31,250 per episode for *Sesame Street*.[24]

A more transparent and arguably more reliable cost figure can be derived from an article that executive producer David Connell wrote for the University of Michigan business school's magazine. Connell itemized CTW's initial budget of eight million dollars in enough detail to separate promotion and distribution—costs borne by the networks but not included in the Pearce's cost figures—from the costs of research and production. Including research and testing would make possible a somewhat more accurate comparison of production under the CTW Model and production under the commercial model. Costs incurred by production companies to create proposals and pilots for programs *not* purchased by the networks appear nowhere in the figures Pearce, or anyone else, used. Using Connell's figures, research, testing, studio production, and film and cartoon segment purchases cost $4,680,000, or $36,000 per one-hour episode. To compare this to Pearce's figure of roughly $20,000 per hour, the number of repeat broadcasts of each segment must be considered. For the stations who played the show only once a day, there would be two plays of any given episode because the seasons were played in their entirety twice in a year. This schedule would mean that the show cost $18,000 per hour per broadcast. Alternatively, for stations that played an episode twice a day and once on Saturday, as many did during the 1970s, the cost per hour would fall to $6,000. Neither of these estimates captures the savings due to the show's reuse of segments across seasons, which is only fair because *Sesame Street*'s form conferred this economy, one that other programs would not have. In any case, *Sesame Street* remained less expensive than the typical $20,000 per hour for network programs. All of these figures would have been available to the participants in the FCC panel hearings.[25]

Even if they had conceded that *Sesame Street* was not more costly, none—other than Johnson—would concede that it had demonstrated the feasibility of noncommercial production. Cooney clearly explained to the commissioners that the program would not have reached the air without basic financial support from the federal government, which had to shoulder the costs of program development because foundations could not. In response to questions from Benjamin Hooks, she saw nothing wrong with public finance of children's programs: "That is an alternative means of broadcasting, Commissioner Hooks." And she offered institutional advertising as a feasible substitute for commercial spot advertisements if the government could not fund production. Later during the same hearing, without addressing her argument, Hooks baldly asserted, "In other words, no panelist so far that I have seen has come up with any viable alternative to advertising as a means of supporting financially children's television." A few months later at the FCC's January 1973 hearings, Charren and Sarson of ACT used the examples of two commercial stations that carried *Sesame Street* without any commercials and at nominal cost because the show had been publicly financed. Even this clear example convinced no one on the commission. By the time of the hearings, apparently all of the commissioners—except Johnson—had come to agree with Burch's remark the previous summer: "If we were to start from scratch, I suspect we'd end up 'inventing' our [existing commercial] system all over again."[26]

Indeed, little changed as a result of the hearings and the neglected example of *Sesame Street*. The regulatory process at the FCC ground on for almost another two years. Burch and Johnson left the agency during 1974, and Richard Wiley took over as chairman. He pressed the networks to reduce further the minutes of commercials to nine and a half per hour, the same as in the adult prime-time slot. Once the NAB agreed to the lower limit, which would go into effect January 1, 1976, the FCC rubber-stamped the industry's self-regulation. Along with the limit, its order also mandated a "reasonable amount" of children's programming. On October 24, 1974, the agency adopted the order without formally closing the case, leaving it open for later commissioners to take it up if they became dissatisfied with the networks' progress. After leaving the FCC, Pearce remarked that the networks had suffered no loss of revenue from the advertising cuts and that, in fact, children's television continued to be more profitable than other parts of their programming schedule. Moving beyond this system of federal regulators' moral suasion and industry self-regulation would have overturned a long-established system. The reform campaign might have succeeded had ACT and the others directed it at Congress. In that case, *Sesame Street* as a model might have played a more effective role, but at the FCC a mere example could be easily brushed aside. Within the bounds of its own commercial system, the television industry found *Sesame Street*'s success hard to replicate but its example easy to dismiss.[27]

While the debate at the commission shaped one image of the show, another dialogue about its value was going on in the press. With the program's premiere, some of television's detractors added to their existing discontents a new question, "Is *Sesame Street* really all that good?"[28] The answers varied greatly, but a short history of the major criticisms of the program suffices to illustrate how *Sesame Street* went from the "most promising and highly praised children's show" to "a modest and amusing step in the 'right' direction."[29] The broader public reaction to the show illustrates the problems that a model program faces in convincing the public to endorse it. Such support would have been critical to convincing other television producers to emulate *Sesame Street*, but a consensus did not emerge readily due to the ambiguities of interpreting an educational program's value.

To fulfill its larger social mission—to help relieve the effects of poverty—*Sesame Street* first had to reach poor and minority children, and one of the earliest criticisms of the show was that it failed to do so. Paul Klein of NBC, known throughout the industry for his expertise in audience measurement, had persuaded CTW to subscribe to the Nielsen ratings service, and the workshop initially turned to ratings to measure its success in attracting African-American youngsters. During the fall of 1969, Nielsen reported that *Sesame Street*'s audience "skews toward upper income [viewers]."[30] Klein read the figures and pointed out that fewer than 10 percent of those watching were low-income and that 11 percent of all American households were so classified. "It can be safely stated that the *true* target audience (low income homes with children under 6)," continued Klein, "have only been marginally exposed." Assuming that the program was as effective as early testing had indicated, he concluded that it "actually has *widened* the difference between blacks and whites."[31] These weak ratings, he argued, had significant ramifications. In retrospect, the shortfall among impoverished viewers seems small for such a summary judgment, but the consequences of his analysis testify to the seriousness with which CTW treated it.

The workshop responded not only to Klein's doubts but also to questions raised earlier and to weaknesses in the ratings themselves. Within the broadcast industry, common wisdom held that the rating services neglected viewers with low incomes because advertisers were less interested in them. Despite the undercount, CTW subscribed to the Nielsen service, but questions raised by Louis Hausman of the U.S. Office of Education during the planning phase lingered. He had doubted that National Educational Television had many viewers in poor urban neighborhoods, and CTW had originally planned a survey to determine if *Sesame Street* was reaching poor children. When the ratings suggested that the show was not reaching them, the workshop commissioned Daniel Yankelovich and

Associates, a major polling and market research firm, to do four audience studies in "ghetto communities."[32]

In the winter of 1970, Yankelovich's pollsters visited poor families at home in several urban neighborhoods and asked about their viewing experiences. They studied four neighborhoods: two in New York City (Bedford-Stuyvesant and East Harlem) and one each in Chicago and Washington, D.C. The firm hired and trained local residents to poll households randomly. They sought out only the homes of preschoolers who would be at home during the day to watch *Sesame Street*. Like the Nielsen ratings, they ignored the children who watched the show at day care or Head Start centers. CTW knew that the early efforts of Evelyn Payne Davis's Community Educational Services department would be overlooked.[33]

The first of the studies strongly contradicted Klein's dire warning. In Bedford-Stuyvesant, 90 percent of mothers reported to Yankelovich that their children watched the show, and 62 percent said the children watched it at least once a day. A quirk of TV station policy contributed to these high percentages. Because the local educational station, WNDT, had previous commitments to carry local school programs, it could not carry the program at 9:00 a.m., so the independent VHF commercial station WPIX offered to do so. WNDT, Cooney's old station, did carry the show at 11:30 a.m. In fact, four New York City stations, two VHF and two UHF, broadcast it at five different times during the day, making it easy for viewers, even those without UHF-capable television sets, to tune in the show.[34]

Two more of the Yankelovich's studies that winter were equally encouraging for CTW. The study in East Harlem, a Hispanic neighborhood, found that 73 percent of those polled had children who had seen the program. The one in Chicago found that 88 percent had watched it, demonstrating that a single VHF station could reach as large an African-American audience as the many stations in New York had. Yankelovich concluded that "the program has attracted such widespread attention and momentum that it does a remarkable job in reaching its target audience even under less favorable conditions than in New York City." So impressive were the results that Yankelovich initially questioned their validity and administered a second round of polling without telling the workshop.[35]

Much less encouraging results, however, came from the Washington, D.C., study, confirming Hausman's original concerns about reaching poor and minority viewers through educational UHF stations. In the nation's capital, a lone educational UHF station (WETA) broadcast the show. Of the 297 mothers with whom the pollsters spoke, only 80 percent had UHF-capable televisions, and only 32 percent of their preschool children at home had watched *Sesame Street*. NET had UHF affiliates carrying it in roughly half of the largest cities. These stations, like those in Washington, could not expect to match the penetration in the two New York City communities or in Chicago.[36]

The question of *Sesame Street*'s minority audience illustrates the problems that a model program confronts with ambiguous data. In subsequent years, Yankelovich performed similar surveys, which showed a growing audience. In fact, Washington's viewership rose to two-thirds of all households by 1973 and to 97 percent by 1978. Judging by these and the Nielsen ratings, the program's audience—across boundaries of class and culture— grew during its early years. In addition, the omission of viewing groups, day care centers, and Head Start preschools from both sources contributed to understating the numbers of minority viewers. *Sesame Street* appears to have been one of the few public television shows with a substantial minority viewership. But the widespread impression that public television was for middle-class white people stubbornly contradicted the data that CTW generated. FCC commissioner Benjamin Hooks's conviction that only a tiny minority of poor, urban African-American children ever watched the program testified to the persistence of this popular belief. In time, however, it became clear to many observers that *Sesame Street* had a distinctly more diverse audience than the rest of public TV.[37]

Sesame Street had other critics who were skeptical of its educational value. They charged that television, especially in a commercial style, could not teach—and by extension that *Sesame Street* would not teach—what preschoolers really needed to learn. Some found the style alone appalling. Typically these critics, like Klein, voiced these objections loudest during the first season. In February 1970, Robert Lewis Shayon, one of the most prominent TV critics, complained that the show suffered from "a compulsive thrust." In his view, it had borrowed "too heavily from the high-pressure patterns of commercial television." Only a month later, Minnie Perrin Berson, a columnist for *Young Children*, a preschool educators' journal, heartily agreed with Shayon and objected to the cartoons, slapstick, and the "high key of pound-it-in didacticism" on *Sesame Street*. Both juxtaposed the show's pace and repetition with a gentler style of television, of *Captain Kangaroo* and *Mister Rogers' Neighborhood*, that, among other things, focused on self-esteem. Education professor Frank Garfunkel similarly considered the "hard sell" of *Sesame Street*'s advertising-inspired style "inappropriate" for preschoolers.[38]

Writing also during the first season, Carl Bereiter agreed with Garfunkel's conclusion that *Sesame Street* did not teach what preschoolers needed to learn. Along with complaining about the show's style, Garfunkel concluded that it only taught through memorization and that it suppressed "real probing and spontaneity." As a mass medium, television could not give the "direct, creative instruction" that preschool children needed. For his part, Bereiter tied the show's curricular failings directly to its acceptance of established television concepts and forms. Because "it's based entirely on audience appeal and is not really teaching anything in particular," Bereiter wrote, it lacked the necessary structure. There was some irony in his criticism because Cooney had drawn inspiration in the project's earliest days from his school's almost military drill–style methods. These probably inspired the boisterous tone of the show and its heavy use of repetition. But Bereiter and the other educational skeptics agreed that a mosaic, televisual style was in fundamental conflict with the educational process. In their view, any instructional concept combined with this style could not work.[39]

Writing just before the second season began, a prominent child development psychologist and a founder of the Head Start program, Urie Bronfenbrenner, added his voice to those who criticized the elements that *Sesame Street* had borrowed from the commercial medium. In his view, TV's two extremes were antithetical to humane teaching. At the one end, he contended that the children and adults on the Street resembled the bland characters typical of situation comedies set in suburban locales. They were all "charming, gentle, smiling and friendly," Bronfenbrenner wrote. They had "no cross words, no conflicts, no difficulties nor, for that matter, any obligations or visible attachments." To this image of the bland and unengaged, he contrasted the puppets and cartoon characters, who have "the problems and the passions . . . [the] color, character, charisma and the seemingly inevitable crash-bang." These livelier, more appealing characters came from the other TV extreme: the heartless world drawn from "American children's television . . . [and] the magic and violent world of Walt Disney." Neither of these opposing realms satisfied Bronfenbrenner's desire that the Street be "a neighborhood—and a society—where *living is human*." Though he readily conceded that the show taught its cognitive goals, it failed to teach children about social relationships. It did not, in his opinion, help a child to integrate herself or himself into society—the greatest lesson TV could impart.[40]

John Holt, a writer and advocate of the Open Education movement, assessed *Sesame Street* near the end of its second season and offered a perspective on TV and education that reversed that of these other critics. Though he agreed with them that *Sesame Street* moved too fast at times, he contended that the show did not go far enough to use the visual capabilities of television. *Sesame Street* did ninety percent of its teaching through spoken language, not images, he asserted. His larger point, however, was a more radical one: *"Sesame Street* still seems built on the idea that its job is to get children ready for school. Suppose it summoned up its courage, took a deep breath, and said, 'We *are* the school.' Suppose it asked itself, not how to help children get better at the task of pleasing first-grade teachers, but how to help them get better at the vastly more interesting and important task—which they are already good at—of learning from the world and people around them."[41]

By the end of the second season in 1971, a journalist trying to answer the question, "How good is *Sesame Street* after all?" could find support for a variety of positions. Holt, like CTW, embraced a televisual form of instruction but rejected the show's mission to prepare children for conventional schooling. Shayon, Berson, Garfunkel, Bereiter, and Bronfenbrenner, in varying degrees and from various preschool pedagogies, rejected TV teaching but had no explicit objection to the academic mission. But none of these experts could offer anything more authoritative than a thoughtful look at the show. The workshop could always point to its own internal research and to Educational Testing Service's evaluations at the conclusion of each of the first two seasons. Underlying the question about *Sesame Street*'s worth remained the fundamental question about TV's capability to educate. Further independent research offered the possibility of a more authoritative verdict, but, in any case, several credible voices had raised doubts about the show from the perspective of established preschool pedagogies.

Over the years since the premiere, *Sesame Street* has spawned many independent research studies. The most important of these during the show's early years came from Herbert A. Sprigle and from a team of psychologists led by Thomas D. Cook. In their studies these researchers argued that *Sesame Street* exacerbated the achievement gap between poor and middle-class children instead of closing the gap, as the backers had originally promised. Sprigle, director of a preschool for disadvantaged children in Jacksonville, Florida, published two much-cited articles in *Young Children*, the same journal in which Berson's column appeared. Cook, a psychology professor at Northwestern University and a major author in the field of educational assessment, published the only independent, book-length evaluation of the show. As of 2001, his work endured as the only early research still being cited by critics of *Sesame Street*. Beyond their prominence, these studies reflect a credible critique probably shared by many preschool educators—but how many actually felt this way remains unclear. When influential individuals, like Bereiter, Bronfenbrenner, and Head Start's director, Edward Zigler, objected publicly to *Sesame Street*, they must have echoed the opinion of less vocal colleagues. But these unvoiced objections to the show did not lead to a campaign to eliminate all funding, for example, and criticism by preschool educators had only a modest impact on the public discussion of the program.[42]

Sprigle's and Cook's critiques apparently started with Zigler's public criticism of *Sesame Street*. Despite disclaimers by Cooney and CTW that they had no ambition to supplant the nation's preschools, some among Head Start's leadership apparently feared that Congress or the Nixon administration would shift money away from their program to support *Sesame Street*. During the show's second season, in February 1971, Zigler attacked *Sesame Street* in the press, saying he feared that *Sesame Street* fed "the tokenistic approach to children's education." When he refused to transfer funds that his agency had promised to the workshop, Head Start became the first of CTW's original backers to end its funding. Sprigle published his first study the month after Zigler's denunciation, and, in his second article the following year, he echoed the Head Start director's thinking: "There are simply no short cuts through the problems of educating poverty children. . . . Sesame Street and other programs with surface appearances of education may be thrust at the public as easy answers to a complicated problem."[43]

Sprigle's articles demonstrated that this opposition to *Sesame Street* was pedagogical as well as political. He contended that it could not provide the rich, personal, verbal interaction that impoverished students like his needed. Television could not substitute for the classroom experience. He arrived at his conclusions from a theory of early intellectual growth already rejected by CTW. Earlier researchers reasoned that only through intensive conversation did children develop the intellectual concepts and verbal skills necessary in school. Citing these previous studies, Sprigle asserted that middle-class children benefited from this kind of interaction with their parents and that poor children did not. The workshop discarded this analysis and labeled it racist. As research director Edward L. Palmer later noted, it relied on the image of the middle-class "educative mother," superior to her poor and black counterpart. While such a "deficit model" buttressed Sprigle's theory of the achievement gap, CTW adviser Gerald S. Lesser had encouraged his colleagues to avoid this logic. Instead, he and others at the workshop hypothesized that impoverished children would interact with loved ones and neighbors and would draw encouragement

from these encounters. Whether he argued that these interactions happened or not, Sprigle believed that much more rigorous instruction—of a
kind television could not undertake—was needed.[44]

Given this fundamental disagreement, it is not surprising that Sprigle
found *Sesame Street* inadequate. In his research, he compared groups of children who had watched only the show to others who had a more interactive preschool curriculum. Two of Sprigle's teachers used the workshop's
adjunct activities, distributed by the Community Education Services
department, to enhance the learning of the children who viewed the show.
The other children, in groups of four, received instruction directly from a
teacher on the same curricular elements. When both groups took the Metropolitan Readiness Test, a standard test for children entering first grade,
those who had watched *Sesame Street* scored significantly worse. Sprigle
added to this testing formal studies of individual children, informal conversations with them, and an analysis of the show's teaching techniques.
He concluded that *Sesame Street* was often pitched at too sophisticated a
level in its vocabulary and concepts. It taught through rote memorization,
he reasoned, which left children with only a superficial familiarity instead
of real understanding. Sprigle considered *Sesame Street* a cheap and inadequate substitute for real preschool and perceived that federal government
decision-makers were planning to foist it on poor children to save money.
His research lent his pedagogical argument credibility with journalists
who wrote assessments of the show.[45]

Lending further credence to doubts about show's ability to eliminate
the achievement gap, Cook's research began around the time of Sprigle's
first article but was not published until 1975. Initially, Cook pursued an
academic, social science task: analyze the Educational Testing Service's
first year study of *Sesame Street* to draw lessons for others who might assess
program reports. He planned to evaluate an evaluation. Initially stymied
in his mission, Cook wrote to ETS: "Quite frankly, the combination of the
Age Cohorts study and your latest analyses of the inferential study leave
little meat on the research carcass for professional vultures like myself—
or is it professional nit-pickers." For one reason or another, he then abandoned his original purpose and decided, instead, to evaluate *Sesame Street*
itself. In the book, he and his sponsoring foundation justified the change
in direction at length and included, as an appendix, a rebuttal from ETS,
whose researchers implied in their response that Cook had made a sudden
shift to a hostile position. Cook's change of direction occurred soon after
Sprigle's first article appeared. Whether Cook chose to follow Sprigle's

lead or simply happened to pursue the same question at the same time, both highlighted the achievement gap.[46]

Unlike Sprigle, however, Cook's team did not do its own research. Instead, they elaborately re-analyzed ETS's data from its two evaluations of *Sesame Street*'s first and second seasons. After re-aggregating the data and calculating new statistical measures, they contended that the show's instructional presentations were not the key factor in whatever it taught. A closer examination of ETS's protocols revealed that researchers had paid regular visits to children's homes and had encouraged them and their parents to watch the show. Cook found that these children did better than others, regardless of social class and IQ scores.[47]

Reasoning from this finding, he proposed a concept not unlike Sprigle's. He speculated that, in these "encouraged" households, parents had interacted with their children more, and the children had learned from these conversations. *Sesame Street* had not taught; it had only supplied the occasion for parental teaching. In his words, the program "mediated the relationship between encouragement and learning."[48] Though he considered the show's instruction more effective than Sprigle had, the two researchers' hypotheses resembled one another. Children learned from adults, their thinking went, not from a TV program. Both research projects cast doubt on television's potential to educate and, consequently, on the show's ability, in a larger sense, to equalize opportunity.

The educational skeptics had raised credible doubts about *Sesame Street*'s ability to teach and provided ammunition for later critics who condemned the show or the medium itself. More than two decades later, only Cook's study was still cited by those who criticized the show; later critics have supplanted these early ones. For example, in 1993, when Billy Tashman, *Village Voice* media critic, wrote on the show, he quoted findings from Cook beside those of a later generation. While earlier criticism from Shayon, Berson, and Bronfenbrenner smacked of cultural elitism, later critics took an apparently culturally neutral and scientific stance. The most prominent of these detractors were child development psychologists Jerome L. and Dorothy G. Singer, who asserted that television—*Sesame Street* in particular—shortened attention spans. Among those who still insisted that television could not teach was Neil Postman, who made a particular point of attacking *Sesame Street* in his popular book *Amusing Ourselves to Death*. Just as the critique of television had shifted grounds between the 1950s and 1970s, it continued to do so into the 1990s, and *Sesame Street* became a prime target for TV's antagonists.[49]

The early critics did not go unanswered. Usually refraining from responses in print to criticism, the workshop, along with ETS and others, occasionally defended the show against its detractors. For instance, of the educational skeptics who simply analyzed the show, only Berson received a public reply. On the other hand, both Sprigle and Cook aroused sufficient anger among the show's proponents that Palmer and ETS, respectively, answered them. Palmer wrote a short paper, "The Deer and the Duck," which he sent to Sprigle but never published. In it, he ridiculed Sprigle's studies as hopelessly biased and described them as though their author posed the following competition: "Look, Sesame Street, we're going to have a race between your television program and my kindergarten program. In this race I'm a duck, and you are a deer. I make the rules and one of them is that the post-training competition will include a test of swimming and a test of diving." As for Cook, ETS's original evaluators, Samuel Ball and Gerry Ann Bogatz, wrote in their rebuttal that Cook had "carried out highly conservative and at times misguided analyses, and arrived at conclusions that are not very sensitive to the positive impact of 'Sesame Street.'"[50]

Independent reviewers also came to the show's defense and made many of the same arguments that Palmer, Ball, and Bogatz had. The only published reply to Sprigle came from four University of Illinois graduate students who pointed out that he had mismatched the experimental groups and surmised that he had biased the study against *Sesame Street* in other significant ways. Of the three academic reviewers of Cook's book, two found that he had taken the ETS data collected for one purpose, turned it to another for which it was not suited, and then exaggerated the certainty of his highly tentative conclusions. They also concurred with Ball and Bogatz that the show had never been designed to eliminate the achievement gap. On the other hand, the third reviewer, Robert M. Liebert, largely agreed with Cook and contended that his research had even understated the way that the show widened the achievement gap. Disgusted with existing commercial programming, Liebert himself had, following Albert Bandura's lead, studied television's effects on children. He coauthored the leading survey of such research. In spite of his prominent position as a critic of TV, he demurred when Cook suggested taking *Sesame Street* off the air. Between the show's critics and its defenders, an observer could choose whom to believe; no undisputed consensus emerged from the independent research.[51]

This stalemate left an opening for *Sesame Street*'s most adept defense from the likeliest of sources, Gerald Lesser, architect of the CTW Model.

He continued through the early 1970s to chair the board of advisers and to write about the show. In *Children and Television: Lessons from Sesame Street,* he published the most complete exposition of CTW's thinking, and the book functions as both a memoir of the show's development and as a response to its critics. On the one hand, he explained the show's logic, its curriculum, and its pedagogy. On the other, he cited roughly thirty individuals and groups and divided the substance of their criticisms into categories like "Questioning Our Premises" and "Other Goals Are Better." Though this presentation made intelligible the essence of the critiques and the variety among them, it also left the reader with no single objection foremost in mind. He rebutted Sprigle and Cook with the same arguments that CTW, ETS, and the independent reviewers had. Setting them apart from the critics, he treated them and the achievement gap thesis only after describing ratings, ETS's evaluations, and other more positive "outcomes." He closed his chapter on the show's detractors with this: "The Workshop staff kept track of all these criticisms, partly from vanity and curiosity, partly in hope that we could discover ways to improve *Sesame Street.* With some exceptions, the criticism was not illuminating. It contained opinions and offered few constructive alternatives."[52]

Without a critical consensus, *Sesame Street*'s detractors had no more success convincing the popular press that the show should be removed from television than the reformers had had convincing the FCC that it should be the model for all children's TV. Instead, the press expressed qualified approval. Some of its assessments came from those thoroughly in sympathy with the show; other journalists adopted a more neutral stance. Prominent among its advocates, Grace and Fred Hechinger, who wrote about education in the *New York Times,* magazines, and books, warned that the show would lose its funding if others did not come to its defense. More detached were two others. James Cass admitted in the *Saturday Review* that, though flawed, *Sesame Street* "should become a model of the creative drive and innovative skill that will be required if television is ever to realize its full potential as the handmaiden of education. . . . We must never forget that no television program, no matter how successful, can take the place of open, innovative classroom instruction." A pseudonymous writer in *Life* concluded that *Sesame Street* "is a modest and amusing step in the 'right' direction: television for children that neither bores them to distraction nor clubs them into insensibility." Gone was the almost utopian enthusiasm. Such measured appreciation would never impel the show's cancellation, but neither could it drive a revolution in children's programming.[53]

Instead, *Sesame Street* became less a model for TV reform and more a vision of multiculturalism. In the show's first months on the air, columnists Les Brown and Jim Fiebig had voiced the hope that *Sesame Street* could help bring about interracial peace. But writers did not drive the shift as much as political activists did when they turned to CTW and demanded that it nurture children's confidence through segments sensitive to ethnicity and gender issues. The media reform movement—of which the workshop saw itself as a member—turned to make demands of *Sesame Street*. In the late 1960s, a series of "second wave" social movements grew from the civil rights and anti–Vietnam War movements. African-American, feminist, Hispanic, gay, and senior citizens groups sought changes in television images as a means to spur larger cultural changes. As the networks and commercial producers faced the criticism of these groups, CTW's executives were surprised to find themselves also a target. Not only did *Sesame Street* represent one example of the cultural power of TV and an institution that could be pressured, but its objectives resonated with the liberation and empowerment focuses of these movements. CTW encountered the activists on the grounds of child development and TV production and thus conceptualized multicultural issues in terms of how effectively *Sesame Street*'s characters and curricular content nurtured the self-esteem of its viewers.[54]

During the 1970s and 1980s, the television industry developed organizations and techniques to minimize the disruptions to their business by placating activists. Standards and practices departments became the primary buffers protecting network, producers, and advertisers from the lobbying of citizens' groups. Hiring script consultants channeled the ideas of these groups through a person that the networks could hire or fire, but the industry found it needed ways to respond more directly to activist organizations. When faced with an array of groups, the networks sought a single organization that made modest demands and seemed a pliable negotiating partner. ACT was one example of an organization that became the "one voice" on its issue. But the broadcasters also found that they had to remain open to comments from many organizations and maintain ongoing relationships with the most useful of these. Ultimately, the networks and production companies found that hiring people from activist organizations and employing them in the standards and practices department protected them from controversy best. CTW did not follow this same path because its production system brought others in from the outside at the beginning. Nevertheless, when it came under fire from Hispanics and feminists, its executives also turned to this last technique of "assimilation."[55]

One of the earliest multicultural critiques came not from Hispanic or feminist activists but from African Americans, and it took a tack unexpected by CTW. Though *Sesame Street* had been praised for its prominent inclusion of African-American actors at a time when their numbers were dwindling on TV, some African-American adults perceived a degrading stereotype in a puppet—one that the workshop did not even consider African-American. CTW had created Oscar the Grouch to dramatize tolerance for those who are different, as a relatively low-priority social goal. In segments about conflicts between Oscar and others on the street, the show taught how children might cope with diversity in the context of school desegregation. But the producers couched the specifics of these conflicts in personal terms—as matters of taste and courtesy—not in explicitly racial terms. For example, skits during the first season established that Oscar had a lifestyle that set him apart; he lived in a trash can, liked trash, spoke and acted rudely. When his behavior—or, occasionally, others' harassment of him—precipitated confrontations, his neighbors found ways to reconcile with him. Sometimes, harmony could not be achieved and only grudging acceptance was possible. Oscar himself often learned greater self-awareness and sensitivity to others, and he became a particular favorite of young viewers during the early seasons.[56]

Some black viewers, however, complained that Oscar represented "the inner-city character," who passively accepted poverty and social injustice. One day care center director asserted: "That cat who lives in the garbage can should be out demonstrating and turning over every institution, even *Sesame Street*, to get out of it." In the eyes of these viewers, journalist Linda Francke reported during the second season, the program socialized their children to submit, not to tolerate. They thought their children would identify with Oscar and not with those around him. These same black parents, day care workers, and other adults also found the show too white and too detached from the grim reality of urban poverty. This latter criticism—that *Sesame Street* was "more Westchester than Watts"—did not surprise Cooney. But when Francke told her about this interpretation of Oscar, she was baffled and frustrated. The pervasiveness of these views remains difficult to assess.[57]

The concerns of these African-American parents and teachers, in any case, challenged not just the characterization of one puppet but the entire orientation of the show. CTW had designed *Sesame Street* with school preparation foremost in mind in the hope that the show could reach a general audience, and there were few African-American staff involved in the design of the show who might have offered a different approach. Jane O'Connor, the lone African-American staffer in early planning meetings, had suggested the oblique approach to racial conflict that Oscar embodied and suggested more research when the workshop added a black Muppet, Roosevelt Franklin, midway through the first season. Franklin's sudden arrival may have been in response to early criticism of the show as too white. But to O'Connor he reinforced white stereotypes of black youth. Ultimately, after several more seasons, Franklin disappeared from the cast but only after he had been transformed twice, once into a teacher and later into a celebrity. This early experiment in nurturing self-esteem based on a distinctive racial and class culture posed problems for holding a broad, largely middle-class, white audience as well. Since 1966, when Cooney had seen *Roundabout*, a program designed especially for poor, urban African-American children, she sought a common, popular culture. She had hoped that the inclusion of African-American music and gesture would appeal to all children, but to African Americans in particular. From the time of the first seasons, it became clear that multiculturalism required balancing culture, identity, and integration.[58]

Hispanic representatives soon added to these challenges. In April 1971—the same month that Francke's article appeared—Evelyn Davis invited Hispanic activists to a conference to discuss expanding *Sesame Street*'s rudimentary bilingual curriculum. During the two days of the San Antonio, Texas, meeting, the Latino representatives locked out the CTW staff, drafted an ultimatum, and demanded a meeting with Cooney. In the words of their press release, the workshop representatives' words and actions "reflected the racist attitude of their employers and this nation towards its Spanish-speaking people." CTW's failure to meet with Hispanics until then, the press release continued, was "reflected in the poor quality and patronizing nature of the current Sesame Street Bilingual Program." They demanded virtual control of this aspect of the show. As shocking as the activists' behavior was to the workshop's executives, the Hispanic representatives challenged CTW in much the same manner that Justicia, a Chicano media group, did the commercial networks.[59]

After initial surprise at the vehemence of these denunciations, the workshop used established strategies to meet the needs of its Latino viewers. It refused to relinquish any control, but, for two years, it did consult a committee drawn partly from the San Antonio group. During an early meeting with these advisers, Cooney conceded that the bilingual elements of the show "were not well thought out," but she expressed shock that the workshop was being treated as "an adversary" and the staff "as evil enemies." Within a year of the first meeting, CTW had hired Hispanic actors, production staff, and researchers who met to enlarge and broaden the "bilingual/bicultural" parts of the curriculum. The workshop contracted with Hispanic filmmakers and animators to produce segments for the show. By the mid-1970s, the show included Chicano and Puerto Rican cast members, films about Mexican holidays and foods, and cartoons that taught Spanish words.[60]

Adding these elements of language and culture arose naturally from the movement that precipitated the San Antonio confrontation. Before the self-styled "National Advisory Committee of *Sesame Street*" could deliver its ultimatum, its members from the Chicano, Puerto Rican, and Cuban communities first had to settle their own differences. In fact, no "Hispanic" movement existed at the time. In the late 1960s Mexican-American activism had overshadowed that of either of the other major national communities and commanded Americans' attention with the United Farm Workers strike in California, land seizures in New Mexico, and student walkouts in Los Angeles.

While these actions focused on civil rights, labor, land, and education grievances, others directed their protest at media targets. Journalist Armando B. Rendon identified the stereotype of the "sleeping giant" as one that reassured white Americans that Chicanos remained "submissive and happy" despite protests to the contrary. African-American parents had feared the effects of an apparently complacent Oscar. Though no similar images of Latinos (or Latinas) appeared on *Sesame Street*, Rendon and other activists found images of lazy, sloppy, irresponsible Mexicans elsewhere on television and contended that these left children without positive models.[61]

Beneath these concerns lay an identity concept typified by the ideas of Pablo Macias, a Chicano media activist, in discussions with CTW before San Antonio. He argued that all children identified with powerful and competent characters and that "Indo-Hispanic" preschoolers dissociated their ethnicity from their ideals when their onscreen models differed from themselves. These children would gain greater self-esteem if Latino characters were added to the show, Macias suggested. Later, others from CTW's advisory committee made a similar case for inclusion of segments about Spanish language, foods, and customs, which would help young viewers see their ethnic culture valued. For example, when the puppet character Big Bird expressed interest in learning Spanish, he demonstrated that others respected the language and the people who spoke it.[62]

Feminists' engagement with *Sesame Street*, like that of Hispanic activists, began quietly and then turned contentious. Like Macias, the women activists initially made only practical suggestions for changing the show.

Though dissuaded by a CTW ally within the leadership, some within the National Organization for Women (NOW) wanted to pass a resolution condemning the program in the spring of 1970. The following December, this anger became public when Ellen Goodman published a newspaper column, "The male, Male, MALE World of Sesame Street." Along with pointing out the preponderance of male characters, Goodman juxtaposed "groovy" Roosevelt Franklin with know-it-all, white, girl cartoon character Alice Braithwaite Goodyshoes. "The idea that comes across," she wrote, "is simply that knowledge in a girl is objectionable, [and] in a boy is groovy." Again, as with both black perceptions of Oscar and Chicano objections to TV Mexicans, Goodman objected to the generally passive roles women and girls played on the show. During the following summer, Jacqui Ceballos, president of the New York City chapter of NOW, threatened a boycott of the products of General Foods (at the time, an underwriter of the show's Saturday morning rebroadcasts) unless it pressured CTW to accede to the women's demands.[63]

Consciousness-raising, a hallmark of the women's movement, became central to the resolution of feminists' demands, but change came slowly. As it had during the Latino encounter, CTW internalized the critique and revised the symbolic and cultural content of the show. A month after the letter to General Foods, NOW representatives met with the predominantly male staff, including executives, producers, and writers. In a consciousness-raising session unlike those experienced by most middle-class women entering the movement, the NOW activists projected photographic slides in a formal presentation to explain to the workshop's staff members what they found offensively stereotypical in children's television. Two rank-and-file members of NOW followed up this meeting with an ongoing series of reports that analyzed shows in detail and assessed progress. The feminist critique became institutionalized when, in keeping with the CTW Model, the research staff—mostly female—routinely worked with the writers and producers—mostly male—to modify the program's content. Producer Jon Stone wrote that he and his colleagues had their "consciousness raised" many times "on the spur of the moment" when women researchers helped them see how their scripts portrayed women and girls in stereotypical ways.[64]

Despite these efforts, however, an important part of the show continued to cause friction with feminists: Jim Henson's all-male puppeteers and their mostly male characters. To remain within its budget, the workshop relied on reusing old segments, and, when these were found to have sexist elements, the inventory of available material—and thus the content of the show—could only change slowly as new, less sexist segments were created. Henson's all-male crew of puppeteers added women to their ranks slowly due to the style and scheduling of their work. To keep costs down, the taping of puppet segments was concentrated into a few long days rather than shorter sessions over more days. Henson and CTW's producers contended that holding the Muppets aloft during these long days exceeded a woman's strength. Though they tried recording female voice-overs and combining these with male puppeteer performances, the improvisational style of the company made it unworkable. The Muppets remained overwhelmingly male. Change came slowly, and tensions between the movement and CTW continued until the mid-1970s. In time, feminists persuaded the workshop to include more female characters and to show them in more active, independent, and nontraditional roles.[65]

One early dispute illustrated a problem that conflicting identity concepts posed for *Sesame Street*. Unlike Latino activists who focused on an ethnic basis for identity, feminists drew attention to the more personal aspects of life: the role of women in families and the kinds of jobs they held, for example. When feminists first criticized the show, they complained that the Street character Susan, an African-American housewife, had no work outside the home. She supported her husband, Gordon, and his career. This portrayal typified the stereotypes that feminists opposed, and CTW scripted Susan to take a job as a nurse near the end of the first season. Creating Gordon and Susan as breadwinner and housewife did not arise from unconscious sexism but from an effort to treat a different problem. Impoverished African-American boys lacked strong adult male role models for their lives, according to the conventional wisdom at the time, and CTW originally conceived of Gordon filling this role as a man capable of supporting his wife.[66] In line with identity theories, the producers hoped his television example would build self-esteem in this particular group of preschoolers.

This dilemma seems typical of multiculturalism, and CTW's solution proved typical as well. Justifying Susan's dependent role in this way apparently infuriated members of NOW. But many African-American women put the needs of African-American men—of their race in general—ahead of those of their gender. Dorothy Height of the National Council of Negro Women had said years earlier, "If the Negro woman has a major underlying concern, it is the status of the Negro man." Other black women echoed the same sentiments through the early 1970s, setting themselves apart from the feminist movement. To resolve such conflicts and to meet the demands of various groups, the workshop embraced these identity hypotheses and simply added or substituted segments and characters. By 1977, when an independent, unmarried, female African-American character named Olivia joined the street cast, it included two African-American men, a Chicano man, two white men, an American Indian woman, a Puerto Rican woman, a deaf white woman, and Susan.[67]

After all these struggles with commercial broadcasters, the FCC, critics, and activists, CTW's leaders pondered the question of yet another journalist, Claire Safran, who asked: "What's the Verdict on 'Sesame Street'?" Her answer to her own question captured the enduring respect which many within the press and public had for the show. The writer cited several critics including Cook but concluded by praising the show for keeping "its basic promise—to be imaginative, to use television to teach as well as amuse young children. If it is not everybody's ideal video classroom, that's because there is no single 'right' way to teach all children. If it has its critics, that's a tribute to its importance. Educators, psychologists, people who care about children take *Sesame Street* seriously—and how many other television programs can make that statement?"[68]

This tone of measured appreciation, however, matched a sense of resignation for those at CTW. "The hope was that *Sesame Street* would inspire other people to go and do likewise, produce quality programs for children," Safran wrote. Cooney offered her own verdict on the show's effectiveness as a model for television reform: "The networks are a *little* better now, but quality programming for children is slow in coming. In part, the very existence of *Sesame Street* has eased the pressure on the networks." Lesser concurred in his book: "Our failure to create a movement toward general improvement in the quality of children's programs forces us to recognize that a single instance of success will not be enough to sustain real progress." Hopes that a TV program could help ease the effects of poverty fared little better. Palmer admitted to Safran that children's "real needs" for food, housing, and schools made the show seem "only a Band-Aid" by comparison.[69]

In truth, each part of defining the meaning of *Sesame Street* came down to a negotiation. In the reform debate, the television and advertising industries refused to recognize the popularity of the show and its distinctly different approach as a rebuke to their system. No data or argument could force them to give up a lucrative part of their businesses. They could simply transform *Sesame Street* into a ratings flop, one extravagantly financed by the government to boot. As is so often the case, no one raised crucial questions that become clearer in historical hindsight. No one separated the issue of production under the CTW Model from the more contentious issue of decommercialization. Had they so desired, the TV industry executives could have hired child development experts and educators to work closely with their producers, write curricula, and systematically test the resulting programs. These could have been financed through advertising revenues; available figures seem to indicate that the workshop's costs were comparable to what the networks were paying. It is impossible to say for sure, but the way that the debate over ACT's proposal shaped broadcasters' perceptions of *Sesame Street* appears to have eclipsed any serious consideration of the Model.

CTW could take heart from the way the other two public debates about the show went. Though some observers could maintain the belief that TV could not teach, *Sesame Street* convinced the public that it had, at least, some modest educational benefits. And by the mid-1970s, the show had become a major symbol of racial, ethnic, and gender tolerance—of multiculturalism. One can only wonder how much of the rosy, illusory quality many Americans perceive in multiculturalism can be traced to *Sesame Street*'s intentionally sweet and innocent vision of community. In the public realm—outside the contention over money and regulation, with much less at stake—the show could hang on to its successes, albeit with reservations. On the whole, it remained a demonstration that television *could* aspire to reach beyond commercialism.

The Many Faces of
SESAME STREET

P sychologist and children's television reformer Dale Kunkel was testifying before Congress twenty years after *Sesame Street*'s premiere. During the intervening years, the 1974 compromise on ACT's petition had fallen apart. As Kunkel pointed out, because children's programming addressed a narrow audience, it "did not generate big enough profits to compete in the marketplace," and educational children's television had disappeared from the networks' schedules. Industry defenders had argued that the new videotape market and cable systems would make up for the dearth of programming. A new children's channel, Nickelodeon, had appeared on cable in 1979 and was reaching half of all American homes at the time Kunkel was testifying. Rebutting the industry's partisans, Kunkel called their logic the "Disneyland Rule." One could similarly insist, he said, that the city of Anaheim, California, no longer needed public parks because the famous amusement park provided "children's needs for open space and recreation. . . . Of course, the fundamental flaw in this logic is that Disneyland charges a price for admission—a price that not all can afford to pay." Even ten years later, one quarter of all American children did not have access to cable programming. The more things changed, the more they remained the same. Reformers continued to struggle against an industry that effectively defended its prerogatives and conceded as little as possible. And *Sesame Street* remained the model of what was possible, but in the 1990s other programs began to emulate it as none had before. The show still stood at the center of American thinking about children's television.[1]

Sesame Street has had many faces, many ways that Americans perceived it. The faces, the masks, the guises that people saw when they looked at the program reveal their complex and conflicted feelings about children and television. When the later history of *Sesame Street* and children's television reform are added to the story already related here, what becomes clear is that the tensions and conflicts seem endemic to American culture, at least in the last decades of the twentieth century and the near future. Taking each face in turn—in historical order and in order of reform, education, and multiculturalism as well—allows us to the see the relationships among these tensions and conflicts, on the one hand, and ideas and arguments about *Sesame Street*, on the other.

The Carnegie Corporation first conceived of *Sesame Street* like a foundation demonstration project. In some ways, its truest face was that of a research project bringing the form and style of popular entertainment together with a serious educational framework of educational and developmental theory, curriculum goals, and systematic evaluation. This face could be called: *Sesame Street* of the CTW Model. When, after its fifth season, Cooney called the show "a perpetual experiment," she wrote about it changing through those years and about the addition of "affective goals."[2] Despite the demise of the reform movement led by ACT, she could write that the show now placed "more emphasis on recognizing, accepting and dealing with such emotions as anger, surprise, fear, pride and happiness." This optimistic, positivist tone of the mid-1960s, which grew directly from the preschool moment, endured to the turn of the twenty-first century. To the question, "Does research have anything to give to art and entertainment?" *Sesame Street* of the Model answers with a confident "yes."

While Cooney wrote about the perpetual experiment, she also expressed disappointment that reform had been thwarted. Of children's programming on commercial TV, she said, "I am disappointed that the general pre–Sesame Street pattern has persisted."[3] This was the reform model *Sesame Street*. These first two faces of *Sesame Street* cannot be fully separated and are not fully compatible. Producers could hardly be expected to adopt the CTW Model voluntarily at the same time that *Sesame Street* was being used by reformers to demonstrate the industry's greed. The broadcasters assisted and applauded the program until its example became an indictment of their commercialism. At that juncture, they turned to obliterate its meaning in defense of their prerogatives, their privilege of self-regulation. In short, the story of the show quickly entered the fray of censorship and the social control of popular culture, an old battlefield littered with the wreckage left by Anthony Comstock, H. L. Mencken, and Joseph Breen. Ultimately, these conflicts always turned on raw political power, and the middle-class reformers of the 1960s and 1970s simply had not mustered the huge popular movement that the Legion of Decency had in the early 1930s.

Once industry executives set out to efface *Sesame Street* as a model, they could describe the show as a lavishly funded government project that attracted only a small audience; it taught no lesson, they contended, to those who had to attract the largest possible audience, to make a profit, and to compete in the marketplace. The problem with the show as a model, however, went beyond the power struggle to the lack of a precise lesson that it was to teach commercial producers. Did the show's creators mean for the industry to try out curricula, producer-expert partnership, and rigorous testing, even if candy companies were paying the bills? Or was *Sesame Street* supposed to show that good television could only come from putting *all* of the control in the hands of the creative staff and researchers, leaving the sponsor and the network out of the system? Did the problem that reformers were complaining about lay in the production system or the profit motive? These were questions that Comstock would never have asked, and they testify to *Sesame Street*'s historical context after the Dodd hearings and the rising discontent of the 1960s. The struggle in the FCC was not just about power; it was also about defining the problem.

The show's educational skeptics would have agreed with the industry on one thing: do not mix entertainment and education. As network executives said, they should stick to their strength, entertaining children, and leave education to the schools. Many critics of *Sesame Street*, like Urie Bronfenbrenner, would have agreed: combining educational goals with slick entertainment only degraded learning. And many teachers would have hastened to add that such TV led its young viewers to demand amusement when they reached the classroom. The history of *Sesame Street* establishes clearly that for many Americans entertainment and education are distinct and that the latter is far nobler. This divide seems to arise from the long-established middle-class urge to shelter children from a harsh, capitalist world and to nurture, prepare, and educate them. A child's domestic world is a sanctum. Though the undiluted, Victorian origins of the sanctuary idea seem quaint in the twenty-first century, the idea itself retains remarkable strength in mainstream middle-class culture. Jim Henson's slapstick segments, in which a baker, arms loaded with desserts, falls down the stairs, stand as one illustration. When educational columnist Minnie Perrin Berson saw the show, she disparaged these segments, asking, "Why debase the art form of teaching with phony pedagogy, vulgar side shows, bad acting, and layers of smoke and fog to clog the eager minds of small children?" Her question is typical of a column whose emotional intensity hints that an important boundary has been breached. For critics like Berson, *Sesame Street* broke down barriers essential to middle-class identity and sullied home and education with low popular culture.[4]

Closely related to buffoon teacher *Sesame Street* was the educational pretender. For many educational skeptics—from Nolan Estes to Thomas Cook—the show pretended to educate when real learning could only take place when two people—teacher and student—encountered each other face to face. CTW refused to accept the contention that television watching was a passive exercise incompatible with active education. In line with this argument, Cook and Herbert Sprigle said all learning connected with *Sesame Street* occurred when adults taught along with it. Workshop spokesmen like Edward Palmer insisted that this charge was false and that it demanded that a television program be fully interactive and personalized in a way that it never could be. These more psychological explorations of the relationship between program and young viewer have been a direction that both hostile critics and sympathetic researchers have followed since the mid-1970s.

The most important hostile critics attacked *Sesame Street* in order to demonstrate that television, in general, hurt children. In 1977, Marie Winn wrote in her bestselling book, *The Plug-In Drug*, that the danger of *Sesame Street* originated with the erroneous belief on the part of parents that it was educational. After citing Cook's study, she explained that the show lulled parents into believing that it was beneficial when it was serving only to get their children addicted to television. If television is harmful to children, in Winn's view, then *Sesame Street* only served to seduce parents into thinking that it could be otherwise. In 1979, developmental psychologists Jerome L. Singer and his wife, Dorothy G. Singer, wrote in *Psychology Today* that "the emphasis in American television on extremely short action sequences, frequent interruptions, and drastic changes in the visual field [such as on *Sesame Street*] . . . are actually creating a psychological orientation in children that leads to a shortened attention span, a lack of reflectiveness, and an expectation of rapid change in the broader environment." Twenty years later after pioneering research in imaginative play, the Singers still recommended that children's TV time be limited because it diverted children "from doing what they ought to be doing—learning to create miniworlds that they can control. Kids who can do this are more cooperative, more likely to become leaders, less likely to be overtly aggressive." In 1985, communications professor Neil Postman argued that television can only tell stories and cannot present a reasoned argument. One of the few programs he specifically addressed was *Sesame Street* because the reading public believed it was educational. Like the rest of television, it simply pumped its young viewers full of facts, according to Postman, without the context necessary to turn them into knowledge. These detractors demonstrated that, by taking on the burden of making TV beneficial to its youngest viewers, *Sesame Street* had become a target for any critic of the medium in general.[5]

While Winn, Postman, the Singers, and others prominently held the public's attention with alarming diagnoses, much less prominent academic researchers constructed a new and more effective paradigm for understanding how children watch television. CTW supported several studies of what could be called the attention-comprehension school. Psychologists like Daniel Anderson, Aletha Huston, John Wright, and Jennings Bryant began to discard ideas of "reflexive responses" by children in favor of learning and literacy. As Anderson put it, "Young children are intellectually active when they watch television; they selectively attend to aspects of program content that they find potentially comprehensible and interesting, ignoring those parts of programs that are uninteresting." This theory grew out of the workshop's approach to crafting their program and has led to a more positive, less polemical posture toward the medium by serious researchers.[6]

If *Sesame Street* had become the Janus of TV education—demon or angel—it had also become a familiar and beloved face of multiculturalism. Thirty years later, it remained the "poster show for respect of every race, creed and color that exists (and several—such as the blue and green cast members—that don't)." And it is the progenitor program that allowed the Public Broadcasting Service's senior vice president of programming, John Wilson, to boast, "We represent all of America, so we portray all of America." The *Economist* magazine applauded the show for representing a "multicultural tolerance," crucial to a diverse nation like the United States, and not mere "political correctness." Communications scholar Ellen Seiter concluded that the program played a significant role in making toy advertising to preschoolers distinctly more multicultural: "*Sesame Street* has created an association between racial integration and educational value that advertisers attempt to use to their advantage. Yet advertisers follow slightly different rules than *Sesame Street* does. While *Sesame Street* frequently has Black or Latino children in single, starring roles, advertisers still tend to use children of color in a crowd."[7]

While, to some, it had become the archangel of multiculturalism, to Speaker of the House of Representatives Newt Gingrich, it had become strong enough to finance all of public television. In December 1994, after a sweeping electoral victory that put a Republican majority in charge of the House for the first time in decades, the speaker promised that he and his colleagues would "zero out" the federal budget for the public broadcasting. The system's defenders quickly invoked *Sesame Street* as its icon and justification. Democratic Congresswoman Nita Lowey brought *Sesame Street* puppets to a committee hearing to speak out against the cuts: "Make no mistake about it, this debate is about Big Bird and Oscar the Grouch and Barney and Kermit and the new Republican majority that would put them on the chopping block." When Gingrich's campaign failed, the *New York Times* headline concluded that the show's star puppet Big Bird was "One Tough Bird, After All." *Sesame Street*, however, became Gingrich's target not just because it represented a government-funded broadcasting network but also because it seemed to hold a key to ending PBS's government support. By the 1990s, CTW drew its financial support from a different mix of sources than it had in the show's early years. To casual observers in the early 1990s, the commercial enterprises among these appeared to be capable of supporting other PBS programs.[8]

Sesame Street's tycoon face deserves some explanation because it has become a part of how some Americans see the show. The workshop's commercial enterprises began almost as soon as the show went on the air and were intended to make the nonprofit company independent of the vicissitudes of government and foundation funding. Lloyd Morrisett served as chairman of CTW's board from the beginning. During the first season, he concluded that "we couldn't count on federal sources, because the political environment changes." Richard Nixon had become president since the original commitments of funds had been made, and he struggled for years to prevent any money from reaching the public broadcasting system. Under his administration, the Office of Education moved to cut the funds for *Sesame Street* as well. If federal money seemed unreliable for political reasons, Morrisett concluded that "foundations could not be counted on in the long run" because foundations did not consider themselves a source of ongoing funds, only of seed money. Around the time that OE tried to cut the federal funds, during the fourth and fifth seasons, the Ford Foundation and the Carnegie Corporation stopped their funding. The workshop had to find other sources of funds.[9]

Before settling on commercial enterprises closely related to its shows, CTW tried a remarkably diverse set of possibilities. In 1973 the company's executives explored direct mail fundraising, selling memberships to viewers and supporters across the country. Morrisett announced this idea at the annual meeting of public television broadcasters. The next day, the workshop's public relations chief, Robert Hatch, and assistant director, Robert Davidson, held a meeting to take questions. Station representatives so vigorously opposed CTW's fundraising proposal that Hatch later said, "They damn near ran us out of the place . . . . It was as close to [a] . . . lynch mob as I've ever seen in public broadcasting." Trying another idea, the workshop convinced the Ford Foundation to make it a grant of money for investment. Earnings from these ventures could then support *Sesame Street* and other productions. The board chose to invest in cable franchises and, later, FM radio stations but found themselves out of their depth in these businesses, so they sold them off. In the early 1980s the workshop built Sesame Place, an amusement park, in a partnership with Anheuser Busch. It never made much money for the workshop, and the two companies abandoned plans to build two more parks. CTW also tried establishing commercial film and video game subsidiaries. The workshop could neither raise money like a public TV station nor manage a media conglomerate like Disney.[10]

Instead, the workshop followed its own distinctive set of businesses. Even before the show had gone into production, a dozen or so companies approached the workshop to license products, and in the first few seasons, the company signed agreements with book, record, and educational toy manufacturers. In those first years, CTW insisted that all products be clearly educational, but, since then, toys like Hokey Pokey Elmo have shifted the purpose of products from learning adjuncts to revenue producers. In the early years, foreign broadcasters—also unsolicited—approached the workshop to export the show to other nations and to produce new versions abroad. As of 2003, it had been seen in more than 140 countries. More than twenty coproductions have been created by the workshop in partnership with foreign producers who have created completely new sets of goals and characters to suit their own cultures. A third source of independent, but closely related, revenue came from publication of magazines, starting from the one directed to viewers of *Sesame Street*. In 1998, for example, the workshop took only $3 million of its roughly $80 million income from the government and earned almost all the rest from commercial ventures. Of the rest, $12 million came from the licensing of products,

$11 million from foreign coproduction and sales of the American show abroad, and $50 million came from magazines.[11]

In time, these ventures have made the workshop financially independent but still unable to support all of public television, as Gingrich and other conservatives had claimed. It was the initial promise of these monies in 1973 that Nixon's Secretary of Health, Education, and Welfare, Caspar Weinberger, used to argue that the commercial revenues should make it possible to begin cutting the federal contributions to CTW. By the 1990s conservatives had expanded this argument to apply to all of public television, suggesting that it be entirely "privatized" and forced to rely on member contributions, corporate image advertising, and product licensing revenues. Quoting gross sales figures of *Sesame Street*-related items of $1 billion, Congressman Philip Crane said that the show needed no federal support. Given the real licensing figures, Crane's figure requires explanation. Between 1991, when the *San Francisco Chronicle* reported that 350 million dollars' worth of merchandise had produced $29 million in licensing fees to CTW and 1995, the figures went through a political transformation. The conservative Family Research Council increased total product sales to $1 billion in 1992 with a royalties yield of $100 million. Journalists began to include *Barney & Friends*, a popular PBS children's show that began broadcasting in 1992, in their articles with its estimated product royalties of $50 million (a more accurate figure was $20 million). By the time that Gingrich's proposal began to encounter opposition, columnist George Will could make the argument that "licensed merchandise related to programs such as 'Barney & Friends,' 'Sesame Street' and 'Shining Time Station' [another children's program] produces hundreds of millions of dollars for the private companies that produce the programs." In fact, between *Barney* and *Sesame Street*—by far the largest earners—figures might reach $80 million, with little chance that other less popular, less marketable shows could bring the total to hundreds of millions. And these two programs needed these monies for their own production. If these funds had been put toward PBS's costs, the producers would have had to replace them. But these inflated figures made plausible Gingrich's claim that public broadcasting's federal contribution of $285 million could be replaced with royalties. Surprisingly strong public support for public broadcasting defeated the conservative proposal. When Senator Larry Pressler, who led the privatization effort in the Senate, ran for reelection the next year, a popular bumper sticker suggested, "Let's keep PBS and 'privatize' Pressler." He lost his bid for reelection.[12]

Not long after the defeat of Gingrich's proposal, children's television reformers won a less decisive victory over the free market approach to programming. After the industry's grudging self-regulation of the 1970s, it took full advantage of the changes that Ronald Reagan's election to president ushered in. Conservative deregulation efforts included an FCC that left broadcasting to marketplace control; viewers could turn to the new media of videotapes and cable channels to find alternatives to the broadcast network programming, Reagan's commissioners argued. To their new chairman, Mark S. Fowler, television was "just another appliance—a toaster with pictures." The industry's favorite new idea involved closely linking children's products and children's television. Corporations produced lines of toys and other products that featured characters, who could in turn become the stars of new programs. Action for Children's Television and other reformers complained that these shows were merely "program-length commercials." However profitable such programs were, the amount of children's programming declined. Fowler concluded that "the reason is no mystery. . . . Other programs may be more profitable or more popular. I don't believe that the FCC should second guess those judgments." The networks could broadcast whatever they pleased to children or nothing at all.[13]

Reformers proposed several responses, out of which grew the Children's Television Act of 1990. They returned to the basic principles of the ACT proposal, beginning with Representative Timothy Wirth's 1983 Children's Television bill, which mandated a minimum number of hours of children's programming. Edward Palmer of CTW proposed, as did others, government funding to pay for programs that the commercial industry would not finance. In 1988, the Children's Television Practices Act set a limit on advertising and required that television stations "serve the educational and informational needs of children in its *overall* programming." After Reagan vetoed the bill, its advocates strengthened their new draft the next year. Their new bill required broadcasters to meet "the educational and informational needs of children through the licensee's overall programming, including programming specifically designed to serve such needs." They also added a National Endowment for Children's Television to make grants to producers. After running as the "education president," Reagan's successor, George H. W. Bush, declined to either sign or veto the bill, and it became law.[14]

The FCC dragged its feet in implementing the law. The commission remained philosophically the same under Bush as it had been under Reagan. The industry, in the first five years after the act, felt free to count many entertainment programs as educational, such as *The Flintstones, America's Funniest Home Videos,* and *Biker Mice from Mars.* According to one station, for example, the cartoon show *Yogi Bear* taught "certain moral and ethical values such as not to do stupid things or you will have trouble." By 1996, public pressure and damning studies of compliance brought President Bill Clinton into the controversy. With his reelection at stake in the fall, the president brought the networks together and persuaded them to accept an FCC "guideline" of at least three hours of educational programming per week. In 2003, a major study of children's educational television found that the act had been effective in providing a real benefit to children.[15]

In the 1990s, a new aspect of *Sesame Street* appeared: parent to a whole new generation of truly educational programs. The most celebrated of these has been *Blue's Clues* (Nickelodeon, 1996–present). On the show, Blue is an animated dog who helps his master Joe, a live-action young man, solve problems by giving him clues. As he collects the clues, Joe also solves logic puzzles in a slow, deliberate pace, somewhat like the "One of these things is not like the others" game on *Sesame Street*. Nickelodeon, the first cable channel dedicated to children, has an entire lineup of preschool shows and programs for older children, many of which utilize parts of the CTW Model. Nickelodeon and PBS remain, as of this writing, the major outlets for educational children's TV. Another program in this new generation is *Between the Lions,* created by veterans from the workshop and designed to teach reading. From the consultants to the curriculum to the testing, they have followed the Model—and articulated it to the public—probably better than any other program since *Sesame Street*. Like Nickelodeon, PBS has a large group of children's shows that, in some places, fill the daytime hours of the schedule. The broadcast networks have not created as many educational programs and remain resistant to the FCC requirements. They have not promoted their educational programs enough and have put them in time slots prone to being preempted by sports programs, according to Daniel Anderson, the primary adviser for *Blue's Clues*. Shelly Hirsch of Summit Media, the producer of a popular network show, *Pokémon,* remarked in a familiar vein, "If you create something really educational, it's the kiss of death with kids. They get enough lessons in school."[16]

The mixed results from the act have nevertheless brought some credible evidence of learning. In 2003, two researchers, Sandra L. Calvert and Jennifer A. Kotler, published in the *Journal of Applied Developmental Psychology* the results of a series of studies with second grade to sixth grade children. They collected their data in both traditional and innovative ways, including asking children to report through the Internet on what they thought they had learned. Calvert and Kotler concluded that 75 percent of all educational shows taught pro-social lessons, not the more academic sort in which *Sesame Street* specialized, and that girls and younger children in the group enjoyed educational programs more than the older boys. This study and the trends in children's TV have made preschool viewers the ones who most often receive the most academic style of TV. This finding seems to imply that *Sesame Street* created a special niche. Along with Calvert and Kotler's results, the same journal published a series of articles—several by major scholars in the field—that celebrated the success, even if limited, of the Children's Television Act. Their study "provides clear confirmation that children are profiting by this law," Dale Kunkel wrote. "Broadcasters can achieve these educational outcomes with programs that attract children's interest and are competitive with other networks that specialize in children's programming." On the other hand, another researcher, Amy Jordan, asked, "How much are they learning?"; were the pro-social lessons, like "Be loyal to your friends," actually imparting anything the children did not already know? More disturbing still in her assessment, Jordan pointed to an important failure at home: "Despite evidence of a causal connection between early educational television viewing and later academic success, parents do not yet seem convinced that television can be an important educational resource in the home." As a parent, *Sesame Street* had not gotten its lesson of cognitive content across either to its programmatic progeny or to the human parents of its viewers.[17]

Sesame Street's most familiar face has not been as prominent in this book as it is to most Americans. That face would be that of Jim Henson's Muppets—including Elmo, Big Bird, Cookie Monster, Grover, Oscar the Grouch, Count von Count, Ernie, and Bert. Their importance to the show grew over time to the point that they have, in some ways, overshadowed much else about it. In the first years, they were an important but not overwhelming part of what made the show popular. In 1970 Ernie's song "Rubber Ducky" made the *Billboard* magazine song charts and sold 700,000 copies. As toy licensing became more important, so too did the Muppets. William Whaley, longtime head of CTW's product licensing group, would later say, "It's the Muppets that sell." Their gentle parodies of mass culture and fairy tales and other innocent fare appealed to adults as well as children. Toys that projected the characters beyond the screen into children's physical bedrooms must have also enhanced their popularity. When Henson, with the help of British television magnate Lew Grade, succeeded in producing *The Muppet Show* (syndicated, 1976–1981) for prime time, Henson's artistry and career took off. Soon he made *The Muppets Movie*, the first of six films; since then, he and his company have made roughly thirty television series and at least fourteen television specials and movies. On *Sesame Street*, CTW added more and more puppet characters because its studies had shown that children easily recognized these brightly colored, stereotypical characters and could learn from them more easily. As Gerald Lesser put it, "Puppets generally remain reliably in character across different episodes (a strong preference of young viewers) and can portray more exaggerated and therefore clearer roles and functions than human figures." Format changes in 2003 that focus even more attention on Elmo, Big Bird, and Ernie have made *Sesame Street* all the more Muppet-centric.[18]

Sesame Street, however, has always been more than a vehicle for the Muppets. It established a niche for serious, educational, preschool television. It became a prominent part of TV across the globe. It proved that education and entertainment could be combined more effectively. In the end, *Sesame Street*'s real strength lay not only in the CTW Model, its style, and its artistry but also in its appeal to deep-seated, long-established strains in American middle-class culture. Middle-class parents demanded that television's programming include shelter from a debased popular culture for their children and a place for their own self-improvement. As long as these desires remain a part of America's dominant class culture, future experiments like *Sesame Street* will find an audience. But these programs will only make it on the air if viewer and citizen activists press for them and if money from organizations outside of the entertainment industry, like the Carnegie Corporation, makes these programs possible. *Sesame Street* showed what was possible, and others have followed—and will follow—its example.

Notes

Introduction

1. This Bert and Ernie skit appeared in episode number 656, broadcast May 6, 1974, near the end of *Sesame Street*'s fifth season.

2. Les Brown quoted in "'Sesame Street': Wunderkind: St. Joan's Click for PTV and UHF," *Variety*, December 24, 1969, 23; "If Kids Act Smarter, 'Sesame Street' May Be the Reason," *Nation's Schools* 87 (March 1971): 34; Jim Fiebig, "Mark My Words," *Bremerton Washington Sun*, July 6, 1970, in July 1970 CTW Clip Report, Box 290, Archives of the Children's Television Workshop, National Public Broadcasting Archives, Hornbake Library, University of Maryland, College Park (hereafter, CTW Archives).

3. Official Report of Proceedings before the Federal Communications Commission, Washington, D.C., October 2, 1972, Public Panel Discussion: Children's Television Programming (Washington, D.C.: CSA Reporting Corp., 1972), Docket no. 19142, in Federal Communications Commission Records, vol. 64, p. 45, Box 28, Acc. 173-90-7, Washington National Records Center, Suitland, Md.; Minnie Perrin Berson, "Ali Baba! What Have You Done?" *Childhood Education* 46 (March 1970): 342; National Advisory Committee to the Bilingual Program of Sesame Street, San Antonio, Texas, April 22, 23, 1971, press release, n.d., file: "Bilingual Educational Sub-Committee Board of Advisers," unprocessed Community Education Services files, CTW Archives; Marie Winn, *The Plug-In Drug: Television, Computers, and Family Life*, twenty-fifth anniversary edition (New York: Penguin, 2002), 63.

4. Martha Wolfenstein, "Fun Morality: An Analysis of Recent American Child-Training Literature," in *The Children's Culture Reader*, ed. Henry Jenkins (New York: New York University Press, 1998), 199–208; Lynn Spigel, *Make Room for TV: Television and the Family Ideal in Postwar America* (Chicago: University of Chicago Press, 1992).

5. Viviana A. Zelizer, *Pricing the Priceless Child: The Changing Social Value of Children* (1985; repr., Princeton University Press, 1994).

6. Heather Hendershot, *Saturday Morning Censors: Television Regulation before the V- Chip* (Durham, N.C.: Duke University Press, 1998); Ellen Seiter, *Sold Separately: Children and Parents in Consumer Culture* (New Brunswick, N.J.: Rutgers University Press, 1993). For active child viewers, see also Daniel R. Anderson, "Watching Children Watch Television and the Creation of *Blues Clues*," in *Nickelodeon Nation: The History, Politics, and Economics of America's Only TV Channel for Kids*, ed. Heather Hendershot (New York: New York University Press, 2004), 241–68.

7. Farber, *The Age of Great Dreams: America in the 1960s* (New York: Hill and Wang, 1994), 17.

8. *Time*, November 23, 1970.

9. "New Bloom on the Wasteland," *PTA Magazine*, May 1968; 26. Lawrie Mifflin, "Move Over, Big Bird: A New Blue Dog's in Town," *New York Times*, March 25, 1998, E1.

Chapter 1. The Problem of Television and the Child Viewer

1. "Preview," *New Yorker*, September 4, 1948, 19.

2. "The Vast Wasteland," in *Equal Time: The Private Broadcaster and the Public Interest*, ed. Lawrence Laurent (New York: Atheneum, 1964), 48–64; Lippmann, as quoted in William Boddy, *Fifties Television: The Industry and Its Critics* (Urbana: University of Illinois Press, 1990), 251.

3. As quoted in Mary Beth Norton et al., *A People and a Nation: A History of the United States*, 6th ed. (New York: Houghton Mifflin, 2001), 312.

4. As quoted in Lawrence W. Levine, *Highbrow/Lowbrow: The Emergence of Cultural Hierarchy in America* (Cambridge: Harvard University Press, 1988), 64.

5. As quoted in Carl N. Degler, *At Odds: Women and the Family in America from the Revolution to the Present* (New York: Oxford University Press, 1980), 98.

6. Shelley Stamp, "Moral Coercion, or The National Board of Censorship Ponders the Vice Films," in *Controlling Hollywood: Censorship and Regulation in the Studio Era*, ed. Matthew Bernstein (New Brunswick, N.J.: Rutgers University Press, 1999), 41–59.

7. As quoted in Paul S. Boyer, *Purity in Print: The Vice-Society Movement and Book Censorship in America* (New York: Charles Scribner's Sons, 1968), 127.

8. As quoted in Michele Hilmes, *Radio Voices: American Broadcasting, 1922–1952* (Minneapolis: University of Minnesota Press, 1997), 123.

9. As quoted in James Baughman, "The Promise of American Television," *Prospects* 11 (1987): 125, 126.

10. Quotes from Lynn Spigel, *Make Room for TV: Television and the Family Ideal in Postwar America* (Chicago: University of Chicago Press, 1992), 44, 45.

11. Christopher H. Sterling and John M. Kittross, *Stay Tuned: A Concise History of American Broadcasting*, 2nd ed. (Belmont, Calif.: Wadsworth, 1990), 657–58.

12. Robert D. Hess and Harriet Goldman, "Parents' Views of the Effect of Television on Their Children," *Child Development* 33 (1962): 413; Gary A. Steiner, *The Peo-*

ple Look at Television: A Study of Audience Attitudes (New York: Knopf, 1963), 82, 83, 85; "The Children's Hour," *Newsweek*, April 26, 1954, 92; Paul Witty, "Studies of Mass Media, 1949–1965," *Science Education* 50 (March 1966): 120.

13. Paul D. Witty and Harry Bricker, "Your Child and TV," *Parents' Magazine*, December 1952, 36.

14. As quoted in Spiegel, *Make Room*, 55.

15. "Stars on Strings," *Time*, January 17, 1949, 70; "Puppets and People," *Newsweek*, December 10, 1951, 55–56.

16. Gary Cross, *Kids' Stuff: Toys and the Changing World of American Childhood* (Cambridge, Mass.: Harvard University Press, 1997), 165.

17. Jack Gould, "Television in Review: 'Ding Dong School,' a Worthwhile Video Program Directed at Children, Stubs Toe on Commercialism," *New York Times*, April 1, 1953, 41.

18. Larry Wolters, "Mistress of 'Ding Dong School': 'Miss Frances' Enthralls Pre-School Youngsters on Weekday Mornings," *New York Times*, January 4, 1953, II–11; "She Rings the Bell: Dr. Frances Horwich Educates Tots by the Millions in Nation's Largest Classroom," *TV Guide*, October 16, 1954, 20–21; "She Battles for Your Children: Dr. Frances Horwich Seeks New Standards for Juvenile Shows," *TV Guide*, December 10, 1955, 18–19; Published letter excerpts, *New York Times*, January 1, 1956, II-9; "Frances Horwich Quits N.B.C. Post: 'Ding Dong School' Director Released from Contract as Show Goes off TV," *New York Times*, December 29, 1956, 29; Jack Gould, "TV: 'Ding Dong School': Dr. Frances Horwich's Series with Ads for Pre-School Children Returns Here," *New York Times*, September 15, 1959, 78; Frances R. Horwich, "Ding Dong School," n.d. [c. 1962], File 261, "Children's Programs," Hedges Collection, Library of American Broadcasting, Hornbake Library, University of Maryland, College Park, Md.

19. As quoted in George W. Woolery, *Children's Television: The First Thirty-Five Years, 1946–1981, Part II: Live, Film, and Tape Series* (Metuchen, N.J.: Scarecrow Press, 1985), 101. For the date I have relied not on Woolery but on Alex McNeil, *Total Television: The Comprehensive Guide to Programming from 1948 to the Present*, 4th ed. (New York: Penguin Books, 1996), 1122.

20. David Connell, *Sesame Street*'s original executive producer, had acted in the same capacity for *Kangaroo*. He told the story of Keeshan's attempts to teach about congressional process in "David Connell," interview by Robert Davidson (New York, July 11, 1990), in "Children's Television Workshop: The Early Years, an Oral History," ed. Robert Davidson (Children's Television Workshop, manuscript, 1993), 77 (hereafter, Davidson oral history); "Captain Kangaroo Explains Modern Art to the Children," *TV Guide*, July 6, 1957, 28–29.

21. Steiner, *People Look*, 104. Sources on *Captain Kangaroo*: Bob Keeshan, *Good Morning, Captain: Fifty Wonderful Years with Bob Keeshan, TV's Captain Kangaroo*, edited by Cathryn Long (Minneapolis: Fairview Press, 1996); Bob Keeshan, *Growing Up Happy: Captain Kangaroo Tells Yesterday's Children How to Nurture Their Own* (New York: Doubleday, 1989), 88, 108–10, 121–24, 179–80; Lucille Burbank, "Children's Televi-

sion: An Historical Inquiry on Three Selected, Prominent, Long-Running, Early Child-hood TV Programs" (Ed.D. dissertation, Temple University, 1992), 18–21, 81–92; J. P. Shanley, "TV: Antidote to Jumping: Capt. Kangaroo Keeps Young Viewers Quiet," *New York Times*, October 15, 1955, 33; "Captain Kangaroo: Bob Keeshan Learns How to Entertain Small Fry—At Home," *TV Guide*, September 8, 1956, 20–21; Gilbert Millstein, "The K Stands for Keeshan Too," *TV Guide*, August 5, 1961, 19; Gilbert Seldes, "Review: Captain Kangaroo and Shari Lewis," *TV Guide*, October 13, 1962, 2.

22. Schramm, Jack Lyle, and Edwin B. Parker, *Television in the Lives of Our Children* (Stanford, Calif.: Stanford University Press, 1961), 174; Elihu Katz and David Foulkes, "On the Use of the Mass Media as 'Escape': Clarification of a Concept," *Public Opinion Quarterly* 26 (1962): 377–88.

23. Delinquent's mother, as quoted in James Gilbert, *A Cycle of Outrage: America's Reaction to the Juvenile Delinquent in the 1950s* (New York: Oxford University Press, 1986), 155. Kefauver committee, as quoted in Willard D. Rowland Jr., *The Politics of TV Violence: Policy Uses of Communication Research* (Beverly Hills, Calif.: Sage, 1983), 104.

24. Bandura and Dodd quotations from Senate Subcommittee to Investigate Juvenile Delinquency, *Effects on Young People of Violence and Crime Portrayed on Television*, pt. 10, Hearings for the Committee on the Judiciary, 87th Cong., 1st Sess., June 15, 1961, 1947–1957, at 1947.

25. Filmed adult model, as quoted in Carmen Luke, *Constructing the Child Viewer: A History of the American Discourse on Television and Children, 1950–1980* (New York: Praeger, 1990), 130; Albert Bandura, Dorothea Ross, and Sheila A. Ross, "Imitation of Film-Mediated Aggressive Models," *Journal of Abnormal and Social Psychology* 66 (1963): 3–11. All quotations except the one from Luke are from the original study report.

26. Albert Bandura, "What TV Violence Can Do to Your Child," *Look*, October 22, 1963, 46–48, 52. Emphasis in original.

27. Ibid., 52. For coverage of confirming and related experiments, see Robert M. Liebert, Joyce N. Sprafkin, and Emily S. Davidson, *The Early Window: Effects of Television on Children and Youth*, 2nd ed. (New York: Pergamon Press, 1982), 54–58, 60–62; Luke, *Constructing the Child Viewer*, 140–41, 145–46.

28. "Crime Shows on TV—A Federal Crackdown Coming?" *U.S. News and World Report*, November 9, 1964, 49–50.

29. National Commission on the Causes and Prevention of Violence, *To Establish Justice, To Insure Domestic Tranquility* (Washington, D.C.: GPO, 1969), 199; Bandura and "entertainment, relaxation" quotations, 196. For a discussion of the impact of the assassination of Robert Kennedy on the industry, see Heather Hendershot, *Saturday Morning Censors: Television Regulation before the V-Chip* (Durham, N.C.: Duke University Press, 1998), 27–32.

30. As quoted in Douglass Cater and Stephen Strickland, *TV Violence and the Child: The Evolution and Fate of the Surgeon General's Report* (New York: Russell Sage Foundation, 1975), 75–76.

31. All quotes are from Eli A. Rubinstein, "The TV Violence Report: What's Next?" *Journal of Communication* 24 (1974): 80, 83, 85.

32. Lazarsfeld, "Why Is So Little Known about the Effects of Television on Children and What Can Be Done? Testimony Before the Kefauver Committee on Juvenile Delinquency," *Public Opinion Quarterly* 19 (Fall 1955): 246; Lesser, *Children and Television: Lessons from Sesame Street* (New York: Vintage Books, 1974), 1.

33. Fred M. Rogers, "Television and Individual Growth," *Television Quarterly* 9 (Summer 1970): 14.

Chapter 2. The Preschool Moment

1. Morrisett, "Preschool Education," *Science* 153 (September 9, 1966): 1197.

2. Stevenson, as quoted in Douglas T. Miller and Marion Nowak, "The Precarious Prosperity of People's Capitalism," in *Major Problems in American History Since 1945: Documents and Essays*, ed. Robert Griffith (Lexington, Mass.: D. C. Heath, 1992), 216. Prosperity statistics are from Alan Brinkley et al., *American History: A Survey*, vol. 2, 8th ed. (New York: McGraw-Hill, 1991), 855–65.

3. I have borrowed John Higham's concept of "American universalism" from "Multiculturalism and Universalism: A History and Critique," *American Quarterly* 45 (June 1993): 195–219. See also Gary Gerstle, *American Crucible: Race and Nation in the Twentieth Century* (Princeton, N.J.: Princeton University Press, 2001), for a more complete exposition of this story.

4. As quoted in Adam Fairclough, *Better Day Coming: Blacks and Equality, 1890–2000* (New York: Viking Penguin, 2001), 230.

5. Harrington, *The Other America: Poverty in the United States*, rev. ed. (Baltimore: Penguin Books, 1971), 188, 2.

6. Ibid., chapter title, 1–19; Oscar Lewis, *The Children of Sanchez: Autobiography of a Mexican Family* (New York: Random House, 1961), xxv, xxiv; Oscar Lewis, "The Culture of Poverty," *Scientific American*, October 1966, 19–25.

7. Land, as quoted in Goldman, *The Tragedy of Lyndon Johnson* (New York: Alfred A. Knopf, 1969), 38; Johnson, "President Lyndon B. Johnson Declares War on Poverty, 1964," in *Major Problems*, ed. Griffith, 310.

8. Kearns, *Lyndon Johnson and the American Dream* (New York: Signet, 1976), 222; AFL-CIO executive council, as quoted in Irwin Unger, *The Best of Intentions: The Triumphs and Failures of the Great Society under Kennedy, Johnson, and Nixon* (New York: Doubleday, 1996), 89.

9. Ralph Nader, *Unsafe at Any Speed: The Designed-in Dangers of the American Automobile* (New York: Grossman, 1965).

10. Edward Zigler and Susan Muenchow, *Head Start: The Inside Story of America's Most Successful Educational Experiment* (New York: Basic Books, 1992), 6; Robert E. Cooke, "Introduction," in *Project Head Start: A Legacy of the War on Poverty*, ed. Zigler and Jeanette Valentine (New York: Free Press, 1979), xxiv.

11. Zigler and Muenchow, *Head Start*.

12. Barbara Beatty, "Rethinking the Historical Role of Psychology in Educational Reform," in *The Handbook of Education and Human Development: New Models of Learn-*

ing, ed. David R. Olson and Nancy Torrance (Malden, Mass.: Blackwell Publishers, 1996), 103.

13. C. B. Lavatelli, "Critical Overview of Early Childhood Education Programs," Head Start Conference, Berkeley, Calif., April 3, 1968 (Washington, D.C.: Educational Resources Information Center, ERIC document ED-019-142), 2.

14. Benjamin S. Bloom, *Stability and Change in Human Characteristics* (New York: John Wiley and Sons, 1964), 88, 89, 90; Hunt, as quoted in Maya Pines, *Revolution in Learning: The Years from Birth to Six* (New York: Harper and Row, 1967), 46.

15. William S. Paley, "Education Is a National Responsibility," *NEA Journal* 53 (May 1964): 10; "Report of the President's Task Force on Education," November 14, 1964, i, "1964–Pres. Task Force on Ed." file, Box 8, Records Relating to the Formulation of National Education Policy, 1959–1980, Record Group 12, National Archives, College Park, MD; EPC, NEA, "Universal Opportunity for Early Childhood Education" (Washington, D.C.: NEA, 1966), 5.

16. Cornelia Goldsmith, "Our Concerns for Young Children Today," *Young Children* 21 (November 1966): 71–77; Norma R. Law, "Are the Public Schools Ready for Preschoolers?" *Young Children* 21 (September 1966): 323–28.

17. Richard I. Miller, Project on the Instructional Program of the Public School, National Education Association, *Education in a Changing Society* (Washington, D.C.: NEA, 1963), 1, 135.

18. EPC, "Universal Opportunity," 4–5.

19. "School for Four-Year-Olds?" *Time*, July 1, 1966, 39; "The Platform of the National Education Association of the United States," in National Education Association, *Addresses and Proceedings*, vol. 104 (Washington, D.C.: NEA, 1966), 464.

20. "Opinion Poll: Big Preschool Problems: Space, Money, and Staff," *Nation's Schools* 77 (June 1966): 68; Rice, "Looking Forward: Let's Not Force Preschool Programs on Everybody," *Nation's Schools* 78 (September 1966): 12. Rice was "editorial adviser to *Nation's Schools* and professor of education at Indiana University, Bloomington," but given the apparent audience of the journal, he undoubtedly spoke for those who actually ran schools. Just the year before, Congress had passed ESEA, a system of categorical grants intended to improve schools in general but particularly those with large numbers of disadvantaged students.

21. Rice, "Looking Forward," 10; "Resolutions Adopted at Miami Beach: 66-3 Expansion of Educational Opportunity," in NEA, *Addresses and Proceedings*, vol. 104, 468.

22. Kenneth B. Clark and Lawrence Plotkin, "A Review of the Issues and Literature of Cultural Deprivation Theory," in *The Educationally Deprived: The Potential for Change*, ed. Clark (New York: Metropolitan Applied Research Center, 1972), 47–73; Herbert Ginsburg, *The Myth of the Deprived Child: Poor Children's Intellect and Education* (Englewood Cliffs, N.J.: Prentice-Hall, 1972).

23. Biber, as quoted in Stacie G. Goffin and Catherine S. Wilson, *Curricular Models and Early Childhood Education: Appraising the Relationship*, 2nd ed. (Upper Saddle River, N.J.: Merrill Prentice Hall, 2001), 76. I have relied on their account of the "Developmental-Interaction Approach" as exemplary of the mainstream of preschool thought

and practice before the preschool moment revolutionized the field. Biber was among the many experts whom Cooney consulted in the early development of *Sesame Street*.

24. Gray, as quoted in Zigler and Karen Anderson, "An Idea Whose Time Had Come: The Intellectual and Political Climate for Head Start," in *Project Head Start: A Legacy of the War on Poverty*, ed. Zigler and Jeanette Valentine (New York: Free Press, 1979), 11; Cynthia P. Deutsch and Martin Deutsch, "Brief Reflections on the Theory of Early Childhood Enrichment Programs," in *The Disadvantaged Child: Selected Papers of Martin Deutsch and Associates*, ed. Martin Deutsch (New York: Basic Books, 1967), 384–85.

25. Jory Graham, "Handbook for Project Head Start," Urban Child Center, University of Chicago, n.p., n.d.; Jeannette Galambos Stone, "General Philosophy: Preschool Education within Head Start," in *Project Head Start*, ed. Zigler and Valentine, 172–73.

26. Pines, *Revolution*, 50; Bereiter and Engelmann, *Teaching Disadvantaged Children in Preschool* (Englewood Cliffs, N.J.: Prentice-Hall, 1966), 120; Bereiter, as quoted in Goffin and Wilson, *Curricular Models*, 101–2.

27. S. T. Moskovitz and E. Weber, respectively, as quoted in Goffin and Wilson, *Curricular Models*, 98, 101; Lavatelli, "Critical Overview," 8–10.

28. Cooney, telephone interview by the author, January 28, 1998, tape recording, transcript, 4; Cooney, "The Potential Uses of Television in Preschool Education," [Carnegie Corporation], [October, 1966], Box 1, The Archives of the Children's Television Workshop, National Public Broadcasting Archives, Hornbake Library, University of Maryland, College Park.

Chapter 3. "A New Bloom on the Wasteland"

1. Cooney, "Joan Ganz Cooney," interview by Robert Davidson (New York, February 13, 1991; April 24, 1991), 1–2, and Morrisett, "Lloyd Morrisett," interview by Robert Davidson (New York, December 5, 1991; April 20, 1992), 33, in "Children's Television Workshop: The Early Years, an Oral History," ed. Robert Davidson (Children's Television Workshop, manuscript, 1993), (hereafter, Davidson oral history). Cooney told the story about Morrisett's daughter and repeated it in Cooney, interview by the author, tape recording, transcript, New York, September 8, 1997, 14.

2. Records of Interview, March 14, March 31, April 1, and April 27, 1966, Freedman to Carnegie Corp., [May 13, 1966], "Educational Television for Preschool Children, Study of (Joan Cooney)" file, 1966–1976, Box 562, Carnegie Corp. Collection, Rare Book and Manuscript Library, Columbia University, New York, N.Y. (hereafter, CC Coll.); Cooney, Davidson oral history, 2–3; Morrisett, Davidson oral history, 33–34. Throughout this book I use the program's title for simplicity and clarity. Until April 1969, however, the program that Cooney, Morrisett, and others were planning had no title. I cover the origins of the title in chapter 5.

3. Les Brown, "'Sesame Street': Wunderkind: St. Joan's Click for PTV & UHF," *Variety*, December 24, 1969, 23; Cooney, as quoted in Michele Morris, "The St. Joan of Television," *Working Woman*, May 1986, 76; Cooney, interview by the author, 5–15; "Resume" of Joan Ganz Cooney, [1967], "Educational Television for Preschool Children, Study of (Joan Cooney)" file, Box 562, CC Coll.; "Cooney, Timothy J.," *Who's Who*

in the East, 14th ed., 1974–1975 (Chicago: Marquis Who's Who, 1973), 151; Jack Gould, "TV Review: Channel 13's Teach-In on Poverty Lively," *New York Times*, June 3, 1965; Val Adams, "8 Emmy Awards Presented Here: WNDT Takes Most Honors—Mayor Also Cited," *New York Times*, December 2, 1966, 79. More coverage of *Poverty* can be found in "WNDT Clippings June 1965" file, Records of WNET, National Public Broadcasting Archives, Hornbake Library, University of Maryland, College Park.

4. "Boss Is Better," *Forbes*, June 1, 1975, 43–44; Cooney, Davidson oral history, 1–2; Brown, "'Sesame Street.'"

5. Carnegie Corporation of New York, "Annual Reports" for 1966, 1967, and 1968 (New York: Carnegie Corp., 1966–68); Morrisett, telephone interview by the author, September 11, 1998, tape recording, transcript, 1–5.

6. Cooney, "The Potential Uses of Television in Preschool Education," [Carnegie Corp.], [October, 1966], Box 1, The Archives of the Children's Television Workshop, National Public Broadcasting Archives, Hornbake Library, University of Maryland, College Park (hereafter, CTW Archives), 38, 9, 10, 38.

7. Ibid., 14.

8. The list appears at the back and includes twenty-six names.

9. [Linda Gottlieb and Cooney], "Television for Preschool Children: A Proposal," February 19, 1968, Box 1, CTW Archives, 1; Cooney, "Potential Uses," 6, 4, 7. Gottlieb was a freelance writer who assisted Cooney with the ideas and prose of the final proposal.

10. Ibid., 20–21.

11. Ibid., 21–23, 27–40; Memo, Research Dept. to Production Dept. et al., "Statement of the Instructional Goals," December 31, 1968, Box 33, CTW Archives.

12. "Section VI—Television and the Disadvantaged Child" appears on pages 45–48 of the 50-page feasibility study; "III. To Reach the Disadvantaged" appears on pages 29–32 of the 52-page final proposal.

13. Cooney, "Potential Uses," 46, 18.

14. Ibid., 45, 47; "TV Show Tuned to Reach City Children of the Poor," *New York Post*, October 29, 1966, bound press clippings, Records of WNET, National Public Broadcasting Archives, Hornbake Library, University of Maryland, College Park.

15. Cooney, Davidson oral history, 4–5; Cooney, interview by the author, September 8, 1997, 15; Richard M. Polsky, *Getting to Sesame Street: Origins of the Children's Television Workshop* (New York: Praeger Publishers, 1974), 25; Channel 13/WNDT Educational Broadcasting Corp., "A Proposal for the Use of Television in Preschool Education," [March, 1967], Box 1, CTW Archives; "Resume" of Joan Ganz Cooney, n.d., "Educational Television for Preschool Children, Study of (Joan Cooney)," file, Box 562, CC Coll.; Carnegie Corp. of New York, "Annual Report 1967" (New York: Carnegie Corp., 1967), 75.

16. Memo, [Pifer] to Finberg, Margaret E. Mahoney, and [Morrisett], December 30, 1966, "Educational Television for Preschool Children, Study of (Joan Cooney)" file, Box 562; Douglas D. Bond to Mahoney, January 6, 1967; Barnaby C. Keeney to Mahoney, February 1, 1967, "Children's Television Workshop 1967" file, Box 489; CC

Coll.; Finberg, interview by Richard Polsky, March 30, 1972, interview 75, microfiche transcript, 8, Columbia University Oral History Collecton, Part IV (Sanford, N.C.: Microfilming Corp. of America, 1979); Polsky, *Getting*, 27. Polsky's oral history interviews at Columbia are hereafter cited as "Polsky oral history." Finberg, telephone interview by the author, July 30, 2003, tape recording.

17. Morrisett, interview by the author, 14–18.

18. "Howe, Harold, 2d," *Current Biography 1967* (New York: H.W. Wilson, 1967), 185–88; Howe, "National Policy for American Education," address at the 71st Annual Convention of the National Congress of Parents and Teachers, May 22, 1967, in *Picking Up the Options* (Washington, D.C.: Dept. of Elementary School Principals, National Education Association, 1968), 182; Polsky, *Getting*, 28; Finberg, Polsky oral history, 1–2; Cooney, Davidson oral history, 7; Howe to Jule Sugarman, June 30, 1967, "Carnegie Corp. Pre-School TV 1967–1968" file, Box 279, Office Files of the Commissioner of Education, 1939–80, Record Group 12, National Archives, College Park, Md. (hereafter, OE Commissioner Files). Sugarman was the director of Head Start.

19. Hausman, interview by Richard Polsky, March 9, 1972, interview 95, Polsky oral history, 1; "Louis Hausman, 59, has been appointed," press release HEW-M17, July 17, 1966, Box 6, Commissioner of Education Press Releases, 1963–1969, Record Group 12, National Archives, College Park, Md.; "Report from Washington," *Nation's Schools* 78 (September 1966): 22; Hausman, "Foreword," in Ralph Garry, F. B. Rainsberry, Charles Winick, eds., *For the Young Viewer: Television Programming for Children . . . at the Local Level* (New York: McGraw-Hill, 1962), v.

20. For accounts of the budget development, see Polsky, *Getting*, passim; Hausman, interview by Polsky, 1–3; Cooney, Davidson oral history, 10. The figure of four to five million dollars appears, for example, in Howe to Morrisett, July 7, 1967, "Carnegie Corp. Pre-School TV 1967–1968" file, Box 279, OE Commissioner Files. Hausman estimated per hour production costs from *Discovery*, *Exploring*, "Children's Theater (NBC)," and "Disney" according to pencilled notes, unsigned, undated, "Carnegie ETV—3–5 Year Olds" file, Box 279, OE Commissioner files.

21. Hausman, interview by Polsky, 2.

22. Cooney, "Potential Uses," 9.

23. Memo, Hausman to Howe, July 5, 1967, "Carnegie Corp. Pre-School TV 1967–1968" file, Box 279, OE Commissioner Files.

24. Cooney, interview by the author, September 8, 1997, 18; Record of Interview, March 15, 1967, "Children's Television Workshop 1967" file, Box 489; Memo, Finberg to Pifer and Morrisett, June 2, 1966, "Educational Television for Preschool Children, Study of (Joan Cooney)" file, Box 562, CC Coll.

25. Morrisett, interview by the author, 18–21; Polsky, *Getting*, 26, 34; [Morrisett], Records of Interview, November 13, 1967, December 12, 1967, "Children's Television Workshop 1967" file, Box 489, February 21, 1968, "Children's Television Workshop (support) 1968" file, CC Coll.; "2 Networks Made Eyes at 'Sesame,'" *Variety*, August 26, 1970, "Clip Reports, July-November 1970" file, Box 290, CTW Archives.

26. Memo, Hausman to Howe, July 19, 1967, Memo, Hausman for the files, July

20, 1967, Hausman to Morrisett, July 24, 1967, Hausman to Morrisett, August 9, 1967, John F. White to Morrisett and Edward J. Meade Jr., January 2, 1968, Morrisett to White, January 10, 1968, White to Hausman, Meade, and Morrisett, January 31, 1968, "Carnegie Corp. Pre-School TV 1967–1968" file, Morrisett to George A. Heinemann, July 28, 1967, Morrisett to George Dessart, August 24, 1967, "Carnegie ETV—3–5 Year Olds" file, Box 279, OE Commissioner Files; Cooney, Davidson oral history, 7–8; Polsky, *Getting*, 31–32.

27. Channel 13, "A Proposal," 4.

28. See, for example: Lesser, Kristine M. Rosenthal, Sally E. Polkoff, and Marjorie B. Pfankuch, "Some Effects of Segregation and Desegregation in the Schools," *Integrated Education* 9 (June-July 1964): 20–26; Lesser, Gordon Fifer, and Donald H. Clark, "Mental Abilities of Children from Different Social-Class and Cultural Groups," *Monographs of the Society for Research in Child Development* 30, no. 4 (1965): 1–115, which is well summarized and analyzed in Herbert Ginsburg, *The Myth of the Deprived Child: Poor Children's Intellect and Education* (Englewood Cliffs, N.J.: Prentice-Hall, 1972), 116–22; Susan S. Stodolsky and Lesser, "Learning Patterns in the Disadvantaged," *Harvard Educational Review* 37 (Fall 1967): 546–93.

29. Lesser, "Gerald Lesser," interview by Robert Davidson (New York, November 28, 1990) in Davidson oral history, 66–67; Hausman to Howe, July 19, 1967, Hausman for the files, July 20, 1967, Hausman to Morrisett, July 24, 1967, Hausman to Morrisett, August 9, 1967, "Carnegie Corp. Pre-School TV 1967–1968" file, Box 279, OE Commissioner files; Morrisett to Hausman, September 15, 1967, "Carnegie Corp.: Meeting for Preschool TV, 1967" file, Box 6, CTW Archives.

30. Lesser, Davidson oral history, 66–67; Morrisett to Wallach, October 4, 1967, Handwritten notes presumably by Hausman, n.d., "Carnegie ETV—3–5 Year Olds," file, Box 279, OE Commissioner files; Finberg, Polsky oral history, 3; Edward Meade, interview by Richard Polsky, April 17, 1972, interview 144, Polsky oral history, 4–5.

31. Channel 13, "A Proposal," 6; Howe to Sugarman, June 30, 1967, Howe to R. Louis Bright, February 16, 1968, "Carnegie Corp. Pre-School TV 1967–1968" file, Box 279, Memo, T. H. Bell to Lewis H. Butler, October 19, 1970, "EM 1-5-2 T.V." file, Box 524, OE Commissioner files; Memo, Morrisett to Pifer, December 27, 1967, "Children's Television Workshop 1967" file, Box 489, CC Coll., emphasis added.

32. Robert J. Blakely, *To Serve the Public Interest: Educational Broadcasting in the United States* (Syracuse, N.Y.: Syracuse University Press, 1979), 147–73.

33. [Gottlieb and Cooney], "Television for Preschool Children: A Proposal," draft version of February 1968 proposal, December 26, 1967, "Carnegie Corp. Pre-School TV 1967–1968" file, Box 279, OE Commissioner Files, 30.

34. Enumerated answers to questions, undated, "Children's Television Workshop 1967" file, Box 489, CC Coll. No author or date appears on this document, but a marginal note at the bottom reads "Probably by Cooney." Other points in this note match things she wrote during that two-year period, such as the use of Schramm's research and the low estimate of *Captain Kangaroo*'s audience among the poor. The enumeration and the topics exactly match those of Hausman to Morrisett, August 9, 1967.

35. [Gottlieb and Cooney], "Television for Preschool Children: A Proposal," February 19, 1968, Box 1, CTW Archives, 48.

36. Hausman to Sugarman, February 5, 1968, Hausman to Edward Meade, February 7, 1968, Estes to Hausman, January 31, 1968, "Carnegie Corp. Pre-School TV 1967–1968" file, Box 279, OE Commissioner files. Meade was the Ford Foundation's representative on the project to whom Hausman was relating the main points of a consultation with Spickler.

37. Hausman, Polsky oral history, 6; Morrisett, interview by the author, 6–10.

38. [Cooney], "Potential Uses," 17, passim.

39. Meade to Morrisett, January 31, 1968, Hausman to Sugarman, February 5, 1968, "Carnegie Corp. Pre-School TV 1967–1968" file, Box 279, OE Commissioner files.

40. Polsky, *Getting*, 51–56, 64–67; John F. White to Morrisett and Meade, January 2, 1968, Memo, Howe to Eli M. Bower, Charles Gershenson, Merrill S. Read, and Sugarman, January 3, 1968, Morrisett to White, January 10, 1968, "Carnegie Corp. Pre-School TV 1967–1968" file, Box 279, OE Commissioner Files; Morrisett, Davidson oral history, 37. White was president of NET; Bower worked for the National Institutes of Health, Gershenson for the Children's Bureau, and Read for National Institute of Child Health and Human Development.

41. Estes to Hausman, January 31, 1968, "Carnegie Corp. Pre-School TV 1967–1968" file, Box 279, OE Commissioner files.

42. Memo, Gorham to Hausman, February 13, 1968, Memo, Lieberman to Hausman, January 31, 1968, Memo, Hausman to Gorham, February 19, 1968, "Carnegie Corp. Pre-School TV 1967–1968" file, Box 279, OE Commissioner files.

43. Memo, Hausman to Estes, February 1, 1968, Hausman to Sugarman, February 23, 1968, "Carnegie Corp. Pre-School TV 1967–1968" file, Box 279, Memo, Hausman to B. A. Lillywhite, August 9, 1968, "EM 1–5 Educational Television" file, Box 349, OE Commissioner files. Lillywhite was Estes's deputy.

44. [Cooney and Gottlieb], "Proposal," 8–9, 52, 16, 19, 25.

45. [Cooney], "Potential Uses," 7; [Cooney and Gottlieb], "Proposal," 7, 11; Morrisett to Heinemann, July 28, 1967.

46. Memo, Morrisett to Pifer, December 27, 1967; Morrisett, "The Age of Television and the Television Age," *Peabody Journal of Education*, January 1971, 118.

47. Press release by Carnegie Corp., Ford Foundation, and United States Office of Education, March 21, 1968, Box 1, CTW Archives.

48. Ibid.

49. Jack Gould, "Educational TV Network to Teach Preschool Child," *New York Times*, March 21, 1968, 1, 94; "Brightening the Boob Tube," *Newsweek*, April 1, 1968, 67; "New Bloom on the Wasteland," *PTA Magazine*, May, 1968, 26; Louise Sweeney, "Joan Cooney's Preschool TV Workshop," *Christian Science Monitor*, April 26, 1968.

Chapter 4. The CTW Model

1. David Connell, "David Connell," interview by Robert Davidson (New York, July 11, 1990), in "Children's Television Workshop: The Early Years, an Oral History,"

ed. Robert Davidson (Children's Television Workshop, manuscript, 1993), 77 (hereafter, Davidson oral history).

2. CTW has defined the CTW Model differently than I have here. I have defined it in a broader fashion—including the interactions of experts as an essential part of the system—and have done so, in part, because it coincides with the historical development of the show.

3. As quoted in Horace Newcomb and Robert S. Alley, *The Producer's Medium: Conversations with Creators of American TV* (New York: Oxford University Press, 1983) 56, 177. For an example of a producer confident in his knowledge of what the viewers would find funny, see James L. Brooks's remarks on 215.

4. *Captain Kangaroo* Show Personnel lists, David Connell Papers, privately held, Sheffield, Mass. (hereafter, Connell Papers).

5. Gilbert Millstein, "The K Stands for Keeshan Too," *TV Guide*, August 5, 1961, 17–21; Edith Efron, "Captain Kangaroo: Social Institution with a Mustache," *TV Guide*, March 19, 1966, 25; Gibbon, "Samuel Gibbon," interview by Robert Davidson (New York, September 19, 1990), in Davidson oral history, 102.

6. "Cooney, Joan Ganz," in *Current Biography Yearbook 1970*, ed. Charles Moritz (New York: H. W. Wilson, 1970), 97–99; Cary O'Dell, *Women Pioneers in Television: Biographies of Fifteen Industry Leaders* (Jefferson, N.C.: McFarland, 1997), 68–69; Cooney, interview by the author, September 8, 1997, New York, tape recording, transcript, 5–15; Christopher Finch, *Jim Henson: The Works* (New York: Random House, 1993), 31–53; Martin Mayer, *About Television* (New York: Harper and Row, 1972), 141–42; David Owen, "Looking Out for Kermit," *New Yorker*, August 16, 1993, 30–43; Jon Stone, "Jon Stone," interview by Robert Davidson (New York, May 29, 1991), in Davidson oral history, 92; Henson, "The Producer's Point of View," in *Action for Children's Television: The First National Symposium on the Effect on Children of Television Programming and Advertising*, ed. Evelyn Sarson (New York: Avon Books, 1970), 25–26.

7. Connell, Davidson oral history, 76–77; Gibbon, Davidson oral history, 103.

8. Cooney, Davidson oral history, 11; Cooney to Lesser, March 7, 1968, Lesser, "Preliminary Outline of Possible Goals and Summer Study Groups," March 15, 1968, "1968 Planning Seminars: General, 1968" file, Box 33, Archives of the Children's Television Workshop, National Public Broadcasting Archives, Hornbake Library, University of Maryland, College Park (hereafter, CTW Archives); Lesser, telephone interview by the author, October 5, 1998, author's notes; Davidson, "Re: Lesser comments," private e-mail message to the author, October 9, 1998; Lesser, "Gerald Lesser," interview by Robert Davidson (New York, November 28, 1990), in Davidson oral history, 69; Davidson, telephone interview by the author, January 14, 1998, author's notes; Lesser, *Children and Television: Lessons from Sesame Street* (New York: Vintage Books, 1974), 42–59; Polsky, *Getting*, 71–84. The topics and titles of the five seminars were: Social, Moral, and Affective Development; Language and Reading; Mathematical and Numerical Skills; Reasoning and Problem Solving; and Perception.

9. Connell, Davidson oral history, 77; [Connell], "Can you tell me how ...," 1, typescript memoir fragment, dated December 13, 1994, Connell Papers.

10. [Connell], "Can," 4–5; Cooney, Davidson oral history, 13; Lesser, Davidson oral history, 72. For an example of a memo in which the head of production specifies three psychologists to consult in reviewing program segments, see Norton Wright to Jon Stone, April 18, 1973, "Fifth Season Curriculum Planning, 1972–1975," Box 35, CTW Archives.

11. Connell's green binder of seminar notes, Connell Papers.

12. Lesser, Davidson oral history, 71–72. Lesser's recollection is confirmed by the internal research study memos, which show no sign of the general board of advisers, as they do of the Hispanic advisers during the period of that committee's greatest activity between 1972 and 1974. See research files in Boxes 34 and 35, CTW Archives.

13. "Report of Seminar II: Language and Reading, New York, New York, July 8, 9, 10, 1968," 13, Box 33, CTW Archives.

14. White, "Perception: Memo to Jerry Lesser," notes from Seminar V: Perception, 1, n.d., Connell Papers.

15. Lesser, *Children*, 88.

16. Gibbon, Davidson oral history, 103; see the reports of the seminars in Box 33, CTW Archives; Lesser, telephone interview by the author.

17. Lesser, *Children*, 59; Davidson, telephone interview by the author, October 5, 1998, transcript, 6; Gibbon, Davidson oral history, 103.

18. "Production Department Recommendations," [n.d.], "Research Staff Goals," [n.d.], R. Davidson, "CTW Goals," [n.d.], Memo, Dan [Ogilvie] to Jerry [Lesser], "Goals for C.T.W.," September 18, 1968, Memo, Lesser to CTW Staff, "Priorities among Goals," September 19, 1968, Shep [White], untitled 11 point list, [n.d.], Connell Papers; [Barbara Frengel], "Goals Meeting, Children's Television Workshop, Sept. 23, 24, 1968," "Preliminary Goal Planning and Documents, September-December 1968" file, Box 33, CTW Archives.

19. When, after the show's third season, the Workshop first compiled the shares of the show's air time devoted to its respective curricular areas, these four areas—"Numbers," "Alphabet," "Relational terms," and "Classification and ordering"—accounted for 51 percent. "Reasoning Skills" accounted for another 9 percent. Curricular area names come from [Frengel], "Goals Meeting" 4–5. Air time figures come from Memo, Bob Emerick to Connell, n.d., "Fourth Season Curriculum Planning, 1971–1972" file, Box 34, CTW Archives.

20. [Frengel], "Goals Meeting," 4, 6, 8; Lesser, *Children*, 182; *Sesame Street* no. 847, Umatic Tape, CTW Tape Library, New York, N.Y. My characterization of the labeling of emotions comes from watching *Sesame Street* episodes. Several files from planning efforts in 1973 and 1974 in box 35 of the CTW Archives cover the development of the affective curriculum. For parental complaint letters about no. 847, see "Criticism: *Sesame Street*, 1971–1976" file, Box 46, CTW Archives.

21. [Frengel], "Goals Meeting," 6; Memo, Sheldon White to Lesser, July 15, 1968, Connell Papers; Polsky, *Getting*, 62–63; Dean Cushman and Rae Paige, eds., "The Muppet Gallery" (New York: CTW, 1978), 16–17, Box 69, PBS Collection 2, National Public Broadcasting Archives, Hornbake Library, University of Maryland, College Park, Md.

22. See the curriculum planning and goals documents in Boxes 33 through 36, which carry the history through the planning of season seventeen in 1985, CTW Archives. Gregory J. Gettas, "The Globalization of *Sesame Street*: A Producer's Perspective," *Educational Television Research and Development* 38 (Fall 1990): 55–63; Charlotte F. Cole, Beth A. Richman, and Susan A. McCann Brown, "The World of *Sesame Street* Research," in *"G" Is for Growing: Thirty Years of Research on Children and Sesame Street*, ed, Shalom M. Fisch and Rosemarie T. Truglio (Mahwah, N.J.: Lawrence Erlbaum Associates, 2000), 147–79.

23. Memo, Scarvia B. Anderson and Samuel J. Messick to M. Martus, April 17, 1968, "Children's Television Workshop (support) 1968" file, Box 488. Carnegie Corp. Collection, Rare Book and Manuscript Library, Columbia University, New York, N.Y.

24. This construction did not immediately emerge but clearly was how CTW's research department thought about the question in the early 1970s. See "Sesame Street" Research, "List of Media Techniques," January 24, 1973, "Fourth Season Research Memos, 1972–1973," Box 34, CTW Archives.

25. Palmer, interview by the author, tape recording, May 6, 1998, Ithaca, N.Y., transcript, 52–55; Palmer, "Edward Palmer," interview by Robert Davidson (Philadelphia, August 1, 1991), in Davidson oral history, 111–12; Palmer to Veryl Schult, November 19, 1968, "Veryl Schult (CTW Project Officer, USOE), Correspondence and Memos, 1968–1980" file, Box 4; "Edward L. Palmer," file biography, n.d., Box 240, CTW Archives.

26. Barbara Frengel Reeves, "The First Year of Sesame Street: The Formative Research," December 1970, 8–9; Leona Schauble, "The Sesame Street Distractor Method for Measuring Visual Attention," July 1976, Box 42, CTW Archives; Valeria Lovelace, *"Sesame Street* as a Continuing Experiment," *Educational Technology Research and Development* 38 (Fall 1990): 20.

27. Palmer, "Can Television Really Teach?" *American Education*, August/September 1969, 3; Gibbon and Palmer, "Pre-reading on Sesame Street," research report prepared for the Committee on Reading of the National Academy of Education (New York: CTW, 1970), 9; Schauble, "Distractor Method," 4, 1.

28. David D. Connell and Edward L. Palmer, "'Sesame Street': A Case Study," 11 (address to the international seminar on Broadcaster/Research Cooperation in Mass Communication Research, University of Leicester, U.K., December 19, 1970), Box 42, CTW Archives.

29. Memo, Frengel to Production Dept., November 8, 1968, "Research for Program Development, 1968–1969" file, Box 33, CTW Archives. For similar memos, see Memo, Barbara Frengel to Production Staff, "Concepts that Could be Taught," n.d., "Research for Program Development, 1968–1969" file, Box 33; Memo, Barbara Frengel to Production, "The ability of four-year-olds from our Day-Care population to deal with NUMBER," February 26, 1969; Memo, Research to Production, June 11, 1969, "A summary report of the performance of four-year-olds on five general ability measures," "Research-Production Memos, 1969" file, Box 34, CTW Archives.

30. Lesser, "Assumptions Behind the Production and Writing Methods in *Sesame*

Street," in *Quality in Instructional Television,* ed. Wilbur Schramm (Honolulu: University of Hawaii Press, 1972), 108 (photocopy in Box 42, CTW Archives); Gibbon and Palmer, "Pre-reading," 8. Copies of Writer's Notebooks from 1970, 1974, and 1975 can be found in Boxes 34 and 35, CTW Archives.

31. "Report of Seminar III: Mathematical and Numerical Skills, New York, New York, July 15, 16, 17, 1968," "Report of Seminar IV: Reasoning and Problem Solving, Cambridge, Massachusetts, July 24, 25, 26, 1968," Box 33; [Frengel], "Goals Meeting," Samuel Ball, "Summative Research at Children's Television Workshop—A Progress Report," [October 14, 1968], Box 43, CTW Archives; Palmer, Davidson oral history, 114; Cooney, Davidson oral history, 11. For correspondence that testifies to this relationship, see "Memos and Correspondence, 1968–1976" file, Box 44, CTW Archives. Ball also spoke at the twentieth anniversary research symposium along with others who had done contract research for CTW; see *20th Anniversary Symposium,* 11–17. Palmer told how Ball "insinuated himself into the process" of hiring a research staff, getting "a longtime friend" hired.

32. Robert K. Yin, "The Workshop and the World: Toward an Assessment of the Children's Television Workshop," report prepared for the John and Mary R. Markle Foundation (Santa Monica, Calif.: Rand, 1973), 29–30; Samuel Ball, "Evaluating Sesame Street: A Research Proposal for Children's Television Workshop," August 1969, Box 44, CTW Archives; Lesser, *Children,* 61; Polsky, *Getting,* 43, 99; Connell and Palmer, "Case Study," 11–12; Gibbon and Palmer, "Pre-reading," 12.

33. Stuart W. Little, "Children's Television Workshop," *Saturday Review,* February 8, 1969, 62.

Chapter 5. "The Itty Bitty Little Kiddy Show"

1. Stone, "Jon Stone," interview by Robert Davidson (New York, May 29, 1991), in Davidson oral history, 93; "Schedule for Wednesday, January 22 Videotaping," n.d., "Scripts and Stopyboards: Sales File, [1969]" file, Box 37, Stone to Tom Cooke, February 7, 1969, Letter, "Operations, 1968–1970" file, Box 36, CTW, Office of Education Progress Report no. 3, March 15, 1969, Box 3, Archives of the Children's Television Workshop, National Public Broadcasting Archives, Hornbake Library, University of Maryland, College Park (hereafter, CTW Archives).

2. Script, n.d., 9, "Scripts and Storyboards: Sales File, [1969]" file, Box 37, CTW Archives; "Sesame Street Pitch Film 1968 No Joan Cooney Intro/Naming Segment," 25 mins., Umatic videocassette, Tape Library, Children's Television Workshop, New York, N.Y. (hereafter, Tape Library); CTW, *Newsletter,* no. 2, February 12, 1969, 1, Box 2, CTW Archives.

3. Schone, "Why 'Sesame Street' Is Not 'Hey, Stupid!'" *Christian Science Monitor,* March 11, 1998, 16, EBSCO Academic Search Elite database; Connell to Schone, November 19, 1969, "Virginia Schone, 1969–1970, 1977" file, Box 36, CTW Archives; Cooney, "Joan Ganz Cooney," interview by Robert Davidson (New York, February 13, 1991, April 24, 1991), in Davidson oral history, 16; Connell, "David Connell," interview by Davidson (New York, July 11, 1990), in Davidson oral history, 82. For the

official story, see CTW, "New TV Program for Preschool Children Combines Education with Entertainment," May 6, 1969, press release, appendix to CTW, Office of Education Progress Report no. 4, September 15, 1969, Box 3, CTW Archives. For show title suggestions, see Connell and R. Polsky, "Show title suggestions," November 11, 1968, January 2 and 3, 1969, "Production Memos, 1969–1971" file, Box 37; Memo, Bob Hatch to Cooney, January 27, 1969, "Show Title Suggestions from Carl Byoir Personnel," "Hatch, Robert A., 1969–1973" file, Box 21, CTW Archives. Demaray's suggestion appears in her note to Connell, n.d., "Barbara Demaray, 1969–[1970]" file, Box 36, CTW Archives.

4. I studied thirty sample episodes to answer questions like: "What is the frequency with which CTW repeated segments?" In these notes, segments are specified by their episode number and the sequential number of the segment within the episode. The segment that begins the book thus would be designated Morrow Sample 656-14.

5. Connell, Davidson oral history, 77.

6. Tim Brooks and Earle Marsh, *The Complete Directory to Prime Time Network and Cable TV Shows, 1946–Present*, 6th ed. (New York: Ballantine Books, 1995), 1264.

7. Ibid., 889–90.

8. Cooney, Davidson oral history, 14; Connell, Davidson oral history, 77–78.

9. Cooney, Davidson oral history, 12; Connell, Davidson oral history, 78; Cooney to Louis Hausman, April 4, 1968, "EM 1-5 Educational Television" file, Box 349, Office Files of the Commissioner of Education, 1939–1980, Record Group 12, National Archives, College Park, Md. The first two seasons' assignment sheets, used to pass the curricular instructions for each episode on to the writer assigned it, are in Box 34, CTW Archives.

10. For one exposition of this basic principle, see Lesser, "Assumptions Behind the Production and Writing Methods in *Sesame Street*," in *Quality in Instructional Television*, ed. Wilbur Schramm (Honolulu: University of Hawaii Press, 1972), 110, in Box 42, CTW Archives.

11. Stuart W. Little, "Children's Television Workshop," *Saturday Review*, February 8, 1969, 60, attested to the long lead time consideration. Samuel Y. Gibbon Jr. and Palmer, "Pre-reading on Sesame Street," research report prepared for the Committee on Reading of the National Academy of Education (New York: CTW, 1970), 9.

12. David Connell's 1968 and 1969 datebooks, David Connell Papers, privately held, Sheffield, Mass. (hereafter, Connell Papers); CTW, "Consultant's Meetings," n.d., "Research for Program Development, 1968–1969" file, Box 33, CTW Archives; Little, "Children's," 60. For examples of scripts and storyboards, see "Counting Scripts, n.d." file, Box 17 and "Scripts and Storyboards" files in Box 37.

13. Cooney, as quoted in Richard M. Polsky, *Getting to Sesame Street: Origins of the Children's Television Workshop* (New York: Praeger Publishers, 1974), 32.

14. Connell, Davidson oral history, 79.

15. Lesser, *Children and Television: Lessons from Sesame Street* (New York: Vintage Books, 1974), 153–58.

16. That is, 438 segments of a total 1192.

17. Little, "Children's," 60; Memo, Barbara Frengel to Production, "J Commercial," n.d., "Research-Production Memos, 1969" file, Box 34, CTW Archives.

18. Frengel to Production, 3.

19. Lesser, *Children*, 82.

20. Early examples of overt behavior documented include: Memo, Palmer, and Sharon Lerner to Production, "Test of 'Man from Alphabet,'" June 6, 1969, "Research-Production Memos, 1969" file, Box 34; Memo, Research to Production, "Report of Research on Five Test Shows," September 24, 1969, Box 33, CTW Archives. For later examples, see Memo, Research to Production, "A, F, and J Spots," June 23, 1969; Memo, Research to Production, "Gessner [*sic*] Film, 'My Own Special TV Show,'" September 30, 1969, "Research for Program Development, 1968–1969 [2]" file, Box 33; Memo, Research to Production, "Observations of Children Watching Shows 126–130," May 28, 1970; Memo, Research to Production, "Larry and Phyllis," December 3, 1970, "Research-Production Memos, 1970" file, Box 34.

21. The idea that children spend much of their early years in front the TV learning to decode it is a common one in the research literature since 1980. For example, see Robert Hodge and David Tripp, *Children and Television: A Semiotic Approach* (Stanford, Calif.: Stanford University Press, 1986), 14–72. An invaluable exploration of "the passive theory of television viewing" by a leading researcher is Daniel R. Anderson, "Watching Children Watch Television and the Creation of *Blues Clues*," in *Nickelodeon Nation: The History, Politics, and Economics of America's Only TV Channel for Kids*, ed. Heather Hendershot (New York: New York University Press, 2004), 242–43.

22. Brooks and Marsh, *Complete Directory*, 635.

23. "The Man from Alphabet," four segments, videocassette copy made from film, privately held by James Thurman, Sheffield, Mass.; David Connell's 1969 datebook, Connell Papers.

24. Palmer and Lerner to Production, "Test of 'Man'"; Memo, Research to Production, "Report of Research on Five Test Shows," Distractor Study appendix, unpaginated, September 24, 1969, Box 33, CTW Archives.

25. Other sources for the "Man" experience include: Cooney, Davidson oral history, 15; Palmer, interview by the author, tape recording, May 6, 1998, Ithaca, N.Y., transcript, 34; Don Monaco, "Cooney and the Kids: Here's TV Your Child Can Watch," *Look*, November 18, 1969, 104; "TV's Switched-On School," *Newsweek*, June 1, 1970, 69; Lesser, *Children*, 128, 158, 162. Of the 1192 segments in the sample, 208 were films. The Mad Painter liked to paint numerals in inappropriate places and always got caught in the act. Slapstick action usually followed. The episode sample included five different Mad Painter films.

26. Stone, Davidson oral history, 92; Cooney, Davidson oral history, 14–15; Christopher Finch, *Jim Henson: The Works* (New York: Random House, 1993), 15–49.

27. Finch, *The Works*, 47–49, 53–54; David Owen, "Looking Out for Kermit," *New Yorker*, August 16, 1993, 30–43, 136, 141; Connell, Davidson oral history, 79–80; Stone, Davidson oral history, 92; Thomas Kennedy, "Thomas Kennedy," interview by Robert Davidson (Key Biscayne, Fla., January 22, 1991), in Davidson oral history, 160;

Carol B. Liebman, "'Sesame Street' Learns It's Paved with Gold," *Village Voice*, July 16, 1970, 8–9.

28. Thurman, interview by the author, tape recording, Sheffield, Mass., May 26, 1998; Stone, Davidson oral history, 96; Finch, *The Works*, passim.

29. Morrow Sample 82-2, 74-26, 257-49; quotations from Finch, *The Works*, 59–61.

30. "Show no. 001 Test Pilot Master," 60 mins., Umatic videocassette, Tape Library). In fact, Bert and Ernie appear several times during the episode, watching the same segment the viewers are seeing. These brief appearances function as segues into another segment. Puppet segments make up 240 of the total 1192 segments in the episode sample.

31. Research to Production, "Report of Research on Five Test Shows"; Leona Schauble, telephone interview by the author, April 27, 1999, tape recording, author's notes. Schauble was a longtime CTW researcher in the 1970s.

32. Research, "Gessner [*sic*] Film, 'My Own Special TV Show,'" September 30, 1969, "Research for Program Development, 1968–1969" file, Box 33, CTW Archives; Stone, Davidson oral history, 90. Emphasis in original. Gesner's films appear in Morrow Sample, 22-13, 22-29, 526-51, 862-28, 939-19, 1030-34, 1075-28, and 1196-39, several of which are repeated as well. His segments are brilliant in their simplicity, building miniature dramas with only animated dots or hands filmed by themselves.

33. Stone, Davidson oral history, 90.

34. For consideration of teachers as performers, see the five file folders of teacher resumes labelled "Teachers, 1968" in Box 39, CTW Archives. For previous careers of the performers, see Martin Mayer, *About Television* (New York: Harper and Row, 1972), 145–46; CTW, "'Sesame Street' Cast Bios," October 20, 1970, "Press Releases, October-December, 1970" file, Box 32, CTW Archives. For a discussion of the fusing of actor and role in the viewers' minds, see John Fiske, *Television Culture* (New York: Routledge, 1987), 151. Of the 1192 segments in the episode sample, 293 were Street studio ones.

35. Stone, Davidson oral history, 90.

36. Although I noted the genders and apparent races or ethnicities of the children in each Street segment, I did not do so in a way that I could easily aggregate the counts. The above statements are based on my impression from studying the sample segments.

37. The earliest five episodes of my sample all open with Gordon addressing the audience and setting the scene; see 22-1, 74-1, 82-1, 176-1, and 202-1, broadcast between December 1969 and February 1971.

38. Stone, Davidson oral history, 91; Cooney to Jo Ann E. Gardner, January 5, 1970, Letter, "Criticism: Feminists, 1969–1971" file, Box 17, CTW Archives; David Borgenicht, *Sesame Street: Unpaved: Scripts, Stories, Secrets, and Songs* (New York: Hyperion, 1998), 122. In keeping with Moynihan's thesis in *The Negro Family: The Case for National Action* (Washington, D.C.: Department of Labor, 1965), 35–37, the Kerner Commission blamed absent fathers for the poor school attendance of poor minority children. See National Advisory Commission on Civil Disorders, *Report*, 1968 (Washington, D.C., 1968), 130.

39. Stone, Davidson oral history, 95; Connell Davidson oral history, 80; John Culhane, "Report Card on Sesame Street," *New York Times Magazine*, May 24, 1970, 62; Lesser, *Children*, 129–30; "Show no. 001 Test Pilot Master."

40. Research to Production, "Report of Research on Five Test Shows," ii–iii; Palmer, "Edward Palmer," interview by Robert Davidson (Philadelphia, August 1, 1991), in Davidson oral history, 122; identification of broadcasting station is from Davidson, note to the author, November 23, 2002.

41. Ibid., Distractor Study appendix, unpaginated. The research department boiled the distractor results for an entire program down to a percentage score of possible perfect attention. *Sesame Street* test episodes numbers 1 and 4 received .90 and .88 scores, respectively. The cartoon shows got these scores: *Yogi Bear* (.88), *Huckleberry Hound* (.81), and *Roger Ramjet* (.63).

42. [Richard Polsky], "Children's Television Workshop, Board of Advisers and Consultants, Meeting in Boston, August 6–8, 1969," August 11, 1969, Box 33, CTW Archives. A second copy of this document in Box 34 identifies it as Polsky's informal notes. As such the quotations are not verbatim but quotations from his notes. For prominent examples of criticism similar to Eisenberg's, see Urie Bronfenbrenner, "Who Lives on Sesame Street?" *Psychology Today*, October 1970, 14, 18, 20; Linda Francke, "The Games People Play on Sesame Street," *New York*, April 5, 1971, 26–29.

43. Ibid.

44. Connell, Davidson oral history, 83–84.

45. Stone, Davidson oral history, 94; Connell, Davidson oral history, 83–84; Robert Davidson, interview by the author, College Park, Md., June 5, 1996, author's notes. Assistant Director Robert Davidson, who has long functioned as CTW's unofficial historian, has emphasized that much of the style and humor of the show came directly from Connell's personal understanding of the audience.

46. Stone, Davidson oral history, 95; Connell, Davidson oral history, 80–81; Cooney, Davidson oral history, 15–16; Lesser, *Children*, 129–30. For the characterizations of Bird and Oscar, see Lewis Bernstein, "Sesame Street Characters: A Position Paper for Discussion," November 22, 1976, "'Sesame Street Position Papers, 1976,' 1976–1977" file, Box 35, CTW Archives; Lesser, *Children*, 126; Dean Cushman and Rae Paige, eds., "The Muppet Gallery" (New York: CTW, 1978), 16–17, Box 69, PBS Collection 2, National Public Broadcasting Archives, Hornbake Library, University of Maryland, College Park, Md.

47. Lesser, *Children*, 126; Schauble, interview by the author.

48. CTW, *Newsletter*, no. 1, January 29, 1969, 2, Box 2, CTW Archives. Cooney began this pitch very early, see Cooney, untitled speech, NET Affiliates Meeting, Statler-Hilton Hotel, New York, April 22, 1968, "Cooney's Speeches" file, Box 33, CTW Archives.

49. Cooney, interview by Sharon Zane (New York, April 9, 1998), transcript, copy obtained from Sesame Workshop, 32.

50. Cooney, Davidson oral history, 16–17; Robert Davidson, interview by the author, College Park, Md., September 10, 1998, author's notes; Lesser, *Children*, 40–41;

"1969/1970 Season: Television Stations which Broadcast Sesame Street," "First Season Broadcast Times by Station, 1969–1970" file, Box 34, Ralph T. Clausen to Palmer, January 20, 1972, "Miscellaneous Files: Weekly Averages, 1969–1973" file, Box 45, CTW Archives.

51. Daniel Yankelovich, Inc., "A Report of Three Studies on the Role and Penetration of Sesame Street in Ghetto Communities," April 1970, Box 44, CTW Archives; "If Kids Act Smarter, 'Sesame Street' May Be the Reason," *Nation's Schools* 87 (March 1971), 34–35. The Yankelovich report is unpaginated.

52. Morrow Sample. Of 1192 segments, 75 were coded as "Miscellaneous." Of these, I lack curricular documents for 22, which I have coded myself. Twenty of the 75 are episode closing segments. Appearances by Stevie Wonder (939-11) and the Pointer Sisters (1059-24) are among the others. Ernie, one of the puppets, sang his hit song "Rubber Ducky" (616-26, though not the original appearance of this segment), which also fell under this rubric.

53. National Commission on the Causes and Prevention of Violence, *To Establish Justice, To Insure Domestic Tranquility* (Washington, D.C.: GPO, 1969), 202; Evan McLeod Wylie, "At Last: A TV Show Good for Children," *PTA Magazine,* May 1970, 13.

54. Morrow Sample 22-23 (this segment, called "Poverty H" internally at the workshop, appears four times in the sample, making it one of the most often repeated segments), 22-43, 384-18.

55. Fourteen times in the sample, including repeats, segments from this series appear. The pieces for numbers 4, 5, 6, 7, and 10 appear. Segments 22-2, 289-18, and 1202-24 are among them. They were heavily used in the first season; three times in each episodes 22 and 74, which may partly explain the alarm of critics like education columnist Minnie Perrin Berson in "Ali Baba! What Have You Done?," *Childhood Education* 46 (March 1970), 339–40.

56. Morrow Sample 862-13.

57. Memo, Hylda Clarke to Production Department, "Program Content in Relation to Viewer Interest or Involvement," March 11, 1969, "Research-Production Memos, 1969" file, Box 34, CTW Archives; Palmer, "Can Television," 5; Lesser, *Children,* 114–15, 128.

58. Palmer, "Can Television," 5; Connell and Palmer, "'Sesame Street,'" 6; Meara's voice is heard in Morrow Sample 521-37 and 641-19.

59. I have not noted in my survey the apparent gender, age group (child or adult), and ethnicity of every voiceover; many are indeterminate to the viewer. The 63 cited here were all clearly children.

60. Morrow Sample 526-37.

61. Morrow Sample 933-11 (auto manufacture), 22-39 (manhole covers), 348-25 (penguins), and 862-23 (birds).

62. Gerald S. Lesser, "Learning, Teaching, and Television Production for Children: The Experience of *Sesame Street,*" *Harvard Educational Review* 42 (May 1972): 239.

63. Cooney, "The Potential Uses of Television in Preschool Education," [Carnegie Corporation], [October 1966], Box 1, CTW Archives, 5; [Linda Gottlieb and

Cooney], "Television for Preschool Children: A Proposal," February 19, 1968, Box 1, CTW Archives, 3.

64. Morrow Sample 526-44, 74-18, 933-25, 698-30.

65. Paul D. Witty and Harry Bricker, "Your Child and TV," *Parents' Magazine*, December 1952, 36–37ff.; quote is from Schramm et al., *Television*, 160.

66. Carmen Luke, *Constructing the Child Viewer: A History of the American Discourse on Television and Children, 1950–1980* (New York: Praeger, 1990), 65; Paul Witty, "Studies of Mass Media, 1949–1965," *Science Education* 50 (March 1966), 119.

67. Cooney, "Potential," 10.

68. Morrow Sample; 200 of 1192 segments were repeats of earlier segments. Of these 126 were cartoons, 33 Muppet segments, 31 films, and the rest studio and hybrid segments.

69. Memo, Ron Weaver to Connell, September 21, 1971, "Budget Documents, 1971–1977 [3]" file, Box 37, CTW Archives, lists particular animated segments and their costs but leaves it difficult to determine a cost per minute of animation because the titles cannot be matched to timed segments. Nevertheless, the oft-repeated generalization that animation is the most expensive of the four segment types is bolstered by budget documents, which consistently show large animation budgets; for examples from the fourth and fifth seasons, see Memo, Bob Dahl to Cooney et al., August 18, 1972; Memo, Ron Weaver to Madeline Anderson et al., September 24, 1973, "Budget Documents, 1971–1977 [3]" file, Box 37, CTW Archives. Other documents in the same file give the same rough impression.

70. Memo, Barbara Frengel to Production, "Re: J Commercial," n.d., "Research-Production Memos, 1969 [2]" file, Box 34, CTW Archives. This memo probably dates from February or early March 1969 based on its position in the file and another memo that refers to this research. This is Memo, Palmer, "Summary of Research Results," March 20, 1969, "Research-Production Memos, 1969 [2]" file, Box 34, CTW Archives.

71. Palmer, "A Pedagogical Analysis of Recurrent Formats on *Sesame Street* and *The Electric Company*" (paper given at the International Conference on Children's Educational Television, Amsterdam, June 1978), 5–7, Box 43, CTW Archives; Lesser, *Children*, 120–21; Connell and Palmer, "'Sesame Street,'" 15; Mayer, *About*, 152–53; "Sesame Street Research, Recurring Formats, Dr. Ed Palmer," May 5, 1978, Umatic videocassette, CTW Tape Library.

72. Joe Raposo, "One of These Things." songbook score, 1970, "*Sesame Street* Sheet Music Folio, c. 1970" file, Box 52, CTW Archives.

73. Morrow Sample 22-16, 82-31, 176-5, 289-15, 348-27, 384-35, 426-10, 526-28, 526-46*, 933-12, 939-22, 939-33*, 1030-10*, 1059-32, 1113-32, 1196-7, and 1287-28*. Marked with an asterisk are those that employ the split-screen films of children. Though the words quoted above are never exactly used in any of these segments, they do relate the gist of the game.

74. Palmer, "Pedagogical Analysis," 3; Palmer covers this format on 3–4 and 8–10 in this paper.

75. Morrow Sample 1113-32.

76. This line of research and analysis continued systematically to include other aspects of the show, such as music, characters, and slapstick. For examples of these elements see: Lesser, *Children*, 99–131; Connell and Palmer, "'Sesame Street,'" 4–10.

77. Edward Zigler and Karen Anderson, "An Idea Whose Time Had Come: The Intellectual and Political Climate for Head Start," in *Project Head Start: A Legacy of the War on Poverty*, ed. Zigler and Jeanette Valentine (New York: Free Press, 1979), 11.

78. [Gottlieb and Cooney], "Proposal," 3–4.

79. Hess and Shipman, "Maternal Influences upon Early Learning: The Cognitive Environments of Urban Pre-School Children," in *Early Education: Current Theory, Research, and Action*, ed. Hess and Roberta Meyer Bear (Chicago: Aldine Publishing, 1968), 91–103. In their article about the different kinds of learning skills exhibited by children in various ethnic groups, Lesser and his coauthor Susan S. Stodolsky called two earlier Hess and Shipman studies "an advance in the direction of explaining the origins of cognitive abilities in young children"; see "Learning Patterns in the Disadvantaged," *Harvard Educational Review* 37 (Fall 1967): 546–93.

80. Palmer, interview by the author, 54–55.

81. Lesser, "Learning," 233. For another, less concise version of this concept, see Lesser, *Children and Television: Lessons from Sesame Street* (New York: Vintage Books, 1974), 80, 89. For the earliest recorded version of the paradigm, see Cooney, untitled speech, 28–29, July 1, 1969, American Association of Elementary/Kindergarten/Nursery Educators at National Education Association, Civic Center, Philadelphia, "Cooney Speeches, 1969" file, CTW Archives.

82. For an indication of the importance of Lesser and Stodolsky, "Learning," see Gary Natriello, Edward L. McDill, and Aaron M. Pallas, *Schooling Disadvantaged Children: Racing Against Catastrophe* (New York: Teachers College Press, 1990), 9.

83. Press release, "Quotes and Anecdotes: Some Reactions to Sesame Street," n.d., "Press Releases, March, 1971" file, Box 31, CTW Archives.

84. Jack Gould, "Television in Review: 'Ding Dong School,' a Worthwhile Video Program Directed at Children, Stubs Toe on Commercialism," *New York Times*, April 1, 1953, 41; Melvin Helitzer and Carl Heyel, *The Youth Market: Its Dimensions, Influence, and Opportunities for You* (New York: Media Books, 1970), 40. The conclusion explores the commercial product aspects of the show's later history in a little more detail.

Chapter 6. "Hope for a More Substantive Future"

1. Senate Committee on Commerce, *Hearings on the Nominations of Dean Burch and Robert Wells, to the Federal Communications Commission*, 91st Cong., 1st Sess., October 27, 1969, 43; http://www.wgbhalumni.org/reunion/mike_amb.htm; http://www.wgbhalumni.org/reunion/lillian.htm.

2. Senate Committee on Commerce, *Hearings of the Communications Subcommittee to Amend the Communications Act of 1934 to Establish Orderly Procedures for the Consideration of Applications for Renewal of Broadcast Licenses*, 91st Cong., 1st Sess., December 4, 1969, 582.

3. Robert Hatch, "Robert Hatch," interview by Robert Davidson (Lakeville,

Conn., June 21, 1991), in "Children's Television Workshop: The Early Years, an Oral History," ed. Robert Davidson (Children's Television Workshop, manuscript, 1993), 166 (hereafter, Davidson oral history).

4. Ibid., 162–68; Cooney, "Joan Ganz Cooney," interview by Davidson (New York, February 13, 1991, April 24, 1991), in Davidson oral history, 17–18. The most thorough presentation of the show's early promotion can be found in Herman W. Land, *The Children's Television Workshop: How and Why It Works* (Jericho, N.Y.: Nassau Board of Cooperative Educational Services, 1972), 137–49.

5. As quoted in Land, *Children's Television Workshop*, 145.

6. Press release, CTW, "New TV Program for Preschool Children Combines Education with Entertainment," May 6 and 23, 1969, 1–5, appendices to CTW, Office of Education Progress Report no. 4, September 15, 1969, Box 3, Archives of the Children's Television Workshop, National Public Broadcasting Archives, Hornbake Library, University of Maryland, College Park, Md. (hereafter, CTW Archives); Land, Children's Television Workshop, 145.

7. "Open Sesame," Newsweek, May 26, 1969, 81; Terrance O'Flaherty, "'J' Is for Junk," San Francisco Chronicle, May 8, 1969, 48. *CTW Newsletter*, no. 4 includes a survey of press reaction.

8. "Experiment in Teaching Children May Make NET's Big Noise Next Fall," *Variety*, April 16, 1969, 39, 48.

9. Allen in [Jon Stone], Script, "This Way to Sesame Street," Catalog no. 11945, Henson Archives, Jim Henson Company, New York City; Hatch and Davidson, Davidson oral history, 168–69; Land, *Children's Television Workshop*, 145. The script includes Allen's words.

10. Les Brown, "'Sesame's' Commercial Friends," *Variety*, December 24, 1969, 33; Norman S. Morris, *Television's Child* (Boston: Little, Brown, 1971), 165; Ray Loynd, "'Sesame Street': NET's $8 Million Teaching Experiment Begins," *Entertainment World*, November 14, 1969, in *CTW Press Digest*, "News from Sesame Street," Box 290, CTW Archives; Allen, "This Way."

11. "Time Out for TV: Children's Television Workshop," *PTA Magazine*, April 1969, 29–30.

12. Cooney, untitled speech, July 1, 1969, American Association of Elementary/Kindergarten/Nursery Educators at National Education Association, Civic Center, Philadelphia, "Cooney Speeches, 1969" file, quotation on 26; Sara E. Drake and Mike Greenwald, "Memo to Pre-First Grade Teachers," n.d., Box 51, CTW Archives.

13. Memo, Hatch to Cooney et al., March 24, 1969, "Press Releases, 1969" file, Box 31, CTW Archives; "Fourth Business Session, July 1, 1966," in National Education Association, *Addresses and Proceedings*, vol. 104 (Washington, D.C.: NEA, 1966), 156–60. An undated galley proof copy of Batchelder's editorial for the Southern Section's magazine is attached to Hatch's memo.

14. Evelyn Payne Davis, "Evelyn Davis," interview by Davidson (New York, February 14, April 26, 1991), in Davidson oral history, 129; Hatch, Davidson oral history, 166. Only one of Booker's articles is preserved in the Workshop's archives, and, in this

one, he points to four African-American members of its staff: James Booker, "'Sesame Street' Series Offers Many TV Jobs," *Afro-American* (Baltimore, Md.) in "Clippings-1968–1969" file, Box 288, CTW Archives. The fact that this is the only article in the clippings and press digest files strongly suggests that Booker's real work was his liaison to black organizations.

15. Land, *Children's Television Workshop*, 152.

16. Cooney to Dorothy Height, NCNW, January 18, 1969, July 18, 1969, Memo, Booker to Hatch, November 11, 1969, "Booker, James E. Associates, 1969–1970" file, Box 14, National Council of Jewish Women organizers' guide, September 26, 1969, in Appendix B, CTW, Office of Education Progress Report no. 5, January 20, 1970, Box 3, CTW Archives. The "vest pocket viewing groups" quotation is from the last of these. For other organizations, see Memos, Booker to Hatch, July 29, 1969, July 31, 1969, December 17, 1969, Memos, Booker to Cooney, n.d., July 31, 1969, and Layhmond Robinson to Booker, December 30, 1969, in the same file.

17. Land, *Children's Television Workshop*, 151–59; Davis, Davidson oral history, 130–34; CTW, Progress Reports to USOE, nos. 3–6, March 15, 1969, to September 1, 1970, Box 3, CTW Archives.

18. Letter, Sugarman to Head Start Directors, October 13, 1969; "Children Shaping New TV Series," Head Start newsletter, photocopy of article clipping, August, [1969], "Head Start Correspondence and Other Documents, 1969–1970" file, Box 4, CTW Archives.

19. Memo, Rossie Drummond to Ken Rashid et al., October 7, 1969, "Head Start Correspondence and Other Documents, 1969–1970" file, Box 4, CTW Archives.

20. Les Brown, *"Sesame's* Commercial Friends," *Variety*, December 24, 1969, 33; Palmer to Paul Klein, July 7, 1969, "Klein, Paul, 1969–1971" file, Box 23, Clausen to Palmer, January 20, 1972, "Miscellaneous Files: Weekly Averages, 1969–1973" file, Box 45, CTW Archives.

21. Klein to Cooney, January 29, 1970, "Klein, Paul, 1969–1971" file, Box 23, Clausen to Palmer, June 22, 1971, "A. C. Nielsen Studies for CTW, 1968–1972" file, Clausen to Palmer, January 20, 1972, Box 45, CTW Archives.

22. Clausen to Edward L. Palmer, January 24, 1975, "Nielsen and Arbitron Ratings, 1969–1977" file, Box 45, CTW Archives; Tim Brooks and Earle Marsh, *The Complete Directory to Prime Time Network and Cable TV Shows, 1946–Present*, 6th ed. (New York: Ballantine Books, 1995), 1265.

23. The CTW Archives contain roughly nine linear feet of viewer mail from 1969 to 1985; James J. Gallagher, deputy assistant secretary of the Department of Health, Education, and Welfare, as quoted in press release, CTW, "Second Season for Sesame Street," April 7, 1970, "Press Releases, April-June, 1970" file, Box 31, CTW Archives; press release, "Quotes and Anecdotes: Some Reactions to Sesame Street," n.d., "Press Releases, March, 1971" file, Box 31, CTW Archives; see the two files labeled "Eric White, 1974," Box 47, CTW Archives; Memo, Lynne to Cooney et al., "Summary of Fan Letters Received and Processed through March 25, 1970," n.d., "Viewer Response, 1969–1970" file, Box 47, CTW Archives. A later memo of the same type shows the pos-

itive and negative letters in largely the same numbers but also indicates that the way they were counted was changed, cutting the count of complimentary letters; see Memo, Pat Tornborgh to Cooney et al., March 8, 1971, "Letters of Protest, 1970–1971" file, Box 45, CTW Archives.

24. For Cookie Monster, see files "Cookie Monster, 1972–1973" (quotation is from Matthew N. Brown Jr. to WHYY, January 17, 1973) and "Nutrition, 1971–1976," Box 45; see "Grammar and Language, 1972–1976," file, Box 45, for that issue (quotation is from Mrs. Richard A. Petrosa to Paul Taff, NET, February 6, 1973); for arousing children's fears see "Grover, Fear of Dark Segment, 1972" and "Muppet Fear, 1973–1975" files, and the *"Sesame Street*, 1971–1976 file"; "Maria, 1973" file, Box 45, includes complaints about her possible career choice (quotation is from Mrs. Noorman Giannukus to CTW, January 10, 1975); the anti-abortion mail is found in Boxes 49 to 51.

25. Memo, Carl Byoir and Associates, "Sesame Street Awards," n.d., "Miscellaneous Awards, 1970" file, Box 32, CTW Archives (Clio quotation is from this memo). Alex McNeil, *Total Television: The Comprehensive Guide to Programming from 1948 to the Present,* 4th ed. (New York: Penguin Books, 1996), 1054, 1125, confirms the Peabody. Cobbett Steinberg, *TV Facts* (New York: Facts on File, 1985), 204, confirms the 1970 Emmys. For the 1998 award count, see David Borgenicht, *Sesame Street: Unpaved: Scripts, Stories, Secrets, and Songs* (New York: Hyperion, 1998), 17.

26. "Educational TV," *TV Guide,* September 13, 1969, 67 (first quotation); "Sesame Street Opens," *Saturday Review,* November 15, 1969, 91 (second quotation); "The Children's Hour," *Newsweek,* December 22, 1969, 91 (third quotation); "The Forgotten 12 Million," *Time,* November 14, 1969, 96, 98; "'Sesame' Opens Up," *Newsweek,* April 20, 1970, 102; "TV's Switched-On School," *Newsweek,* June 1, 1970, 68–71; Don Monaco, "Cooney and the Kids: Here's TV Your Child Can Watch," *Look,* November 18, 1969, 100–104; John Leonard, "On the Street Where Kids Live: *Sesame Street,*" *Life,* folder of loose clippings, 1968–1975, Box 290, CTW Archives; Carroll Terry, "Learning Can Be Fun," *Good Housekeeping,* April 1970, 48, 50; "A Toddle Down 'Sesame Street,'" *Ebony,* January 1970, 36–39; Stuart W. Little, "From A to Z on *Sesame Street,*" *Saturday Review,* May 9, 1970, 62–64. Documenting the early newspaper coverage is *CTW Press Digest,* "News from Sesame Street," Box 290, CTW Archives. Byron Scott, "Turning on Tots with Educational TV," *Today's Health,* November 1969, 28–32; "'Sesame Street' Asks: Can Television Really Teach?" *Nation's Schools* 85 (February 1970): 58–59; Evan McLeod Wylie, "At Last: A TV Show Good for Children," *PTA Magazine,* May 1970, 13–14; Alan Caruba, "Marshall McLuhan Lives on *Sesame Street,*" *Publishers Weekly,* April 20, 1970, 28–31.

27. Fred Ferretti, "Women's Group Urges Network to Take Ads off Children's TV," *New York Times,* January 7, 1970, 87.

28. For Cooney's support of ACT, see Cooney, "Educational Crossroads: Madison Avenue and Sesame Street," in *Action for Children's Television: The First National Symposium on the Effect on Children of Television Programming and Advertising,* ed. Evelyn Sarson (New York: Avon Books, 1970), 15–19, and Cooney, "Financing," ACT Third National Symposium; Official Report of Proceedings before the Federal Communica-

tions Commission, Washington, D.C., October 4, 1972, Public Panel Discussion: Children's Television Programming (Washington, D.C.: CSA Reporting Corp., 1972), Docket no. 19142, in Federal Communications Commission Records, vol. 64, Box 28, Acc. 173-90-7, Washington National Records Center, Suitland, Md. (hereafter, FCC Panels). Palmer to Lillian Ambrosino, April 20, 1970, "Action for Children's Television: Memos and Correspondence, 1970–1981," file, Box 13, CTW Archives.

29. Charren as quoted in Joan Barthel, "Boston Mothers Against Kidvid," *New York Times Magazine*, January 5, 1975, 40; editorial, "Draining the Bog," March 24, 1970, *Christian Science Monitor*, photocopy in "Action for Children's Television: Memos and Correspondence, 1970–1981" file, Box 13, CTW Archives.

30. William Melody, *Children's Television: The Economics of Exploitation* (New Havan, Conn.: Yale University Press, 1973) is the most complete articulation of ACT's rationale. But elements of it appear in Barthel, "Boston Mothers" and in their FCC testimony. Stanley E. Cohen, "Tendency to Turn Off Is Evident by 2nd Grade Level," *Advertising Age*, July 19, 1971, 1, 59, covers Harvard business professor Scott Ward's study of children's understanding of advertising. Speech, Cooney, "Financing for Children's Television," Action for Children's Television's Third National Symposium on Children and Television, New Haven, Conn., October 17, 1972, "Cooney Speeches, 1972" file, Box 33, CTW Archives.

31. The age groups specified were 2–5 years old, 6–9, and 10–12. With regard to *Sesame Street*'s fulfillment of ACT's recommended hours of children's programming, all stations that carried the show received at least one daily hour-long episode for five hours per week. Many repeated the daily episode in the afternoon, for a total of ten hours. And a few, like WTTW in Chicago, also carried the five weekly episodes back to back on Saturday mornings, for a total of fifteen hours. These totals, of course, do not include the hours added by *Mister Rogers' Neighborhood* (2.5 hours per week), *The Electric Company* (2.5 hours per week, beginning October 1971), and *Zoom* (2.5 hours per week, beginning in 1972), the other children's programs that PBS broadcast during the FCC debate about the petition.

32. "'Sesame Street': Wunderkind: St. Joan's Click for PTV and UHF," *Variety*, December 24, 1969, 23, 33.

33. John Leonard, "Since the Kiddies Are Hooked—Why Not Use TV for a Head Start Program?" *New York Times Magazine*, July 14, 1968, 5ff.; Norman S. Morris, "What's Good about Children's TV," *Atlantic*, August 1969, 68. Emphasis in original.

34. Leonard, "On the Street"; Morris, *Television's Child*, 232.

35. Samuel Ball and Gerry Ann Bogatz, *The First Year of Sesame Street: An Evaluation* (Princeton, N.J.: ETS, 1970), 53ff. For examples of coverage generated by the ETS report, see "Sesame at One," *Newsweek*, November 16, 1970, 71; "Sesame Street Report Card," *Time*, November 16, 1970, 70; Alan Rosenthal, "The Sesame Street Generation Arrives," *Today's Health*, December 1970, 42–45, 64–65; James Cass, "Sesame Street and Its Critics," *Saturday Review*, December 19, 1970, 49; Fred M. Hechinger, "Sesame Street: Learning from the 'Cookie Monster,'" *New York Times*, November 8, 1970, in *CTW Newsletter*, no. 11, November 18, 1970, Box 2, CTW Archives. For news-

paper coverage of ETS evaluation, see William Doolittle, "'Sesame' Top Teaching Tool," *Newark Evening News*, November 5, 1970, 18; "Tests Show TV's 'Sesame' Helps Kids," *San Francisco Chronicle*, November 5, 1970, 48; "*Sesame Street* Is Evaluated," *Tulsa Daily World*, November 7, 1970; and others in "Clip Reports July–Nov. 1970" file, Box 290, CTW Archives. *Time*'s cover story was Stefan Kanfer, "Who's Afraid of Big, Bad TV?" *Time*, November 23, 1970, 60–73.

36. "Big Sister on *Sesame Street*," *Seventeen*, July 1970, 112, 146; Gilstrap as quoted in Rosenthal, "*Sesame Street* Generation," 44; "If Kids Act Smarter, 'Sesame Street' May Be the Reason," *Nation's Schools* 87 (March 1971): 34–35. Teacher fears of restless students appeared in Stanley and Janice Berenstain, "It's All in the Family: New School Year," *Good Housekeeping*, October 1970, 96, 98, 99; "Sesame at One," *Newsweek*, November 16, 1970, 71; Richard K. Doan, "Kindergarten May Never Be the Same Again," *TV Guide*, July 11, 1970, 6–9.

37. For examples of early critics, see Robert Lewis Shayon, "Cutting Oedipal Ties," *Saturday Review*, February 14, 1970, 50; Minnie Perrin Berson, "Ali Baba! What Have You Done?" *Childhood Education* 46 (March 1970): 339–40; Frank Garfunkel, "Sesame Street: An Educational Dead End?" *Bostonia*, March 1970, 19–21, "Criticism: General *Sesame Street*, 1969–1973," file, Box 17, CTW Archives. In chapter 7, I detail these and other important criticisms of *Sesame Street*.

38. Brown, "'Sesame Street,'" 23; Jim Fiebig, "Mark My Words," *Bremerton Washington Sun*, July 6, 1970, in July 1970 CTW Clip Report, Box 290, CTW Archives; Benjamin Spock, "Children, Television, and *Sesame Street*," *Redbook*, July, 1970, 24, 28.

39. David Fleiss and Lillian Ambrosino, "An International Comparison of Children's Television Programming," NCCB, Washington, D.C, July 1971, in Federal Communications Commission Records, vol. 31, acc. 173-90-8, Washington National Records Center, Suitland, Md.; Stanley E. Cohen, "Kids in Other Lands See Better TV, Study Reveals," *Advertising Age*, July 5, 1971, 36; Cooney, FCC Panels, October 4, 1972, 398; Alan Pearce, "The Economics of Network Children's Television Programming," staff report submitted to the Federal Communications Commission, [July 1972], Washington, D.C., ERIC ED 066882; Melody, *Children's Television*.

40. Newton N. Minow and Craig L. Lamay, *Abandoned in the Wasteland: Children, Television, and the First Amendment* (New York: Hill and Wang, 1995), 9–10. Minow's recollections of the fruits of the Burch-Cooney connection are not wholly consistent with the documentary record, but, in addition to their letters in the CTW archive, the article "Drugs on TV: Next in Line for Federal Suppression?" *Broadcasting*, July 24, 1972, 16–18 testifies to their friendship. As a member of the National Commission on Marijuana and Drug Abuse, Cooney bantered in a notably friendly manner with Burch when he appeared before the commission. Burch, as quoted in Barry Cole and Mal Oettinger, *Reluctant Regulators: The FCC and the Broadcast Audience* (Reading, Mass.: Addison-Wesley, 1978), 263.

41. Johnson, *How to Talk Back to Your TV Set* (Boston: Little, Brown, 1970). Examples of articles that testify to broadcasters' antipathy for Johnson include "Editorial: The Case Against Nicholas Johnson," *Broadcasting*, February 24, 1969, 94; "Nicholas

Johnson's Private Demons," *Broadcasting*, September 1, 1969, 38–40. Although *Broadcasting*'s reaction seems little short of hysterical, Stanley E. Cohen, "Nick Johnson's Book Shows Why FCC Commissioner Worries Broadcasters," *Advertising Age*, March 16, 1970, 122, gives a significantly more balanced assessment. Johnson, "Beyond Sesame Street," *National Elementary Principal*, April 1971, 6–13; quotations on 9, 11.

42. Gary H. Grossman, *Saturday Morning TV* (New York: Delacourt Press, 1981), 258; Stone, "Jon Stone," interview by Davidson (New York, May 29, 1991), in Davidson oral history, 100; George W. Woolery, *Children's Television: The First Thirty-Five Years, 1946–1981, Part II: Live, Film, and Tape Series* (Metuchen, N.J.: Scarecrow Press, 1985), 227–28, 133–35; McNeil, *Total*, 390, 189.

43. Woolery, *Children's Television: The First Thirty-Five Years, 1946–1981, Part I: Animated Cartoon Series* (Metuchen, N.J.: Scarecrow Press, 1983), 99–100; McNeil, *Total*, 280; "Two Academics in CBS-TV Picture as Consultants on Kid Programming," *Variety*, June 6, 1973, 35, 45; "How Networks Are Upgrading Weekend Shows," *Broadcasting*, November 20, 1972, 46; "NBC to Feed Affils and O&O's Pre-School Kidvid Series in Feb.," *Variety*, December 1, 1971, 27, 43; "Kidvid '72: Quality Replacing Quantity," *Television/Radio Age*, September 4, 1972, 17–19, 60–62; Langbourne W. Rust, "Do Children Prefer Junk on TV?" *Variety*, September 13, 1972, 38; Edith Efron, "The Children's Crusade that Failed," *TV Guide*, April 7, 1973, 8. Show dates for other programs from McNeil, *Total*, 5, 509, 813, 930, except *Schoolhouse Rock*, the dates for which are drawn from http://www.davemackey.com/animation/schoolhouserock, June 27, 2004, and the *ABC Afterschool Specials* from http://mtr.inet7.com/PressRoom/pressRelease/05132003.htm, June 27, 2004. For a behind-the-scenes look at *Fat Albert*, see Heather Hendershot, *Saturday Morning Censors: Television Regulation before the V-Chip* (Durham, N.C.: Duke University Press, 1998), 193–216.

44. "NBC to Feed Affils," 27, 43; Ducovny, as quoted in Rosenthal, "Sesame Street Generation," 64; Unnamed "television executive," as quoted in "Networks Are Upgrading," *Broadcasting*, 46; Larry Harmon, "How to Pacify Parent and Educator Groups: Give Them Better Kids' Programming," *Television/Radio Age*, March 20, 1972, 37; "Advertiser Group Asks TV Clean-up, Plans Research," *Advertising Age*, September 25, 1972, 2.

45. "Academics," *Variety*.

Chapter 7. "The Verdict on SESAME STREET"

1. Speech, Cooney, "Financing for Children's Television," Action for Children's Television's Third National Symposium on Children and Television, New Haven, Conn., October 17, 1972, "Cooney Speeches, 1972" file, Box 33, Archives of the Children's Television Workshop, National Public Broadcasting Archives, Hornbake Library, University of Maryland, College Park, Md. (hereafter, CTW Archives).

2. Lee Mendelson, producer of *Hot Dog*, as quoted in Gary H. Grossman, *Saturday Morning TV* (New York: Delacourt Press, 1981), 260.

3. Edmond M. Rosenthal, "No Losers in This 'Pro-social,' Live-action Year of Kids' TV; Three Networks in Tight Race," *Television/Radio Age*, November 11, 1974, 29.

4. Norm Prescott, "Filmation co-owner," as quoted in Grossman, *Saturday*, 160.

5. The end date for *Afterschool* is unclear. I am using the one that the Museum of Television and Radio used in 2003. This excludes several years during the early 1990s when Oprah Winfrey took over production of the shows. As of 2004, the series is apparently off the air.

6. Grossman, *Saturday*, 275. Dates for *Pop Ups* are from George W. Woolery, *Children's Television: The First Thirty-Five Years, 1946–1981, Part I: Animated Cartoon Series* (Metuchen, N.J.: Scarecrow Press, 1983) and Jack Gould, "Saturday Morning TV 'Spots' Help Teach Children to Read," *Cleveland Plain Dealer*, October 3, 1970, in "Clip Reports July-Nov. 1970," Box 290, CTW Archives; http://www.school-house-rock .com/history.htm, February 28, 2005. For *Schoolhouse Rock*, the dates are drawn from http://www.davemackey.com/animation/schoolhouserock/, March 18, 2005.

7. Hogan and Golog, as quoted in Edmond M. Rosenthal, "Pro-profit Conquers Pro-social, in Network Kids' Programs," *Television/Radio Age*, August 18, 1975, 92. George A. Heinemann, "Children's Programming," *Journal of Broadcasting* 25 (Summer 1981): 309–11. Heinemann had consulted with Carnegie at one of the 1967 seminars, was NBC's first vice president of children's programming, and produced *Take a Giant Step*, which some called *Heinemann Street* because it was his response to CTW's show. See Wesley Hyatt, *The Encyclopedia of Daytime Television* (New York: Billboard Books, 1997), 421.

8. Robert Lewis Shayon, "Act with ACT," *Saturday Review*, March 7, 1970, 22. For another similar prediction, see Stanley E. Cohen, "Broadcast Men Wary, But Are Reassured by Conservative FCC," *Advertising Age*, November 2, 1970, 47–50.

9. Burch, as quoted in Barry Cole and Mal Oettinger, *Reluctant Regulators: The FCC and the Broadcast Audience* (Reading, Mass.: Addison-Wesley, 1978), 263 and in "Forget Profits on Kid Shows: Burch," *Television Digest*, September 21, 1970, 2. For other indications of Burch's rhetoric, see "Better Children's Programs Urged by FCC Chairman Burch," *Highlights* (National Association of Broadcasters), April 13, 1970, 13; "Burch's Commitment to Children's TV," *Television Digest*, September 20, 1971, 2–3; "Children's Programming. . . ," *Highlights*, April 6, 1970, 1; Henry R. Bernstein, "Broadcasters, Admen Hit Proposed Ban on Kids' Shows Commercials," *Advertising Age*, April 6, 1970, 1.

10. Duffy, as quoted in Cole and Oettinger, *Reluctant Regulators*, 257; Bernstein, "Broadcasters," 1, 81.

11. "Cutbacks in Commercials for Young," *Broadcasting*, January 10, 1972, 32; Pearce, "The Economics of Network Children's Television Programming," staff report submitted to the Federal Communications Commission, [July 1972], Washington, D.C., ERIC ED 066882, 57–58.

12. Maurine Christopher, "ANA Guidelines for Kids' TV Will Reveal Increased Social Area Awareness," *Advertising Age*, July 3, 1972, 2, 44; Stanley E. Cohen, "Tendency to Turn Off Is Evident by 2nd Grade Level," *Advertising Age*, July 19, 1971, 1, 59; "Clustering Ads, Banning Stars as Pitchmen in Offing," *Advertising Age*, July 19,

1971, 1, 59. For a subsequent synthesis of the developmental studies, see Scott Ward and Daniel B. Wackman, "Children's Information Processing of Television Advertising," in *New Models for Communication Research*, ed. Peter Clarke (Beverly Hills, Calif.: Sage Publications, 1973), 119–46.

13. Pearce, "Economics," 34–42, 58–68.

14. William Melody, *Children's Television: The Economics of Exploitation* (New Haven, Conn.: Yale University Press, 1973), quotations on 126, 119.

15. Eisner, 133, Silverman, 49, and Thurston, 33, in Official Report of Proceedings before the Federal Communications Commission, Washington, D.C., October 2, 1972, Public Panel Discussion: Children's Television Programming (Washington, D.C.: CSA Reporting Corp., 1972), Docket no. 19142, in Federal Communications Commission Records, vol. 64, Box 28, Acc. 173-90-7, Washington National Records Center, Suitland, Md. (hereafter, FCC Panels); O'Brien, 759, in Official Report of Proceedings before the Federal Communications Commission, Washington, D.C., January 8, 1973 (Oral Argument), (Washington, D.C.: CSA Reporting Corp., 1973), Docket no. 19142, in Federal Communications Commission Records, vol. 65, Box 20, Acc. 173-90-8, Washington National Records Center, Suitland, Md. (hereafter, FCC Hearings). Suitland holds only the last three volumes of the original six Oral Arguments.

16. FCC Panels, October 2, 1972, 9–13.

17. Ibid., 36–41.

18. Quaal in FCC Panels, October 4, 1972, 422. The same sentiment was voiced by a network executive when Burch, speaking to the International Radio and Television Society, pointed to *Sesame Street* as a great show that the networks had rejected; see "Burch's Commitment," 3.

19. Quote is from Grossman, *Saturday*, 101. For the content and format of *Garfield*, see Daniel D. Calibraro, ed., "The Wonderful World of WGN," (Chicago: Bassett Publishing, 1966) in "WGN, Chicago, Illinois" file, Library of American Broadcasting, Hornbake Library, University of Maryland, College Park, Md.; Kenan Heise, "Frazier Thomas [host of *Garfield*], Kids' TV Pal for 35 Years," obituary, *Chicago Tribune*, April 4, 1985, sect. 4, 10; Bill Granger, "Frazier Thomas: Friend and More," *Chicago Tribune*, April 15, 1985, sect. 1, 1; Patricia Best, "The Children's 'Prime Minister,'" *Chicago Tribune*, May 19, 1985, sect. 5, 2. Fondly remembered by many, *Garfield* occasionally included educational tidbits. As a child, I watched this show regularly. To any regular viewer, likening it to *Sesame Street* was transparent humbug.

20. Koehler in FCC Panels, October 2, 1972, 166.

21. Thurston in FCC Panels, October 2, 1972, 36; Daley in FCC Panels, October 2, 1972, 141; Hooks in FCC Panels, October 2, 1972, 141–53, October 3, 200–201; October 4, 405, 408; Pierce in FCC Panels, October 4, 1972, 406. Hooks's biographical information is from Cole and Oettinger, *Reluctant*, 20

22. FCC Panels, October 4, 1972, 406–7.

23. Francis in FCC Panels, October 2, 1972, 13; Cooney in FCC Panels, October 4, 1972, 401. For coverage of the Pearce report's release, see "Asked at FCC: Should Children's Programming Make Profit?" *Broadcasting*, July 24, 1972, 23–24.

24. Pearce, "Economics," 10–14; quotation on 14.

25. "The Dollars and Sense of Sesame Street," *Dividend*, Winter 1971, reprint, 4, in Box 18, CTW Archives. From Connell's figures for "creation and production of what was seen on the air," I have taken the expenses for "studio and technical staff," "raw videotape stock," "props," and "153 animated and 112 live action pieces" as the figures analogous to the production figures that Pearce used. Because the production costs Connell itemized do not add up to the $4.6 million for that largest section of the budget, I have taken the only part I am excluding, distribution, from that figure to arrive at a figure of $4,080,000. Added to the costs of "pre-production research and post production studies" ($600,000), that yields a total cost of $4,680,000, which divided by 130 episodes results in my $36,000 figure. The trade press covered Pearce's report to the commission: "Asked at FCC," 23–24; "FCC Released Study by Communications Economist," *Television Digest*, July 24, 1972, 2.

26. Cooney in FCC panels, October 4, 1972, 399–403; Hooks in FCC panels, October 4, 1972, 416; Charren and Sarson in FCC Hearings, January 8, 1973, 631–34; Burch, as quoted in "Drugs on TV," 18.

27. "FCC's Children's Policy Statement," appendix C in Cole and Oettinger, *Reluctant*.

28. Walter Goodman, "Is *Sesame Street* Really All that Good?" *Redbook*, October 1973, 98–99, 200ff.

29. "The Children's Hour," *Newsweek*, December 22, 1969, 91; Cyclops, "Wrong Way down *Sesame Street*," *Life*, October 15, 1971, 18–19.

30. Letter, Ralph T. Clausen [of Nielsen ratings service] to Palmer, January 24, 1975, "Nielsen and Arbitron Ratings, 1969–1977" file, Box 45, CTW Archives.

31. Klein to Cooney, January 29, 1970, "Klein, Paul, 1969–1971" file, Box 23, CTW Archives.

32. Memo, Palmer to Klein, "Subject: Viewing-rate Survey," August 20, 1968, "Klein, Paul, 1969–1971" file, Box 23, CTW, Progress Report to USOE, no. 3, March 15, 1969, Box 3, CTW Archives; Les Brown, "'Sesame Street': Wunderkind: St. Joan's Click for PTV and UHF," *Variety*, December 24, 1969, 23, 33.

33. Memo, Daniel Yankelovich, Inc. to Robert Hatch, March 1970, "A Report of Three Studies on the Role and Penetration of Sesame Street in Ghetto Communities," 2–3, April 1970, Box 43, CTW Archives.

34. Yankelovich, [Bedford-Stuyvesant study], in "Role and Penetration," [unpaginated]; "1969/1970 Season: Television Stations which Broadcast Sesame Street," "First Season Broadcast Times by Station, 1969–1970" file, Box 34, CTW Archives.

35. Memo, Daniel Yankelovich, Inc. to Robert Hatch, "Survey Results on Viewing of Sesame Street by Pre-School Aged Children," March 1970, "Ghetto audience study, survey instruments, miscellany" file, Box 43, CTW Archives; Yankelovich, "Report of Three Studies"; Robert Hatch, "Robert Hatch," interview by Robert Davidson (Lakeville, Conn., June 21, 1991), in "Children's Television Workshop: The Early Years, an Oral History," ed. Robert Davidson (manuscript, Children's Television Workshop,

1993), 171–72 (hereafter, Davidson oral history). The Chicago study appears along with the other three in the same file. The quotation is from page 1 of that report.

36. "Television Stations which Broadcast *Sesame Street*"; U.S. Bureau of the Census, "Table 20: Population of the 100 Largest Urban Places: 1970," http://www.census .gov/population/documentation/twps0027/tab20.txt. By the 1970 census, of the top 10, Los Angeles, Detroit, Baltimore, Washington, and Cleveland had UHF stations, but of the top 25, only 2 others (San Diego and Columbus, Ohio) had UHF stations. The rest had VHF stations.

37. "A Report of Three Studies on the Role and Penetration of Sesame Street in Ghetto Communities," June 1971; "A Report on the Role and Penetration of Sesame Street in Ghetto Communities," April 1973; "A Trend Report on the Role and Penetration of Sesame Street in Ghetto Communities," July 1978, Boxes 43 and 44, CTW Archives. The Washington figures appear on pages 62 and 14 of the 1973 and 1978 reports, respectively. Memo, Allen R. Cooper to Program Managers, All PBS Member Stations, "November-December 1974 Nielsen Cumes and Demographics," December 5, 1975, 5–6, "Nielsen and Arbitron Ratings, 1969–1977" file, Box 45, CTW Archives. Cooper, in charge of audience measurement for PBS, found that the show attracted children fairly evenly across racial, ethnic, and class boundaries. Hooks in FCC Panels, October 2, 1972, 143. For a discussion of *Sesame Street*'s audience divergence from PBS, see Laurie Ouellette, *Viewers Like You?: How Public TV Failed the People* (New York: Columbia University Press, 2002), 79–84.

38. Robert Lewis Shayon, "Cutting Oedipal Ties," *Saturday Review*, February 14, 1970, 50; Minnie Perrin Berson, "Ali Baba! What Have You Done?" *Childhood Education* 46 (March 1970): 339–40; Frank Garfunkel, "Sesame Street: An Educational Dead End?" *Bostonia*, March 1970, 21, in "Criticism: General *Sesame Street*, 1969–1973" file, Box 17, CTW Archives.

39. Garfunkel, "Dead End?" 21; Bereiter, as quoted in Everett Groseclose, "Educational TV Turns to Hard Sell in Series Aimed at Preschoolers," *Wall Street Journal*, November 10, 1969, from Press clippings, "Clippings 1968–1969" file, Box 288, CTW Archives.

40. Urie Bronfenbrenner, "Who Lives on Sesame Street?" *Psychology Today*, October, 1970, 14, 18, 20. Emphasis in original.

41. John Holt, "Big Bird, Meet Dick and Jane: A Critique of *Sesame Street*," *Atlantic Monthly*, May 1971, 72–74, 77–78.

42. Thomas D. Cook, Hilary Appleton, Ross F. Conner, Ann Shaffer, Gary Tamkin, and Stephen J. Weber, *"Sesame Street" Revisited* (New York: Russell Sage, 1975). A perusal of ERIC attests to Cook's position in the field of evaluation.

43. Zigler, as quoted in wire service news story text, United Press International, n.d., "Office of Education Correspondence, Memos, and Other Documents, 1971" file, Box 4, CTW Archives. I have dated the story from a letter, Cooney to Lesser, February 8, 1971, in the same file. For documentation of the lack of Head Start funds beginning with the second season, see "Children's Television Workshop Budget for the Period July 1, 1970 to June 30, 1971," April 1, 1970, Box 1, CTW Archives. Sprigle,

"Can Poverty Children Live on *Sesame Street,*" *Young Children* 26 (1971): 202–17 and "Who Wants to Live on *Sesame Street?*" *Young Children* 28 (1972): 109.

44. Sprigle, "Can," 209–11; Palmer, interview by the author, May 6, 1998, tape recording, Ithaca, N.Y., transcript, 54–55; [Barbara Frengel], "Goals Meeting, Children's Television Workshop, Sept. 23, 24, 1968," 2, "Preliminary Goal Planning and Documents, September-December 1968" file, Box 33, CTW Archives; Lesser, *Children and Television: Lessons from Sesame Street* (New York: Vintage Books, 1974), 51–52.

45. Sprigle, "Can," 204–207, 211–15.

46. Cook, as quoted in Samuel Ball and Gerry Ann Bogatz, "Some Thoughts on this Secondary Evaluation," in Cook et al., *Revisited,* 389; Howard E. Freeman, "Foreword," in ibid., xi–xiv; ibid., 1–4.

47. Ibid., 1–4, 12–13, 142–53.

48. Ibid., 153.

49. Billy Tashman, "E-Z Street: 25 Years and Still Counting," *Village Voice,* November 23, 1993, 55–56; Jerome L. Singer and Dorothy G. Singer, "Come Back, Mister Rogers, Come Back," *Psychology Today,* March 1979, 56; Neil Postman, *Amusing Ourselves to Death: Public Discourse in the Age of Show Business* (New York: Penguin Books, 1985), esp. 142–48.

50. "Reader Reaction to *Sesame Street,*" *Childhood Education* 46 (May 1970): 429. Palmer, "The Deer and the Duck," 1973, Box 42, CTW Archives. He may have sent it to journalists assessing the show and its detractors. See Goodman, "All that Good?" 99, 200, which includes much of the argument from "Deer." Ball and Bogatz, "Some Thoughts," 402.

51. For review of Sprigle, see Marilyn Martin, Irene Dowdy, Stephen Kemmis, and Kathleen Brophy, *"Sesame Street* Revisited: A Response to Inadequate Criticism," *Educational Products Information Exchange Report* no. 53 (New York: Educational Products Information Exchange Institute, 1973), unpaginated. For reviews of Cook, see Herbert A. Terry, book review, *Journalism Quarterly* 53 (1976): 162–63; Gladys Engel Lang, book review, *Contemporary Sociology* 6 (1977): 612–13; Liebert, "Evaluating the Evaluators," *Journal of Communication* 26 (1976): 165–71. For the survey of effects research, see Liebert, John M. Neale, and Emily S. Davidson, *The Early Window: Effects of Television on Children and Youth* (New York: Pergamon Press, 1973). Liebert and his coauthors produced two more editions of this book, in 1982 and 1988, testifying to its popularity.

52. Lesser, "Criticism," 174–201 and "Outcomes," 227–28 in *Children and Television;* final quotation on 201. Lesser had access to a pre-publication version of Cook's report given to Russell Sage Foundation in 1972. *Revisited* did not come out until after Lesser own book.

53. Grace and Fred Hechinger, "Meanwhile, on Sesame Street . . . ," *New York,* October 25, 1971, 39–40; James Cass, "Sesame Street and Its Critics," *Saturday Review,* December 19, 1970, 49; Cyclops, "Wrong Way down *Sesame Street.*" Other summaries of criticism in the popular press appeared in Betty Baer, "The Secrets of *Sesame Street,*" *Look,* September 22, 1970, 56–58, 62; "'Sesame' Under Attack," *Newsweek,* May 24, 1971, 52; Goodman, "All that Good?"; and Claire Safran, "What's the Verdict on 'Sesame

Street'?" *TV Guide*, October 2, 1976, 4–8. Another, more scholarly survey was Janet M. Rogers, "A Summary of the Literature on 'Sesame Street,'" *Journal of Special Education* 6 (1972): 43–50.

54. "Second wave movements" comes from Terry H. Anderson, *The Movement and the Sixties* (New York: Oxford University Press, 1995), 294, 343, 356.

55. I have closely followed Kathryn Montgomery's analysis in "Managing Advocacy Groups," in *Target: Prime Time: Advocacy Groups and the Struggle over Entertainment Television* (New York: Oxford University Press, 1989), 51–74.

56. Praise for the show's inclusion of African-American cast members appeared in "New York Beat," *Jet*, December 18, 1969, 63 and "A Toddle Down 'Sesame Street,'" *Ebony*, January 1970, 36–39. J. Fred MacDonald in *Blacks and White TV: African Americans in Television Since 1948*, 2nd ed. (Chicago: Nelson-Hall, 1992), 196, observes that the numbers of African-American characters had begun to dwindle when *Sesame Street* premiered. For the development of Oscar the Grouch, see Memo, Sheldon White to Lesser, July 15, 1968, Connell Papers; "Goals Meeting, Children's Television Workshop, September 23, 24, 1968," 7, "Statement of Instructional Goals for Children's Television Workshop," December 31, 1968, 9, "Preliminary Goal Planning and Documents, September-December 1968" file, Box 33, CTW Archives. Viewer mail testifies to Oscar's popularity; see for example Joyce Oliver, "Summary of Fan Letters Received and Processed," October 20, 1972, "Viewer Response, 1970–1973" file, Box 47, CTW Archives. The Yankelovich reports found Oscar to be the character most often mentioned when children were asked what they liked about the show in 1970 and second only to Big Bird in 1971. For my impressions of Oscar's role on the show, I have relied on the seven segments in my sample involving Oscar and the curricular goal of "Differing Perspectives," the forty segments for any curricular goal in which he appears, and a survey of first season Program Information Sheets, Box 23, NET Program Files, PBS-2 Collection, National Public Broadcasting Archives, Hornbake Library University of Maryland, College Park, Md.

57. Grace Richmond, "director of education at the West 80th Street Day Care Center," and Dorothy Pitman Hughes, as quoted in Linda Francke, "The Games People Play on *Sesame Street*," *New York*, April 5, 1971, 28. The "Westchester" characterization comes from Cooney herself in Memo, Cooney to Jane O'Connor, February 10, 1970, "Cooney's Production Miscellany, 1968–1971" file, Box 36, CTW Archives.

58. Jane O'Connor to David Connell, Jon Stone, Lu Horne, Sam Gibbon, Memo, February 10, 1970, "Cooney's Production Miscellany, 1968–1971" file, Box 36, CTW Archives. The vicissitudes of Roosevelt Franklin can be followed in part through CTW records, but only a closer look at his segments would really tell the whole story; see LaMarian Hayes and Ana Herrera, "Cultural Diversity: Curriculum on Multicultural Awareness," "Sesame Street Position Papers, 1976" file, November 22, 1976, Box 35, Lewis Bernstein, "Sesame Street Characters: A Position Paper for Discussion," in "Sesame Street Position Papers, 1976" file, November 22, 1976, Box 57, and the entire "Greene, Dr. Carolyn J., 1976," file, Box 20, CTW Archives.

59. Press release, "National Advisory Committee to the Bilingual Program of

Sesame Street, San Antonio, Texas, April 22, 23, 1971," n.d., Daniel J. Gomez to Diego Castellano, April 27, 1971, "Bilingual Educational Sub-Committee Board of Advisers" file, unprocessed Community Education Services files, CTW Archives; Davis, "Evelyn Davis," interview by Davidson (New York, February 14, 1991, April 26, 1991), in Davidson oral history, 141–43; Robert Davidson, telephone interview by the author, July 1, 1999, tape recording, author's notes. For an account of the campaign by a major Chicano media group, Justicia, see Montgomery, *Target: Prime Time*, 55–65.

60. Cooney, as quoted in "Report on CTW Subcommittee on Bilingual Education Meeting, Friday, December 10, 1971," [January 19, 1972], "Bilingual Subcommittee" file, Box 241, Robert Davidson, "Report on Bilingual/Bicultural Activities May 1971–November 1972," 3, January 5, 1973, "Bob Davidson" file, Box 247, "Fact Sheets," in *Sesame Street* Press Information Kits, Oversize Documents Box 3, and documents in the following files: "Community Education Services: Bilingual Project, 1970–1971," Box 16, "Miscellaneous Research Reports, 1970–1971," Box 34, "Bilingual Subcommittee," Box 241, and "Bilingual Educational Sub-Committee Board of Advisers," unprocessed Community Education Services files, CTW Archives; Davis, Davidson oral history, 137, 141–43; Davidson, interview by the author, July 1, 1999.

61. Armando B. Rendon, *Chicano Manifesto*, twenty-fifth anniversary edition (Berkeley, Calif.: Ollin and Associates, 1996), 41–51.

62. Pablo Macias, "Television Role Models and the Chicano," college essay, December 28, 1970, "Second Season Preparations, 1970" file, Box 34, CTW Archives; Palmer, interview by the author, transcript, 20–21.

63. For early encounters with feminists, see correspondence among Cooney, Jo Ann E. Gardner, and Muriel Fox, dated from late 1969 through 1970, in "Criticism: Feminists, 1969–1971" file, Box 17, CTW Archives. Gardner was a psychologist and a "long-time activist in the women's movement," according to Winifred D. Wandersee, *On the Move: American Women in the 1970s* (Boston: Twayne Publishers, 1988), 26. Fox was a vice president at Carl Byoir, CTW's public relations firm, and her name appears on NOW's letterhead as a top officer at the time. Ellen Goodman, "The male, Male, MALE World of Sesame Street," *Boston Globe*, December 17, 1970 in January 1971 CTW Clip Report, Box 290, Jacqui Ceballos to Richard Aszling [of General Foods], July 26, 1971, "Criticism: Feminists, 1969–1971" file, Box 17, press release, Corporation for Public Broadcasting, "General Foods Grants Total $370,000 for Saturday 'Sesame Street' Rebroadcasts," September 18, 1970, Box 31, CTW Archives.

64. Anne Grant West to Aszling, August 29, 1971, "Criticism: Feminists, 1969–1971" file, Box 17, Patricia Hayes O'Donnell, "Sex Roles on Sesame Street," 2, January 1977, Box 43, CTW Archives. See reports and letters in "Criticism: National Organization for Women, Cynthia Eaton, Susan Chase, 1971–1973" file, Box 17, CTW Archives. For accounts of the researcher-producer encounters, see Palmer, "Edward Palmer," interview by Davidson (Philadelphia, August 1, 1991) in Davidson oral history, 123–24; Samuel Gibbon, " Samuel Gibbon," interview by Davidson (New York, September 19, 1990) in Davidson oral history, 106; Leona Schauble, telephone interview by the author, April 27, 1999, tape recording, author's notes; "Jon Stone notes,"

n.d., "Criticism: Feminists, 1970–1972" file, Box 17, CTW Archives. Gibbon was producer of *Sesame Street* for only its first season but was executive producer of *The Electric Company*, CTW's second TV show, for its entire run. Schauble was a senior member of the research department and close to the encounters between the women of her department and the largely male production department.

65. [Children's Television Workshop], press release, "*Sesame Street* Efforts Toward a Fuller Portrayal of Women," March 30, 1972, "Criticism: Feminists, 1970–1972" file, Box 17, CTW Archives; Stone, "Jon Stone notes"; Cooney, telephone interview by the author, January 28, 1998, tape recording, transcript, 10–11; Schauble, interview by the author. Stone's testimonial follows the press release closely enough that it was undoubtedly a source, thus dating it to early 1972.

66. Cooney to Gardner, January 5, 1970, "Criticism: Feminists, 1969–1971" file, Box 17, CTW Archives. For an example of the conventional wisdom, see the notorious Moynihan report, *The Negro Family: The Case for National Action* (Washington, D.C.: Department of Labor, 1965), 35–37.

67. Height, as quoted in Woloch, *Women*, 520. For feminists' anger with the opposition of needs of women and African Americans, see correspondence in "Criticism: Feminists, 1969–1971" file, Box 17, CTW Archives. For cast see press release, "Fact Sheet: 'Sesame Street' Ninth Season 1977–78," November 1977, "*Sesame Street* Press Information Kits: Season 9, 1977" file, Oversize Documents Box 3, CTW Archives.

68. Safran, "Verdict?" 8.

69. Cooney and Palmer as quoted in ibid.; Lesser, *Children*, 241.

Conclusion: The Many Faces of SESAME STREET

1. Kunkel in U.S. Congress, Senate, Subcommittee on Communications, *Children's TV Act of 1989*, Hearings for the Committee on Commerce, Science, and Transportation, 101st Cong., 1st Sess., 1989, 76–77. Statistics about Nickelodeon are from Tim Brooks and Earle Marsh, *The Complete Directory to Prime Time Network and Cable TV Shows, 1946–Present*, 6th ed. (New York: Ballantine Books, 1995), 749–50. Cable penetration statistic is from Kunkel, "The Truest Metric for Evaluating the Children's Television Act," *Journal of Applied Developmental Psychology* 24 (August 2003): 351.

2. Joan Ganz Cooney, "Sesame Street at Five: The Changing Look of a Perpetual Experiment" (New York: Children's Television Workshop, 1974), Box 42, Archives of the Children's Television Workshop, National Public Broadcasting Archives, Hornbake Library, University of Maryland, College Park, Md. (hereafter, CTW Archives).

3. Ibid.

4. Berson, "Ali Baba! What Have You Done?" *Childhood Education* 46 (March 1970): 342.

5. Marie Winn, *The Plug-In Drug: Television, Computers, and Family Life*, twenty-fifth anniversary edition (New York: Penguin Books, 2002), 58–63. Roni Beth Tower et al., "Differential Effects of Television Programming on Preschoolers' Cognition, Imagination, and Social Play," *American Journal of Orthopsychiatry* 49 (April 1979): 265–81; Singer and Singer, "Come Back, Mister Rogers, Come Back," *Psychology Today*,

March 1979, 56; Jerome Singer, quoted in John Leland, "The Magnetic Tube," in "Your Child's World," *Newsweek*, special edition, May 1997, 89, NexisLexis; Shannon Brownlee, "The Case for Frivolity," *U.S. News and World Report*, February 3, 1997, 45, 48. Neil Postman, *Amusing Ourselves to Death: Public Discourse in the Age of Show Business* (New York: Penguin Books, 1985).

6. Daniel R. Anderson, "Cognitive Effects of Sesame Street," in *Sesame Street Research: A 20th Anniversary Symposium* (New York: Children's Television Workshop, 1990), 20–24; preface in *Children's Understanding of Television: Research on Attention and Comprehension*, ed. Jennings Bryant and Anderson (New York: Academic Press, 1983), xiii–xiv; Anderson, "Educational Television Is Not an Oxymoron," *Annals of the American Academy of Political and Social Science* 557 (May 1998): 24ff., Infotrac article A20556099, quotation on 3.

7. Mary Maddeve, "Get Real," *Kidscreen*, October 1, 1999, 1; Wilson, quoted in Paige Albiniak, "Via Con Demos," *Broadcasting and Cable*, March 22, 2004, 34; "Sesame Street, the Acceptable Face of Political Correctness," *Economist*, January 18, 1992, 30; Ellen Seiter, *Sold Separately: Children and Parents in Consumer Culture* (New Brunswick, N.J.: Rutgers University Press, 1993), 88.

8. Gingrich and Lowey, quoted in Jerry Gray, "House Committee Discusses Public Broadcasting Budget," *New York Times*, January 20, 1995, A22; Irvin Molotsky, "One Tough Bird, After All: How Public Broadcasting Survived the Attacks of Conservatives," *New York Times*, November 27, 1997, E1.

9. Morrisett, "Lloyd Morrisett," interview by Davidson (New York, December 5, 1991, April 20, 1992), in "Children's Television Workshop: The Early Years, an Oral History," ed. Robert Davidson (Children's Television Workshop, manuscript, 1993), 43 (hereafter, Davidson oral history). The story of the threat to *Sesame Street*'s funding from the Office of Education and Caspar Weinberger can be traced in Boxes 524, 574, 575, 645, 683, 701, 758, Office Files of the Commissioner of Education, 1939–1980, Record Group 12, National Archives, College Park, Md.

10. Hatch, "Robert Hatch," interview by Davidson (Lakeville, Conn., June 21, 1991), in Davidson Oral History, 183–84; Morrisett, Davidson oral history, 45–49, 51; Morrisett, "Beyond Foundations: Why CTW Is Asking the Public for Money," *Public Telecommunications Review* 1 (August 1973): 50–56; David Britt, "David Britt," interview by Robert Davidson (New York, October 17, 1991), in Davidson oral history, 55–58; Franz Allina, "Franz Alina," interview by Robert Davidson (New York, July 12, 1990), in Davidson oral history, 184–89; Joan Ganz Cooney, "Joan Ganz Cooney," interview by Robert Davidson (New York, February 13, 1991, April 24, 1991), in Davidson oral history, 29; Thomas Kennedy, "Thomas Kennedy," interview by Robert Davidson (Key Biscayne, Fla., January 22, 1991), in Davidson oral history, 154–55.

11. Financial figures come from Paul Arnsberger, U.S. Internal Revenue Service, telephone interview by the author, January 8, 2001, author's notes. Arnsberger quoted from the workshop's income reports to the IRS for the most recent year then available, 1998.

12. Crane, quoted in Ellen Edwards, "Is Public TV a Purple Dinosaur? GOP

Renews Attack on Funding," *Washington Post,* December 22, 1994, D1, LexisNexis; Carl T. Hall, "The Marketing of Nonprofit 'Sesame Street' Licensing Contracts Bring in Millions," *San Francisco Chronicle,* December 30, 1991, B1, LexisNexis; Dick Williams, "Big Bird and 'Sesame Street'— Welfare Cheats," *Atlanta Journal-Constitution,* September 29, 1992, A6, LexisNexis; Edwards, "PBS Missing Out on 'Barney' Bucks; Tie-ins Reap Millions for Creators," *Washington Post,* September 13, 1993, A1; Will, "The Culture of Entitlement," *Washington Post,* February 2, 1995, A27. The more accurate *Barney* figure and Pressler bumper sticker are from Robert K. Avery and Alan G. Stavitsky, *A History of Public Broadcasting* (Washington, D.C.: Current, 2000), 89, 82.

13. Fowler, quoted in Caroline E. Mayer, "FCC Chief's Fears: Fowler Sees Threat in Regulation," *Washington Post,* February 6, 1983, K6; Dale Kunkel and Bruce Watkins, "Evolution of Children's Television Regulatory Policy," *Journal of Broadcasting and Electronic Media* 31 (Fall 1987): 379.

14. Law quotation (1988) from Naeemah Clark, "These Dames Are Bananas: The History of Action for Children's Television, 1969–1992," Ph.D. dissertation, University of Florida, Gainesville, Fla., 2002. Emphasis is apparently Clark's. 1990 law quotation from Dale Kunkel, "Policy Battles over Defining Children's Educational Television," *Annals of the American Academy of Political and Social Science* 557 (May 1998): 41.

15. *Yogi Bear* quote is from Kunkel, "Policy Battles," 45.

16. James Collins and Jeanne McDowell, "Tube for Tots: Move Over, Barney, You've Got Some Company," *Time,* November 24, 1997, 96, Academic Search Elite; Gloria Goodale, "TV *and* Reading? Yes!" *Christian Science Monitor,* September 1, 2000, 13, 16; Anderson, "The Children's Television Act: A Public Policy that Benefits Children," *Journal of Applied Developmental Psychology* 24 (August 2003): 339; Hirsch, quoted in Eric Schmuckler, "Sit Still Now, Class: It's Time to Get Serious," *New York Times,* February 27, 2000, Arts and Leisure, 47. I have consulted the Nickelodeon and PBS Kids websites for their information on production-research apparatus: http://www.nick.com and http://pbskids.org, June 12, 2004.

17. Calvert and Kotler, "Lessons from Children's Television: The Impact of the Children's Television Act on Children's Learning," *Journal of Applied Developmental Psychology* 24 (August 2003): 275–335; Kunkel. "The Truest Metric for Evaluating the Children's Television Act," 350; Amy B. Jordan, "Children Remember Prosocial Program Lessons But How Much Are They Learning?" 342, 345.

18. "Author Squeezes a Hit out of 'Rubber Ducky,'" *Boston Globe,* December 13, 1970, Press Notice Compilations 1969–1972, Box 290, CTW Archives; Whaley, "William Whaley," interview by Robert Davidson (New York, April 19, 1990), in Davidson oral history, 201; Lesser, *Children and Television: Lessons from* Sesame Street (New York: Vintage Books, 1974), 125–26. I have relied on the Jim Henson Company's web site for counts of movies and television shows: http://www.henson.com, June 12, 2004.

Essay on Sources

■■

The archival sources for the history of *Sesame Street* are rich. Recently opened and only partially processed are the Archives of the Children's Television Workshop (National Public Broadcasting Archives [NPBA] Hornbake Library, University of Maryland, College Park). This large collection (525 linear feet) does not include personnel or financial records but does extensively document production, audience, research, and many other aspects of *Sesame Street*, the Workshop, and its other shows up to the early 1980s. For the records of the earliest work on the project, the researcher should consult the Carnegie Corp. Collection (Rare Book and Manuscript Library, Columbia University, New York, N.Y.). The Office Files of the Commissioner of Education, 1939–1980 (Record Group 12, National Archives, College Park, Md.), supply much of the story of the dialogue between the show's creators and its government and foundation backers. The records for the Action for Children's Television petition before the Federal Communications Commission (Federal Communications Commission Records, Docket No. 19142, various accessions, Washington National Records Center, Suitland, Md.) are available in an unprocessed form. David Connell's papers remain privately held in Sheffield, Mass. Of peripheral use are the WNET and various Public Broadcasting Service collections also at NPBA.

There are three sources of oral histories and interviews. Complementing the CTW archive is an oral history, "Children's Television Workshop: The Early Years, an Oral History," Robert Davidson, ed. (Children's Television Workshop, manuscript, 1993). Davidson, the original assistant director and corporate secretary of the Workshop, interviewed sixteen major CTW figures in the early 1990s and edited them into this unofficial collection. Richard M. Polsky, an early member of the research staff, interviewed eight people, both Workshop personnel and others (microfiche transcripts, Columbia University Oral History Collection, Part IV, Microfilming Corp. of America, Sanford, N.C., 1979) for his 1974 dissertation. My interviews of Edward L. Palmer and Lloyd N. Morrisett are available at the National Public Broadcasting Archives. In addition, there is a video oral history with Cooney at the Archive of American Television.

Although no history similar to this one exists, there are several books that are basic to any study of *Sesame Street*. Most important is Gerald S. Lesser's *Children and Television: Lessons from* Sesame Street (New York: Vintage Books, 1974). Written by the show's leading academic adviser, it is the most complete exposition of the educational logic of the show, the relationship of children to television, and the program's early history. Polsky's dissertation became the first history of the pre-broadcast period: *Getting to* Sesame Street: *Origins of the Children's Television Workshop* (New York: Praeger Publishers, 1974). It is based on the papers of the Carnegie Corporation and Polsky's own interviews. Rounding out this short list of usable histories is a study written for the Office of Education analyzing CTW, with an emphasis on "how and why it works." The author, Herman W. Land, a significant public broadcasting figure in his own right, brought a sympathetic outsider's perspective, and his study includes promotion and administrative aspects not covered by these other authors: *The Children's Television Workshop: How and Why It Works* (Jericho, N.Y.: Nassau Board of Cooperative Educational Services, 1972). Attractive but not very useful is David Borgenicht, *Sesame Street: Unpaved: Scripts, Stories, Secrets, and Songs* (New York: Hyperion, 1998).

The many battles over culture started with the formation of the middle-class family as explained in Steven Mintz and Susan Kellogg, *Domestic Revolutions: A Social History of American Family Life* (New York: Free Press, 1988); Stephanie Coontz, *The Social Origins of Private Life: A History of American Families, 1600–1900* (London: Verso, 1988); Marilyn Dell Brady, "The New Model Middle-Class Family (1815–1930)," in *American Families: A Research Guide and Historical Handbook*, ed. Joseph M. Hawes and Elizabeth I. Nybakken (Westport, Conn.: Greenwood Press, 1991), 83–123. In addition to Lawrence W. Levine's classic *Highbrow/Lowbrow: The Emergence of Cultural Hierarchy in America* (Cambridge: Harvard University Press, 1988), Richard Butsch, *The Making of American Audiences: From Stage to Television, 1750–1990* (New York: Cambridge University Press, 2000), helps explain the bifurcation of the American audience along lines of social class.

Among the sources on the social control of media, print media and film are better covered than radio and television. Accounts of nineteenth- and early-twentieth-century print censorship can be found in Nicola Beisel, *Imperiled Innocents: Anthony Comstock and Family Reproduction in Victorian America* (Princeton, N.J.: Princeton University Press, 1997), Alison M. Parker, *Purifying America: Women, Cultural Reform, and Pro-Censorship Activism, 1873–1933* (Urbana: University of Illinois Press, 1997), and Paul S. Boyer, *Purity in Print: The Vice-Society Movement and Book Censorship in America* (New York: Charles Scribner's Sons, 1968). On the protection of children, see Viviana A. Zelizer, *Pricing the Priceless Child: The Changing Social*

Value of Children (1985; repr., Princeton University Press, 1994) and Linda Gordon, *Heroes of Their Own Lives: The Politics and History of Family Violence, Boston 1880–1960* (New York: Viking Penguin, 1988). For film censorship, the two classic histories of the industry are still a good starting point: Robert Sklar, *Movie-Made America: A Cultural History of American Movies* (New York: Vintage Books, 1975; updated, 1994), and Garth Jowett, *Film: The Democratic Art* (Boston: Little, Brown, 1976). Also valuable are two essay collections: *Movie Censorship and American Culture*, ed. Francis G. Couvares (Washington, D.C.: Smithsonian Institution Press, 1996) and *Controlling Hollywood: Censorship and Regulation in the Studio Era*, ed. Matthew Bernstein (New Brunswick, N.J.: Rutgars University Press, 1999). Radio censorship is covered briefly in Michele Hilmes, *Radio Voices: American Broadcasting, 1922–1952* (Minneapolis: University of Minnesota Press, 1997), and TV censorship is treated more extensively in Heather Hendershot, *Saturday Morning Censors: Television Regulation before the V-Chip* (Durham, N.C.: Duke University Press, 1998). For the Payne Film Studies, the three narrative chapters in Garth S. Jowett, Ian C. Jarvie, and Kathryn H. Fuller, *Children and the Movies: Media Influence and the Payne Fund Controversy* (New York: Cambridge University Press, 1996), are invaluable.

For the general trends in television during the 1950s and 1960s, the researcher should start with William Boddy, *Fifties Television: The Industry and Its Critics* (Urbana: University of Illinois Press, 1990); Erik Barnouw, *Tube of Plenty: The Evolution of American Television* (New York: Oxford University Press, 1975); and Christopher H. Sterling and John M. Kittross, *Stay Tuned: A Concise History of American Broadcasting*, 3rd ed. (Belmont, Calif.: Wadsworth Publishing, 2001). Sterling and Kittross include useful statistics in their appendices.

For views of the reform debate the following are useful: James L. Baughman, *Television's Guardians: The FCC and the Politics of Programming, 1958–1967* (Knoxville: University of Tennessee Press, 1985), and "The National Purpose and the Newest Medium: Liberal Critics of Television, 1958–60," *Mid-America* 64 (April–July 1982): 41–55. Though Baughman recounts well the story of Newton Minow's various reform efforts, his characterization of the reformers as exclusively liberal elitists probably does not apply to critics of children's TV. Mary Ann Watson, *The Expanding Vista: American Television in the Kennedy Years* (New York: Oxford University Press, 1990), covers both Minow's and Dodd's reform crusades. For Dodd's corrupt scuttling of the delinquency hearings, see James Boyd, *Above the Law* (New York: New American Library, 1968). Michael Curtin also touches on reform in the early pages of *Redeeming the Wasteland: Television Documentary and Cold War Politics* (New Brunswick, N.J.: Rutgers University Press, 1995). For material on the reconsideration of ratings in the early 1960s, see Sydney W. Head, *Broadcasting in America: A Survey of Television and Radio*, 2nd ed. (Boston: Houghton Mifflin, 1972), 308–10.

For the trends in 1950s and 1960s children's TV, George W. Woolery's introduction to his encyclopedia of programs is concise: *Children's Television: The First Thirty-Five Years, 1946–1981, Part II: Live, Film, and Tape Series* (Metuchen, N.J.:

Scarecrow Press, 1985), ix–xxvi. Joseph Turow also covers general trends in *Entertainment, Education, and the Hard Sell: Three Decades of Network Children's Television* (New York: Praeger Publishers, 1981), as does Maurice E. Shelby Jr. in "Children's Programming Trends on Network Television," *Journal of Broadcasting* 8 (Summer 1963): 247–56. For a polemical version from the advertising executive's point of view, see Cy Schneider, *Children's Television: The Art, the Business, and How It Works* (Lincolnwood, Ill.: NTC Business Books, 1987). Jeff Kisseloff adds some nice recollections in a chapter of *The Box: An Oral History of Television, 1920–1961* (New York: Viking, 1995), 452–60. Gary Cross provides a useful perspective on TV advertising in *Kids' Stuff: Toys and the Changing World of American Childhood* (Cambridge, Mass.: Harvard University Press, 1997).

Several books supply invaluable summaries of individual shows. The standard work, Tim Brooks and Earle Marsh, *The Complete Directory to Prime Time Network and Cable TV Shows, 1946–Present*, 8th ed. (New York: Ballantine Books, 2003), covers only prime-time programs and, thus, misses most of children's TV and includes only commercial shows. More useful is Alex McNeil, *Total Television: The Comprehensive Guide to Programming from 1948 to the Present*, 4th ed. (New York: Penguin Books, 1996), which covers non–prime-time and public broadcasting programs. Like McNeil, Wesley Hyatt's *Encyclopedia of Daytime Television* (New York: Billboard Books, 1997) is useful for children's shows because it covers those outside prime-time. In a narrative format and not as complete is Gary H. Grossman, *Saturday Morning TV* (New York: Delacourt Press, 1981), but it makes up for its selectivity with anecdotes and quotations. Best of all for children's programs is Woolery's authoritative two-volume work: *Children's Television: The First Thirty-Five Years, 1946–1981, Part I: Animated Cartoon Series* (Metuchen, N.J.: Scarecrow Press, 1983) and *Part II* (1985).

There are several useful works for the issue of TV violence and children: Willard D. Rowland Jr., *The Politics of TV Violence: Policy Uses of Communication Research* (Beverly Hills, Ca.: Sage, 1983); Douglass Cater and Stephen Strickland, *TV Violence and the Child: The Evolution and Fate of the Surgeon General's Report* (New York: Russell Sage Foundation, 1975); and Eli A. Rubinstein, "Television Violence: A Historical Perspective," in *Children and the Faces of Television: Teaching, Violence, Selling*, ed. Edward L. Palmer and Aimee Dorr (New York: Academic Press, 1980), 113–27. (Note that editor Palmer is unrelated to the Sesame Street research director of the same name.) James Gilbert sets the Kefauver and Dodd considerations of media violence in the larger debate about delinquency in *A Cycle of Outrage: America's Reaction to the Juvenile Delinquent in the 1950s* (New York: Oxford University Press, 1986).

Two books set Bandura in the context of children and television. Carmen Luke's *Constructing the Child Viewer: A History of the American Discourse on Television and Children, 1950–1980* (New York: Praeger, 1990) is an impressive compendium of all the social science research and puts Bandura in that context. For a narrower and more sympathetic treatment of Bandura and the other behaviorists, see Robert M. Liebert, Joyce N. Sprafkin, and Emily S. Davidson, *The Early Window: Effects of Television on Children and Youth*, 2nd ed. (New York: Pergamon Press, 1982).

There is a small but growing literature on noncommercial broadcasting. Basic to the story told here are: Robert W. McChesney, *Telecommunications, Mass Media, and Democracy: The Battle for Control of U.S. Broadcasting, 1928–1935* (New York: Oxford University Press, 1993); Robert J. Blakely, *To Serve the Public Interest: Educational Broadcasting in the United States* (Syracuse, N.Y.: Syracuse University Press, 1979); George H. Gibson, *Public Broadcasting: The Role of the Federal Government, 1912–76* (New York: Praeger Publishers, 1977); Donald N. Wood, "The First Fifteen Years of the 'Fourth Network,'" *Journal of Broadcasting* 13 (Spring 1969), 131–44; Robert M. Pepper, *The Formation of the Public Broadcasting Service* (New York: Arno Press, 1979). A newer source that brings the reader up to the twenty-first century and includes the Gingrich campaign against public broadcasting is Robert K. Avery and Alan G. Stavitsky, *A History of Public Broadcasting* (Washington: Current, 2000).

In addition to the sources cited in the notes, I found several sources useful for the culture and politics of the Great Society period. Charles A. Valentine's *Culture and Poverty: Critique and Counter-Proposals* (Chicago: University of Chicago Press, 1968) concisely covers the ideas about poverty. Besides Gilbert's *Cycle*, which explains delinquency's link to theories about poverty psychology, Irwin Unger's *The Best of Intentions: The Triumphs and Failures of the Great Society under Kennedy, Johnson, and Nixon* (New York: Doubleday, 1996) also covers the cultural basis for the Great Society as well as, more generally, the legislation and politics. For the War on Poverty, see Mark I. Gelfand, "The War on Poverty," in *Exploring the Johnson Years*, ed. Robert A. Divine (Austin: University of Texas Press, 1981), 126–54 and Bruce E. Altschuler, *LBJ and the Polls* (Gainesville: University of Florida Press, 1990).

For Head Start, the following essays in *Project Head Start: A Legacy of the War on Poverty*, ed. Edward Zigler and Jeanette Valentine (New York: Free Press, 1979), are useful: Robert E. Cooke, "Introduction"; Zigler and Karen Anderson, "An Idea Whose Time Had Come: The Intellectual and Political Climate for Head Start"; and Barbara Biber, "Introduction" to "Part II: The Preschool-Education Component of Head Start." Zigler's memoir, cowritten with Susan Muenchow, *Head Start: The Inside Story of America's Most Successful Educational Experiment* (New York: Basic Books, 1992), is readable and includes particular attention to his objections to *Sesame Street*.

For early education history and theory, Barbara Beatty's *Preschool Education in America: The Culture of Young Children from the Colonial Era to the Present* (New Haven, Conn.: Yale University Press, 1995) is a concise history, and Stacie G. Goffin and Catherine S. Wilson, *Curricular Models and Early Childhood Education: Appraising the Relationship*, 2nd ed. (Upper Saddle River, N.J.: Merrill Prentice Hall, 2001), provides a basic grasp of the pedagogical approaches. Rochelle Selbert

Mayer, "A Comparative Analysis of Preschool Curriculum Models," in *As the Twig Is Bent: Readings in Early Childhood Education*, ed. Robert H. Anderson and Harold G. Share (Boston: Houghton Mifflin, 1971), 286–314, also helps with the teaching theories. Hamilton Cravens, *Before Head Start: The Iowa Station and America's Children* (Chapel Hill: University of North Carolina Press, 1993), gives a sense of the mounting evidence for an environmental view over a genetic one. For useful insights into cultural deprivation theory, see Kenneth B. Clark and Lawrence Plotkin, "A Review of the Issues and Literature of Cultural Deprivation Theory" in *The Educationally Deprived: The Potential for Change*, ed. Clark (New York: Metropolitan Applied Research Center, 1972), 47–59; Herbert Ginsburg, *The Myth of the Deprived Child: Poor Children's Intellect and Education* (Englewood Cliffs, N.J.: Prentice-Hall, 1972); and Gary Natriello, Edward L. McDill, and Aaron M. Pallas, *Schooling Disadvantaged Children: Racing Against Catastrophe* (New York: Teachers College Press, 1990), 3–8.

There is a small set of basic secondary sources for the Workshop, its development, and the show. For biographical information on Joan Ganz Cooney, see Cary O'Dell, "Joan Ganz Cooney" in *Women Pioneers in Television: Biographies of Fifteen Industry Leaders* (Jefferson, N.C.: McFarland, 1997). Ellen Condliffe Lagemann provides good background on the Carnegie Foundation in *The Politics of Knowledge: The Carnegie Corporation, Philanthropy, and Public Policy* (Middletown, Conn.: Wesleyan University Press, 1989). For treatments of the CTW Model, see: Edward L. Palmer, *Television and America's Children: A Crisis of Neglect* (New York: Oxford University Press, 1988); Keith W. Mielke, "Research and Development at the Children's Television Workshop," *Educational Technology Research and Development* 38 (Fall 1990): 7–16; and Land, *Children's Television Workshop*, 6. For Jim Henson and the Muppets, the most useful sources are Christopher Finch, *Jim Henson: The Works* (New York: Random House, 1993), and David Owen, "Looking Out for Kermit," *New Yorker*, August 16, 1993, 30–43.

Though the literature on commercial broadcasting is dauntingly vast, the works on commercial producers and the control and testing of commercial programming are few: Horace Newcomb and Robert S. Alley, *The Producer's Medium: Conversations with Creators of American TV* (New York: Oxford University Press, 1983); Muriel G. Cantor, "The Role of the Producer in Choosing Children's Television Content" in *Television and Social Behavior: Reports and Papers*, vol. 1: *Media Content and Control, Technical Report of the Surgeon General's Scientific Advisory Committee on Television and Social Behavior*, ed. George A. Comstock and Eli A. Rubinstein (Washington, D.C.: U.S. Government Printing Office, 1972) and *The Hollywood TV Producer: His Work and His Audience* (New York: Basic Books, 1971); Todd Gitlin, *Inside Prime Time* (New York: Pantheon Books, 1985); Herbert J. Gans, "The Audience for Television—and in Television Research" in *Television and Social Behavior: Beyond Violence and Children, A Report of the Committee on Television and Social Behavior Social Science Research Council*, ed. Stephen B. Withey and Ronald P. Abeles (Hillsdale, N.J.: Lawrence Erlbaum Associates, 1980), 55–81.

Theoretical works are also plentiful. Three that I found insightful were: Robert Hodge and David Tripp, *Children and Television: A Semiotic Approach* (Stanford, Ca.: Stanford University Press, 1986; John Fiske, *Television Culture* (New York: Routledge, 1987); and Grant Noble, *Children in Front of the Small Screen* (London: Constable, 1975).

A few secondary sources exist for the post-premiere part of this book. For the story of the Action for Children's Television campaign, see Hendershot, *Saturday Morning Censors*; Barry Cole and Mal Oettinger, "Part IV: The Kidvid Controversy" in *Reluctant Regulators: The FCC and the Broadcast Audience* (Reading, Mass.: Addison-Wesley, 1978); and Naeemah Clark, "These Dames Are Bananas: The History of Action for Children's Television, 1969–1992," (Ph.D. dissertation, University of Florida, Gainesville, Fla., 2002). The standard history of media activism by a host of groups is Kathryn Montgomery, *Target: Prime Time: Advocacy Groups and the Struggle over Entertainment Television* (New York: Oxford University Press, 1989). For the broader context of this activism, see Terry H. Anderson, *The Movement and the Sixties* (New York: Oxford University Press, 1995). For the second-wave feminist movement, see Nancy Woloch, *Women and the American Experience* (New York: Knopf, 1984); Sara M. Evans, *Personal Politics: The Roots of Women's Liberation in the Civil Rights Movement and the New Left* (New York: Vintage Books, 1979) and *Born for Liberty: A History of Women in America* (New York: Free Press, 1989); and Winifred D. Wandersee, *On the Move: American Women in the 1970s* (Boston: Twayne Publishers, 1988). For the Hispanic movements, see Carlos Munoz Jr., *Youth, Identity, Power: The Chicano Movement* (London: Verso, 1989); Juan Gomez-Quinones, *Chicano Politics: Reality and Promise, 1940–1990* (Albuquerque: University of New Mexico Press, 1990); and Armando B. Rendon, *Chicano Manifesto*, twenty-fifth anniversary edition (Berkeley, Calif.: Ollin and Associates, 1996).

For coverage of the story after the defeat of ACT's 1970 petition, there are a number of good sources. Although he was both partisan and scholar, Dale Kunkel's articles give the best overview of the issues surrounding the Children's Television Act of 1990: with Bruce Watkins, "Evolution of Children's Television Regulatory Policy," *Journal of Broadcasting and Electronic Media* 31 (Fall 1987): 367–89; "Crafting Media Policy: The Genesis and Implications of the Children's Television Act of 1990," *American Behavioral Scientist* 35 (November/December 1991), 181–202; "Policy Battles over Defining Children's Educational Television," *Annals of the American Academy of Political and Social Science* 557 (May 1998): 39–53; "The Truest Metric for Evaluating the Children's Television Act," *Journal of Applied Developmental Psychology* 24 (August 2003): 347–53. Daniel R. Anderson is also a major researcher, advocate, and television show adviser; see his "Educational Television Is Not an Oxymoron," *Annals of the American Academy of Political and Social Science* 557 (May 1998): 24–38. Another useful introduction to this subject is J. Alison Bryant et al., "Curriculum-Based Preschool Television Programming and the American Family: Historical Development, Impact of Public Policy, and Social and Educational Effects" in *Television and the American Family*, ed. Jennings Bryant and

J. Allison Bryant, 2nd ed. (Mahwah, N.J.: Lawrence Erlbaum, 2001), 415–33. The children's cable channel Nickelodeon is covered well in a collection of essays, *Nickelodeon Nation: The History, Politics, and Economics of America's Only TV Channel for Kids*, ed. Heather Hendershot (New York: New York University Press, 2004). Avery and Stavitsky, *A History of Public Broadcasting*, is also useful for period after 1975.

Index

Brown, Les, 2, 49, 122, 124, 152
Burch, Dean, 110, 125–26, 133, 141
Bush, George H. W., 168

California Teachers Association, 115
Calvert, Sandra L., 169–70
Captain Kangaroo, 20–21, 29; and parents, 97, 112; and *Sesame Street*, 55, 67–68, 72, 87, 144
Carl Byoir and Associates, 112
Carnegie Corporation (foundation), 30, 47–48, 161, 165, 171; CTW launch press conference, 64–65; and educational and social reform, 49; support for developmental research, 49. *See also Sesame Street*, planning
Cass, James, 151
CBS, 54, 127; promotional help for *Sesame Street*, 114; refusal to fund *Sesame Street*, 56–57; viewer survey, 16–17
censorship, 3, 4, 10–12, 14–15, 29; of books, newspapers, and comic books, 24; of motion pictures, 13–14, 23; of radio, 15; of television, 19, 23–24, 133, 152–58, 161–62
Chalfen, Judith, 112
Channel 13/WNDT, 47–49, 50, 143; 1967 *Sesame Street* proposal, 53
Charren, Peggy, 112, 121
Chauncey, Henry, 52
child development science, 36–38; cultural deprivation, 41–42, 107; environmentalist theories, 37–38, 41–42; hereditary theories, 37
children: and media, ideas about, 11, 22–26; middle-class protection of, 3–4; 9–12, 29, 162–63, 171; public education of, 10
children and television, 4, 7, 81; ACT's ideas, 121–22; advertising, 134–35; attention-comprehension school of research, 164; *Sesame Street*'s insights into, 86–87, 89–91, 95–99, 102–6, 108.
See also Captain Kangaroo; censorship; *Ding Dong School*; Lesser, Gerald S.; Palmer, Edward L.; parenting, and television; *Sesame Street*
Children and Television: Lessons from Sesame Street (Lesser), 150–51
Children's Bureau, 60
Children's Television Act of 1990, 168–70
Children's Television Workshop (CTW), 5; African-American staff, 75; commercial enterprises, 165–67; creation of, 61, 64–65; relations with Henson Associates, 93–94; *Sesame Street* distribution, 99–100, 103. *See also Sesame Street*, production; *Sesame Street*, promotion
Clark, Kenneth, 32, 41
Clausen, Ralph T., 118
Clinton, Bill, 169
Comstock, Anthony, 10–12, 14, 162
Connell, David, 67–68, 97, 113, 137, 140; author, *Sesame Street*'s humor, 191n. 45; career, 72; and "The Man from Alphabet," 91–92; production design, 85, 87–89, 98–99; and summer seminars, 73–75; and show title, 86
Cook, Thomas D., 146, 147, 148–49, 163
Cooney, Joan Ganz, 30, 31, 54, 113, 154; and ACT, 120–22; in ACT petition debate, 111, 129, 138, 140–41, 161; ambition of, 48–49; appointed CTW director, 67; career, 48–49; and Dean Burch, 125; at Channel 13, 47–49, 53; Community Education Services, 116; self-esteem theory, 106–7; *Sesame Street* distribution, 99–100; and *Sesame Street* promotion, 115; views on Bereiter's curriculum, 46, 52; verdict on *Sesame Street*, 158. *See also Sesame Street*, planning
Crane, Philip, 167
CTW Model, 83–84, 161–62; compared to commercial production, 68–72, 127, 130–32; costs, 139–41; curriculum, 75–78; defined, 68; expert-producer part-

Harmon, Larry, 127

Hatch, Robert A., 112–13, 166

Hausman, Louis, 106, 142, 143; career, 54–55. *See also Sesame Street*, planning

Head Start, 4, 30, 36, 46, 51, 138; creation of, 35–36, 42; curricular models, 42–46; financial backing for *Sesame Street*, 54, 61, 147; "Handbook for Head Start" (1965), 43–44

Hechinger, Grace and Fred, 151

Height, Dorothy, 157

Hendershot, Heather, 4

Henson, Jim, 74, 156–57: baker segments, 101, 162–63; career, 72–73, 93; *Hey, Cindarella*, 93; relations with CTW, 93–94

Hess, Robert, 16, 107

Hirsch, Shelly, 169

Hogan, William, 132

Holt, John, 145–46

Hooks, Benjamin, 138, 140–41, 144

Hot Dog, 126–27, 130

Howe, Harold, II, 54, 59, 77

Hunt, J. McVicker, 38, 39

J commercial ("The Story of J"), 88–91

Johnson, Lyndon, 38, 125; and universal preschool, 40; War on Poverty, 31, 33, 34

Johnson, Nicholas, 126, 133, 141; lone FCC defender of *Sesame Street*, 136, 138, 140

Jones, James Earl, 104–5

Kagan, Jerome, 49, 51, 98–99

Keeshan, Robert, 20–21, 72

Kennedy, Thomas, 93

KERA, 116

Klein, Paul, 117, 142, 144

Koehler, George, 138

Korg: 70,000 B.C., 130

Kotler, Jennifer A., 169–70

Kunkel, Dale, 160, 170

Laugh-In, Rowan and Martin's, 87, 91

Law, Norma R., 39

Lazarsfeld, Paul F., 23, 28

Legion of Decency, 14, 23, 28, 162

Leonard, John, 122–23

Lesser, Gerald S., 28, 65, 77; career, 58; *Children and Television*, 150–51; defense of *Sesame Street*, 150–51; on Muppets, 99, 171; self-esteem theory, 107–8, 147–48; and summer seminars, 68, 74–75; verdict on *Sesame Street*, 158

Lewis, Oscar, 33, 35–36

Liebert, Robert M., 150

Lippmann, Walter, 8, 18, 19

Lyons, Leonard, 7

Macias, Pablo, 155

Mad Painter film series, 92

"Man from Alphabet, The," 91–92

Maria (character in street skits), 119

Meade, Edward, 61

Melody, William 135

Mencken, H. L., 15, 162

Minow, Newton N., 7–8, 51, 58, 125

Mr. Hooper (character in street skits), 95, 106

Mister Rogers' Neighborhood, 28–29, 198n. 31; and *Sesame Street*, 96, 97, 138, 144

Mitchell, Mabel M., 41

Morris, Norman, 122–23

Morrisett, Lloyd N., 31; career, 49–50; and CTW commercial enterprises, 165–66; *Science* magazine editorial, 30; and television reform, 64. *See also Sesame Street*, planning

motion pictures, early development, 12–14. *See also* censorship, of motion pictures

Moynihan, Patrick, 96

Muppets, 170–71; Anything Muppets, 94; Bert and Ernie, 1–2, 94, 97, 171; Big Bird, 74, 96–97, 99, 106, 171; character development, 93–94; Cookie Monster, 119; Elmo, 108, 166, 171; feminist criticism, 156–57; Kermit, 86, 93; Oscar the Grouch, 76, 99, 119, 153; Roosevelt

Schramm, Wilbur, 23, 104

Seiter, Ellen, 4, 164–65

Sesame Street, 28; advertisers' reactions, 2; and advertising, 51, 104, 164–65; and as anti-poverty program, 31, 46; appeal to middle class, 35; awards, 119; basic concept, 1; and behaviorism, 81–82, 91; commercial broadcasters' reactions, 2, 126–28, 130–32, 136–40, 141; and commercial television veterans, 72–73; and cultural deprivation debate, 41–42; cultural roots of, 3–4, 8–9, 12, 15–16, 22–23, 29, 88; and early childhood education, 31, 128; as an experiment, 57–60, 108, 113, 161; as funder of PBS, 165, 167; and later children's programs, 6; and *Mister Rogers' Neighborhood*, 28–29; and 1960s, 4–5, 152, 155; as "plug-in drug," 3, 163; products, 108; psychologists' reactions, 6, 98; and Republican attack on PBS (1994), 165, 167; titling the show, 85–86, 179n. 2; and violence, 100–101. *See also* CTW Model

Sesame Street, audience, 86–87, 95–97, 101–3, 163–64; African-American, 76, 95–07, 118, 142–44; Hispanic, 143; ratings, 117–18, 142–43; viewer mail, 118–19

Sesame Street, distribution, 53, 56–57, 198n. 31; National Educational Television, 59–60, 85, 99–100, 112–13; problems, 117–18

Sesame Street, and education, 111, 128, 159; achievement gap, 146–51; assessments in popular press, 151, 158; educational criticisms, 124, 141–42, 144–51, 162–63; educators' reactions, 2, 6, 118, 124; *Sesame Street*'s defenders, 150–51

Sesame Street, and multiculturalism, 2–3, 6, 35, 111, 128, 151–58, 159, 164–65; African-American criticism, 152–54; bilingual/bicultural curriculum, 154–55; feminist criticism, 155–58; Hispanic criticism, 2–3, 154–55; National Advisory Committee of *Sesame Street*, 155; pro-

moting racial tolerance, 124–25; self-esteem theories, 152, 154, 155, 157

Sesame Street, planning: achievement gap goal, 53, 65; advisers, 51; audience, 50–51, 52–53, 54, 55–56, 59, 60–64; budget, 55; dinner party, 47; educational potential of television, 51; finding financial backers, 53–54, 60, 62; format ideas, 52; independent educational evaluation, 57–58, 77; independent production unit, 53, 55–57; initial concept, 47–49; opposition within Department of Health, Education, and Welfare (HEW), 60, 61–63; 1966 feasibility study, 48, 50–53; 1967 Channel 13 proposal, 53. *See also* Cooney, Joan Ganz; CTW Model; Hausman, Louis; Morrisett, Lloyd N.

Sesame Street, and the press, 2, 6, 83; broadcast trade press, 112–14; educational assessments, 151, 158; as example for ACT petition, 111; magazines and newspapers, 113–15, 119–20, 124–25; *Time* magazine cover, 6, 124. *See also Sesame Street*, promotion

Sesame Street, production: 86; cartoons, 88–91, 101, 103, 136–37; cast, 95–97, 154, 157–58; children in studio skits, 96; children in voiceover, 102–3; costs, 139–41; and curriculum, 92, 94, 99; films, 88, 91–92, 102–4; format and style, 87–88; miscellaneous segments, 100; and multiculturalism, 153–58, puppet skits, 88, 92–95; set design, 95–96; studio skits, 88, 95–97, 103, 104–6; test episodes (July 1969), 97–99

Sesame Street, promotion: and African Americans, 112, 115–16; campaign before premiere, 112–17; CTW launch press conference, 64–65; and educators, 112, 114–15; and Head Start, 117; live press conference, 112–13; message, 113, 120, 127–28

Sesame Street, research and testing: ETS